The Abraham Lincoln Lecture Series

This series aims to reflect the principles
that Abraham Lincoln championed:
education, justice, tolerance,
and union.

*Smart*Jews

The Construction of the Image of Jewish Superior Intelligence

Sander L. Gilman

University of Nebraska Press

Lincoln and London

The lectures on which this book is based
were sponsored by the University of Nebraska
Press and the College of Arts and Sciences, the
Norman and Bernice Harris Center for Judaic
Studies, and the Departments of English and
Modern Languages at the University of
Nebraska–Lincoln.

♾ The paper in this book meets the minimum
requirements of American National Standard for
Information Sciences–Permanence of Paper for
Printed Library Materials, ANSI Z39.48-1984.

First Bison Books printing: 1997
Most recent printing indicated by the last digit below:
10   9   8   7   6   5   4   3   2   1

Set in the Carter and Cone version of Galliard
type. Book design by R. Willis Eckersley

Library of Congress
Cataloging-in-Publication Data

Gilman, Sander L.
Smart Jews : the construction of the image of
Jewish superior intelligence / Sander L. Gilman.
p. cm.–(The Abraham Lincoln lecture series)
Includes bibliographical references and index.
ISBN 0-8032-2158-4 (cloth : alkaline paper)
ISBN 0-8032-7069-0 (paper : alkaline paper)
1. Jews – Intelligence levels – Public opinion.
2. Jews – Public opinion.   3. Jews – Intel-
lectual life.   I. Title.   II. Series.
DS143.G43 1996 155.8'4924–dc20
95-45639 CIP

For Dr. Willis Regier, in Friendship

Signum reprobationis in vultu gerens

Goethe, in his autobiography *Dichtung und Wahrheit,*
commented that a poor portrait of Spinoza, one of the
standard figures evoked in the eighteenth century to
prove "Jewish superior intelligence," was used by his
detractors to prove that Spinoza "bore the sign
of corruption in his face."

CONTENTS

PREFACE

IN THE SPRING of 1994 I was called by Willis Regier, then the director of the University of Nebraska Press, who asked if I could come to Lincoln and deliver the inaugural Abraham Lincoln lectures under the auspices of the press as well as other programs and divisions of the University of Nebraska. Having had a long and positive relationship with the press, which publishes my series Texts and Contexts and is the home for my study *Inscribing the Other* (1992), I accepted with great pleasure. But when asked what I wanted to speak about, I was a bit puzzled as to a potential topic.

I had just finished a major book project on the *fin de siècle* and was struck by an ongoing discussion that I found in the psychological and philosophical literature about the superior/inferior intelligence of the Jews in an age of growing anti-Semitism. Initially, I felt that this discussion was of little real interest, as I first saw it as a simple function of the envy that I (a "smart Jew") assumed that the British, Americans, French, or Germans felt about Jewish achievement. The more I read on the topic, the more complex were the rationales for Jewish superior intelligence presented and the more complex the response of Jewish intellectuals to the question of their own superior intelligence. I decided to begin to work on this topic in earnest for the lectures, even though the question of the relationship between race and intelligence was, I was certain, truly an old-fashioned one, one well researched and commented on in the 1960s by a number of colleagues including my dear friend the late Harry Levin at Cornell. His work and that of others had put a stake through the topic's heart.

In the fall of 1994 the rotting corpse walked again. *The Bell Curve* appeared on the bookshelves throughout America, and an issue that I was convinced was quite dead began to move again like a movie monster across the intellectual horizon. The numerous stakes driven through its heart had not killed it in the '60s, and it was lumbering again through the American political and cultural scene! It was a scene out of the *Night of the Living Dead. The Bell Curve,* however, was

Preface

also a text with real political impact in the newly elected Republican Congress in 1995. It articulated a political position of the 1990s using an argument of the 1960s and even earlier. And I found my work suddenly and sadly "relevant."

This volume on "Smart Jews" is the result of Dr. Willis Regier's invitation and the sudden interest shown in the topic of race and intelligence in the mid-1990s. I was able to gather material for this not only in the normal scholarly paths of library research and scholarly publications, but also through the informal contributions from a number of colleagues on the "net." Where I cited this material, I did so anonymously, as it functions quite often as a sociological litmus test for my more scholarly readings. I am especially grateful to my friend Jo Miller for her help in this project. My assistant at Chicago, Hillary Hope, undertook library research and read the manuscript of the study.

I am, however, especially grateful to the friends and colleagues at the University of Nebraska and the University of Nebraska Press for their positive response to this material. This book is dedicated to Dr. Willis Regier, whose tenure at Nebraska came to an end while these talks were being held, but whose presence on the American cultural scene remains strong and powerful.

Chicago, April 1995

I

A Problem Still

The Bell Curve, INTELLIGENCE, AND VIRTUE

T
HE APPEARANCE of Richard J. Herrnstein and Charles
Murray's book *The Bell Curve: Intelligence and Class Structure
in American Life* again drew attention to the debate about
the relationship between inheritance and intelligence, a debate that
in the American context is read as a comment on "race" (read: Blackness) and lower intelligence.[1] (In my discussion of the idea of the "bell
curve," it is important to understand that the very existence of such
a "curve" can be drawn into question once the definition of what is
being plotted on it is examined.) There is no question that *The Bell
Curve* was (and is) read as a book on race and intelligence. When the
book appeared, Charles M. Madigan of the *Chicago Tribune* noted
that "it adds a layer of scientific glaze to a collection of racial attitudes that seems to have escaped from the 19th century. In that sense,
this huge tome is the perfect Thinking Bigot's Beach Book. If you're
looking for data to back up your prejudices, it's all here; David Duke
will find much to borrow."[2] Madigan clearly read the book as a book
about race, and race in the American context is defined by Blackness.
In *The Bell Curve,* intelligence becomes a discussion of character and
virtue. And it is this red thread throughout the debates about race and
intelligence that has been little acknowledged over the past decades.
During this debate about the relationship between "race" and "IQ,"
sporadically carried out over the past three decades around the work
of Arthur Robert Jensen, William Shockley, and J. Philippe Rushton,
little attention has been paid to the ethical and moral questions that
permeate these studies.[3] As Richard Lacayo noted in a *Time* magazine
essay on the book (24 October 1994),

> *The Bell Curve*'s explosive contentions detonate under a cushion
> of careful shadings and academic formulations. Even so, they ex-
> plode with a bang. To give credence to such ideas—even when
> doing so with loud sighs of alas!—is to resume some of the most
> poisonous battles of the late 1960s and '70s, when the sometimes
> cranky outer limits of the IQ debate were personified by Arthur

A Problem Still

Jensen, the Berkeley psychologist who stressed the link between race, genes and IQ, and William Shockley, who proposed paying people with low IQs to be sterilized. Murray says the reaction against them shut off a necessary discussion. "The country has for a long time been in almost hysterical denial that genes can play any role whatsoever."

All these writers of the 1960s implicitly or explicitly raised the question of the relationship between "intelligence" and "race" as defined by skin color. They have also implied (explicitly or implicitly) that race and intelligence are related in very specific ways to questions of morality and virtue. Herrnstein and Murray's presentation in this regard is neither the most extensive nor the most hotly contested. Even though it deals with "cognitive class" and not explicitly with race as defined by skin color, it repeats the collateral question addressed by much of the earlier literature on this topic. Virtue and morality are the real objects of *The Bell Curve,* and these qualities are posited positively or negatively at both ends of the curve.

For there are two ends to Herrnstein and Murray's "bell curve," each thin and rare. As rare as is the lowest end of the curve—those of lowest intelligence—according to the classic argument, the upper end of the curve is also rare. Little or no attention is given in the analysis of such studies to the "normal" center. The thin ends define the problem—the "normal" center is understood as the model of intelligence and therefore also as the model of virtue. These investigations erroneously assume that only the deviant, following the model of the pathological in medicine, can provide insight into the normal. And thus the center—the two standard deviations from the norm in this model—is invisible. It remains the implicit site of virtue through (or because of) its "average" intelligence.

Given the American political climate of the mid-1990s, one can understand why the Herrnstein and Murray book has attracted much attention in its evocation of the myth of the permanent underclass (read: African Americans) whose high rate of reproduction, low intelligence, and degenerate sociopathic genes have led to an America where it is dangerous to walk the streets of the big cities. Or as Herrnstein and Murray note, "high intelligence also provides some protec-

tion against lapsing into criminality for people who otherwise are at risk" (235). According to this model, criminals are dumb and dumb people are criminals. This ahistorical reconstruction ignores the complex reading of the relationship between "intelligence" and "crime" (however the two concepts are defined).[4]

According to contemporaries, New York's "Hell's Kitchen" in the 1860s was full of atavistic Irish who made the streets unsafe. They too were literally seen as a race apart and were accused of reproducing at an uncomfortably high rate. The racial sign of their lower intelligence could be seen in their simian brow and saddle nose! Such myths about the relationship of "low intelligence" and "race" are stock in the repertory of Western science, at least since the mid–eighteenth century, in attempting to dispel the anxiety of an established society about the source of social instability. Identify your potential enemy and you can control your anxiety! Thus the focus on the lower end of the "bell curve" has been an attempt to locate the origins of anxiety in a stereotyped category.

But what about those who are too smart? Little attention has been paid to the other end of the spectrum, to the thin line at the other end of the "bell curve." It is this end that serves as a prophylaxis against crime. Herrnstein and Murray devote only one page to the highest group in terms of intelligence: "Ashkenasic Jews of European origins" who "test higher than any other ethnic group." Based on this model that equates intelligence with virtue, we would come to expect that the higher the intelligence, the greater the protection against criminality and the greater the virtue of the group. According to Herrnstein and Murray, "Jews in America and Britain have an overall IQ mean somewhere between a half and a full standard deviation above the mean, with the source of the difference concentrated in the verbal component" (275). Such test scores, however, are not sufficient for them to establish the superior intelligence of the Jews; they also rely on "analyses of occupational and scientific attainment by Jews, which constantly show their disproportionate level of success, usually by orders of magnitude, in various inventories of scientific and artistic achievement." Jews are not only smart but also creative—and following Max Weber's reading of American-Protestant culture, this is a sign of their virtue, for worldly success is a sign of a virtuous life. This combination of the two instruments employed to measure intelligence—catalogs of accomplishments and multiple-choice testing—mirrors the history of the construction of the image of Jewish superior intelligence from the mid–nineteenth century to the present.[5] But, equally important, *the implication of such studies is the identification and quantifiability of virtue,* and such rather crude types of analogies are just as likely to draw the virtue of the Jews into question as to posit them as the site of virtue. Such arguments are variants on the myths that attribute superior intelligence to the Jews as a cohort.

The myth of Jewish superior intelligence has its origin in the age of biological racism. It is part of the discussion of Jews as a racial category.[6] This myth is quickly absorbed in the discourse of racial science and continues to hold power even today. In *The Bell Curve,* Herrnstein and Murray describe the "Jews" as "Ashkenasic Jews of European origins," labeling them as what historically has been a racial category. The arguments about who is smarter than whom reflect the general debates in the world of nineteenth-century scientific racism. The superiority of northern Jews (Ashkenasic) over southern Jews (Sephardic) is an argument from the general realm of scientific racism in the nineteenth century about the improvement of the race the farther north or east (to a point!) one goes ("Caucasians" versus "Semites"). By the late twentieth century, the social situation in Israel seemed to present this superiority as a given.[7] Jewish scientists of the late nineteenth century often reversed this argument, seeing the Sephardic Jew as the better type.[8]

In the recent literature on the intelligence of the Jews, written after the post-Shoah constitution of the State of Israel with its "Eastern" and "Western" Jews, the idea of the superior intelligence of the Ashkenasic Jew has reappeared.[9] One can turn to the studies of the perception of intelligence in Israel today, for example, to see how social status and distance creates the illusion of Ashkenasic superior intelligence. A revealing Israeli study looked at the meaning attributed to the intelligence of the Jews in present-day Israel. Moshe Zeidner interviewed sixty Jewish and sixty Arab Israeli college students about their perceptions of the modal intelligence and social distance of five Israeli ethnic groups: European Jews, Eastern Jews, Christian Arabs, Moslem Arabs, and Druze.[10] He also explored the determinants to which the subjects attributed differences in ability between the ethnic groups. The perceived modal intelligence profiles for the ethnic groups varied as a function of the subject's ethnic group membership. There was consensus among the subjects that Jews of Western extraction (Ashkenasic) were the most intelligent of the subgroups. Arab informants were more prone than Jewish informants to give environmental reasons for differences in group ability. In an Israeli context, Jewish superior intelligence is a function of the position and the self-definition of the observer.

A careful examination of the literature on Jewish superior intelligence reveals that a unitary category of "the Jews" is always imagined. This category is divided by those who wish or need to identify with one subclass or another, such as in Zeidner's case. Nineteenth-century Central European Jews, such as Theodor Herzl, wishing to relativize their relationship both to Eastern European Jews (understood as primitive) and to Central/Western European Jews (understood as assimilated), postulated the Sephardic Jewish experience as the "real" world of the Jews. Arabs in contemporary Israel see the politically most visible Jews in Israel, the Jews of Western (Eastern European) extraction, as the most intelligent. The distinction among subsets of the "Jews" is, however, more frequently found among Jewish savants writing about racial science of the nineteenth and early twentieth centuries.

When "Jewish" superior intelligence is assumed to be positive it is rarely seen as "biological." Rather it is understood as a quality that can be attained by any group if only the "right" rules are followed. If Jewish superior intelligence is seen as a negative quality, as merely cleverness or "the cultivation of a single faculty, that of hair-splitting judgment, at the cost of the rest, narrow[ing] the imagination, [without] a single literary product appear[ing] . . . deserving the name of poetry. . . . A love of twisting, distorting, ingenuous quibbling"[11] (so said the late-nineteenth-century Jewish German scholar Heinrich Graetz about *Polish* Jewish intelligence), then superior intelligence is often seen by Jews as inherited but by non-Jews as acquired. Forms of creativity such as writing poetry come to be indicators of the virtue of a specific group, as aesthetics come to have the position of marking "high" as opposed to "low" values and culture in the post-Enlightenment era. Thus the pseudointelligence of the Polish Jews, according to Graetz, is a form of instrumental or functional rationality rather than substantive rationality. Substantive rationality is marked by aesthetic creativity, which in turn marks the creator as able to both comprehend and represent the beautiful and the true, that is, the virtuous. Virtue (or its absence) is thus a quality ascribed to or implicit in nineteenth-century racial categories. While the nineteenth-century concept of race, with its stress on the perfected prototype, is obviously different from the contemporary biological view of race as a probabilistic aggregate, Murray's views blur this distinction.[12] In a discussion at the Aspen Institute after the appearance of *The Bell Curve,* the following exchange took place: "An Israeli cellist asks if Murray draws any conclusions about Africa's shortage of ancient literature. Murray says he does, and as the veal chops sizzle, he offers the Israeli a national compliment: 'In terms of IQ, you guys are off the charts.'"[13] The "guys" who are "off the charts" are the "Ashkenasic Jews of European origins" who make up a minority of Jews in Israel today. This distinction is countered in Murray's source ("Storfer 1990") for these comments in *The Bell Curve.* The "compliment" is not a national one but a racial one. It is also, as we shall see, a gendered argument—for the "guys" really are men. The relationship of categories of gender to those of morality must be kept in mind as we read through the texts that represent Jewish superior intelligence.

The slipperiness and interrelationship of the racial categories that haunt the discourse on Jewish superior intelligence—Jew, Hebrew, Israeli, Ashkenazi of European Heritage, and Sephardic—present one aspect of the complexity of the "bell curve" as a model for representing the difference of the Jew. Are "Jew" and "Hebrew" religious designations encompassing the widest range of Jews from all corners of the world and of every possible "racial" label? Is "Israeli" a label of national identity or (as it has been among German left-wing anti-Semites for decades) a hidden code referring to "the Jews" as a homogenous racial group? Are "Ashkenasic" and "Sephardic" ethnic or

A Problem Still

cultural labels or the designation of racial cohorts? Who exactly belongs to what category and why? And why is it that, when all is said and done, we are left with the idea of a homogenous "Jew" who is the embodiment of Jewish superior intelligence?

The image of the Jew in *The Bell Curve* comes to haunt the reception of the work in a direct manner. In the collected volume of essays on *The Bell Curve* edited by Steven Fraser, as well as in that edited by Russell Jacoby and Naomi Glauberman (both published a year after the volume appeared), there is a series of readings of the image of Jewish superior intelligence as presented by Herrnstein and Murray.[14] Needless to say, this passage is given very minor notice (with three exceptions, all by Jewish commentators) in the wide range of essays published in this volume. Virtually all the essays deal with African Americans and intelligence, and one by the Queens College sociologist Andrew Hacker rather pointedly ignores the Jews when tabulating "immigrant groups" (F 105). These readings reflect a wide range of the positions taken over the past century when scientists, both Jewish and non-Jewish, are confronted with the question of Jewish intellectual superiority.

A number of the commentators, such as Alan Wolfe, stressed that IQ testing had its "original use against Jews and Catholics" (F 119). The American experience is the source of the understanding of Jewish superior intelligence in such a view. These commentators see the procedure of testing these groups (and by extension others) as inherently flawed at its American origin, regardless of its present use. John Carey notes that "social scientists 'proved' that the new Americans, many of them Jewish, would drag down the nation's average intelligence. . . . Jews now score some 10 points higher than the white average."[15] Among the non-Jewish essayists, conservative African-American intellectual Thomas Sowell sees Jewish superior intelligence as the result of the marked improvement of Jewish intelligence from 1914 to the 1930s (F 75). Sowell does not accept the idea that Jews were mismeasured, as Herrnstein and Murray state, or that the measurements of the later period reflect the real, unalterable state of Jewish intelligence. Instead he argues for a theory of adaptation, stating that the measurement of Jewish intelligence that placed the Jew at the lower end of the

A Problem Still

bell curve was remedied in a relatively short period of time through acculturation rather than intermarriage or the elimination of bias in IQ tests. Here the equation of the victim status of American Jews and African Americans provides a reading that would parallel the increase in Jewish intelligence with the potential increase in African American intelligence that Sowell sees as possible in the American system of acculturation. Jews became smarter because they became Americans.

Jewish savants see the matter very differently. Nathan Glazer, the Harvard sociologist, postulates that the inherent reason for Jewish achievement and intelligence was the "urban and commercial background of many Jewish immigrants in the late nineteenth century and early twentieth century compared to the predominately peasant background of other immigrant groups of the period" (F 143). Jews were smarter than other immigrant groups because they were already advantaged to deal with urban capitalism in *fin-de-siècle* America. Here the distinction is a social one, but one that goes much farther back in history to the oppression of the Jews and the limitation of their ability to own and till the land. Rather than an artifact of American adaptation, Jewish superior intelligence and achievement are seen to compensate for prior stigmatization.

For the Jewish commentators, intelligence and creativity are interchangeable. Martin Peretz, editor of the *New Republic,* stresses the cultural background of the Jews in commenting that "a population which listens to Midori or Itzak Perlman is likely to produce violinists from among its children, and one that doesn't won't. . . . A similar process helps explain why some American ethnicities (like Jews and subcontinent Asians) disproportionately produce physicians and physicists and why others (like Italians and Greeks) also disproportionately produce restaurateurs" (F 152). The evident flaw in such a view is the assumption that Jews and Japanese were always part of Western high culture. When and how do Eastern Jews and Japanese move from liturgical music or klezmer or traditional Japanese music to Western high culture? Peretz's view stresses that creativity and intelligence are linked through a context that expects the ethnic group to produce specific occupations. Cultural expectations seem to dominate. Yet he is tempted by the notion that Jews are biologically somehow dif-

A Problem Still

ferent. All Jews "are consistently close in genetic constitution" (F 153), a "fact" that may (if we only knew enough about the human genome, he cries) eventually provide a genetic basis for Jewish superior intelligence. Indeed, Peretz argues that while Jewish genetic diseases, which we shall discuss in chapter 3, may well be a result of collecting information among highly educated (and hypochondriacal?) Jews, the actual desire to collect data (read: science) "has genetic origins."[16] Conservative scholar Nathan Glazer states this without hesitation: "We take these differences in intelligence for granted in the case of families, and it stands to reason that such differences might also characterize larger groups that share some common features in genetic inheritance and culture. Otherwise we would have no explanation for the disproportionate presence of Jews and Asians in selective high schools and selective colleges, or in the disproportionate presence of these groups in such occupations as medicine, law, and college teaching."[17] Jews are smarter than the average non-Jew and are predisposed to become scientists.

Of the Jewish commentators, it is finally Leon Wieseltier, the literary editor of the *New Republic*, who points the finger directly at the source of the problem and at his own anxiety about the question of Jewish superior intelligence. Commenting on the discussion of Jewish superior intelligence in *The Bell Curve*, Wieseltier is "repelled" because he wishes to believe that he is responsible for his own achievements rather than accept them as a property of a group to which he happens to belong. Earlier IQ studies in which Jews "did not 'test higher'" led to "consequences that were catastrophic." (F 159) (One assumes he is referring to the Shoah. As we shall see, the role of the Shoah in framing the question of Jewish superior intelligence is a most complex one.) And Wieseltier makes the appropriate gesture: "What if the 'generalizations' that Murray takes from the study that he calls 'Storfer 1990' had turned out differently? How would he explain my failure to express the limitations of my group? Or would it be more appropriate, in the event of psychometric embarrassment, that I stop pretending and start tailoring?" (F 159). Does the question asked by the Jewish savant about Herrnstein and Murray's source ("Storfer 1990") draw the "Ashkenasic Jew of European origins" (Wieseltier's

A Problem Still

self-description) to ask about his own role as an intellectual? What is there in "Storfer 1990" that provides Herrnstein and Murray with the certainty of their argument and generates anxiety in Leon Wieseltier, the Jew who could be only pretending to be a "smart Jew," but of course knows that he really is one?

The Bell Curve's SOURCE ON JEWISH SUPERIOR INTELLIGENCE

No clearer example of the pitfalls of romanticizing the "Jewish intellect" and its problematic relationship to the concept of virtue can be found than in the cited source for Herrnstein and Murray's one-page digest of the upper end of the bell curve, Miles D. Storfer's *Intelligence and Giftedness: The Constitutions of Heredity and Early Environment*.[18] Published by a legitimate academic publisher, Jossey-Bass, in San Francisco in 1990, this volume contains a summary of the positive, century-long search for the source for the improvement of the human condition, using the Jews as its model. It is thus different from many of the more questionable sources of the Herrnstein and Murray volume which are published in clearly ideologically biased journals.[19] Much like the nineteenth-century discussions concerning the improvement of the human condition through the adoption of Jewish ritual practices such as circumcision (which accounts for the wide practice of this ritual as a medical prophylaxis in the United States among non-Jews) and ritual slaughter (as a prophylaxis against tuberculosis, an argument not generally accepted but put forth in the same period), the question of the duplicable source of Jewish intelligence lies at the heart of Storfer's long chapter on "the nurturing of verbal/conceptual reasoning abilities in Jewish families."[20] Although my discussion of Storfer comes at the beginning of this book, Storfer self-consciously places himself in the tradition of the testing studies from the 1920s, such as those by Lewis Terman, that will be discussed in chapter 2 (320). He thus sees his work as a continuation of the "scientific" discourse about Jewish superior intelligence that has its roots in nineteenth-century science.

In his chapter on Jewish superior intelligence, Storfer summarizes the bulk of the post-Shoah statistical studies of Jewish superior intel-

A Problem Still

ligence based on various modalities of intelligence testing and notes, as Herrnstein and Murray's summary reflects, the superiority of Ashkenasic over Sephardic Jews. But Storfer's summary of the literature that employs this distinction actually draws his conclusion into question. First, he makes sure his reader knows that his idea of "the Jew" has little or nothing to do with religious belief, faith, or practice by removing "Jewishness" from the realm of religion: "The overall intellectual proficiency of American Jewish children does not appear to depend on whether or not their families adhered to the Orthodox Jewish traditions" (321). Orthodoxy is for Storfer the only legitimate form of Jewish religious practice as it is evidently the most authentic and the least polluted by "non-Jewish" traditions. According to this argument, whatever virtue is to be associated with Jewish superior intelligence has nothing to do with religious practice or belief. For Storfer, Jewish superior intelligence is the result of child-rearing practices, the linguistic matrix of the child, and the specific areas of Jewish accomplishment. None of these are, at least in his initial discussion, seen as aspects of religious practice.

Storfer's Lamarckian, ethnopsychological model of organic memory that defines "the Jews"[21] destroys any distinction between the Ashkenazi and the Sephardic Jew. The "verbal precocity of the Jewish people" can dissipate "after several generations of 'intellectual neglect,'" which he defines as living in "backward Arab lands for ten or twenty generations and [being] *assimilated into the Arab child-rearing customs*" (his emphasis). But Jewish intellectual superiority is so resilient that "exposure to a cognitively enriched (primarily Ashkenazi) kibbutz environment may be able to restore as much as two-thirds of this loss in a single generation" (321). The underlying Jewish psyche is the "source" of the superiority of the Jew, whether or not that psyche is found in Ashkenazi or Sephardic form. It is clearly "the Jew" as a unitary, racial category about whom Storfer is speaking.

Storfer's sources for the practices to which he ascribes the origin or perpetuation (or both) of Jewish superior intelligence are as romanticized as his own discussion. For Storfer, "Jewish infant care taking practices" shape the ethnopsychology of "the Jew" and are themselves shaped by the resulting superior intelligence of the Jews who develop

13

A Problem Still

it. Such tautologies are not uncommon in studies of Jewish superior intelligence. Storfer's view of "Jewish infant care taking practices" is rooted in a post-Shoah textual tradition. His primary source is Mark Zborowski and Elizabeth Herzog's *Life Is with People* (1952), a work that reflects immediately post-Shoah passionate memories of the sole authenticity of the Eastern Jewish experience in the form of narratives about the world of European Jewry lost in the destruction of the Shoah.[22] Storfer's "Jews" are universal (all Jews everywhere) and are also the most "authentic of the Ashkenazi Jews," Yiddish-speaking *Ost-juden*. Rooted in fieldwork among survivors of the Shoah, Zborowski and Herzog's text collected post-Shoah legends, myths, and memories of the pre-Shoah world of Eastern Jewry and presented them as fieldwork about the actual daily reality of the shtetl. But the image of the shtetl that Zborowski and Herzog retrospectively construct was already an invention of late-nineteenth- and early-twentieth-century Yiddish high culture by writers such as Sholem Aleichem. Sitting in the south of France or New York City at the turn of the century, these authors evoked, at the moment after its dissolution, a lost world of an integrated, authentic Jewish experience located in the East. Such a construction was shared by German Jews during World War I, who also "found" in the East the authenticity they seemed to lack in their own culture.[23]

The world of the Eastern Jews imagined during World War I and after the Shoah was a constructed image that fulfilled specific ideological needs. The shtetl was a product of the Pale of Settlement and land-settlement practices in the Austro-Hungarian Empire, and it was certainly not paradise. As soon as Jews were able to move into urban areas in Russia and Central Europe or to leave for North America, England, France, South Africa, or Australia—anywhere but that "perfect world"—they fled in overwhelming numbers. The image captured in the narratives in Zborowski and Herzog were early-twentieth-century myths about the idyllic nature of the shtetl that evolved retrospectively after the dissolution of the shtetl through urbanization and immigration. Certainly such an idealized image also tended to stress the virtuousness of such communities. Zborowski and Herzog's discussion of the verbal environment of the child, of swaddling

A Problem Still

practices, and of a favorable caretaker ratio based on an extended family (Storfer's terms) is part of their image of coherent extended families with specific child-rearing rituals. The existence of analogous practices among Russian, Ukrainian, and Polish "peasants" seems never to be invoked to make an argument about the origin of rural Russian, Ukrainian, or Polish superior intelligence. Rather, such practices seem to be proof of the "primitive" status of the peasant in an agrarian society barely three generations out of serfdom.

Such stereotypes can be used both in "negative" and "positive" manners. Zborowski and Herzog's image of the Jewish family, borrowed by Storfer, certainly does not overlap with the inchoate, complex, difficult world of the widely divergent Jewish Diaspora experiences in the nineteenth and twentieth centuries in the world of the Ashkenazi Jew. It certainly does not reflect the four generations of the Jewish experience of American life, which, according to the contemporary anxieties expressed in the Jewish community, is moving toward precisely the opposite pole in becoming too American.

The romanticizing that results from Storfer's appropriation of Zborowski and Herzog's world is evident in Storfer's idea of language, one of the core concepts in his model for the origin of Jewish superior intelligence. The question of the nature of Jewish language and discourses is an extended trope in Western thought.[24] One can see the transvaluation of Eastern European language use and practices following Graetz's comment on the stultifying mental set reflected in "Talmudic" discourse. Graetz, internalizing the anti-Semitic Enlightenment view of a universal Jewish linguistic particularity, projected comments about the intrinsic nature of "Jewish language" and therefore "Jewish thought" onto the *Ostjude* and into the world of Polish Jewry. He saw this discourse as irrational and limiting. The origin of this argument lies with Kant's distinction between the rational and the crafty man. Kant's example of craftiness, cunning, and slyness is the Jews, a "nation of deceivers" who use their special command of language for their economic advantage.[25] Kant associates little or no virtue with the image of the Eastern (Polish) Jew. Indeed, the Eastern Jew becomes the model for the rapaciousness and destructiveness of the Jew. The language of the Jews in this context becomes the measure of their craftiness, not of their intelligence.

A Problem Still

Storfer reverses this negative image of the "natural" language of the Jews and sees "the highly repetitive use of specific words and phrases" as capturing specific "expressions of emotions" (327). It is for him the "linking of words, melody and strong emotions . . . in the liturgy of the Jewish rituals" (328) that represents the ethnopsychological sensitivity of the Jews to the nuances of language. But again, such a view is tautological in its basic argument, for is it the liturgy (religious practice) that makes the Jew so positively sensitive to language or is it the Jewish predisposition to language manipulation that generated the liturgy?

According to Storfer there is no specific link between religious belief and Jewish superior intelligence. There is, however, an ancient tradition that has imprinted itself on the Jewish psyche so that the liturgical practices of the Temple account for the contemporary Jewish facility with language. Such an argument would be analogous to the arguments of the nineteenth and twentieth centuries (well past midcentury) that Jews—at least Jewish males—have a much higher incidence of congenital circumcision than non-Jews because Jews have practiced circumcision over such an extensive period of time.[26] The argument is of interest because it links two areas in the nineteenth-century discussion of Jewish superior intelligence: "creativity" (music) and "intelligence" (verbal ability). But Storfer is not original in this linkage.

Given his heavy reliance on studies that illustrate Jewish superior intelligence through statistical proof based on multiple-choice testing, Storfer still does not feel that this wide range of "scientific" studies of intelligence based on testing is sufficient to make his point. Jews, according to the psychological testing literature, are smarter and better at most tests that measure verbal and numerical ability. Thus Storfer cites P. M. Sheldon's 1954 study in which, of twenty-eight children in New York City with Stanford-Binet tests of 170 or higher, "*twenty-four . . . were Jewish*" (his emphasis).[27] Storfer cites this and dozens of other studies to show that Jews are much smarter, at least in terms of verbal and numerical ability, than non-Jews. *But is smarter better?* For Storfer, the discussion of Jewish superior intelligence ("cleverness") is an answer to the more traditional European view of Jewish superior

A Problem Still

intelligence as a negative sign, a view found even in the psychological literature of the early twentieth century that Storfer evokes. Storfer needs to equate Jewish superior intelligence with virtue if, as he and Herrnstein and Murray argue, the transmission of low intelligence must be linked to vice. Storfer's view equates Jewish superior intelligence with virtue in unusual ways.

Storfer employs a model of Jewish superior intelligence from the age prior to psychological testing. This model catalogs Jewish achievements in order to correlate Jewish intellectual ability with "the contribution of the Jewish people to human progress." Jews are smarter, Storfer notes, but they are also better. Jews' "verbal and/or numerical (conceptually based) mechanism for analyzing and integrating knowledge" (319) enables them to "attain proficiency in conducting and playing classical music, acting, selling, and practicing psychotherapy" (314). These are—well, most of these are—good occupations. They are a sign of the "educated man," the *Bildungsbürger,* whom Western Jews since the Enlightenment have taken as the model for the "good" (and "smart") Jew. High culture is the mark of accomplishment in this model.

Storfer catalogs examples of "Jewish genius," to use the nineteenth-century term. He begins with the paradigmatic smart men who are also good "Jews": Albert Einstein and Sigmund Freud (322). As we shall see in the discussion of Freud and the question of Jewish genius in chapter 3, such attributions are fraught with problems, because the question of what "Jewish superior intelligence" means to the individual so characterized is complex. Storfer and other American conservatives concerned with intelligence and race at the close of the Cold War abridged the normal catalog of smart Jews as either positive and negative examples: Marx suddenly vanishes from the triumvirate, leaving only Einstein and Freud. Storfer then turns to the tabulation of Nobel Prizes in science (including economics) and follows the Jewish scholar Raphael Patai's tabulation of "Jews" who have been awarded prizes. Patai, author of the major study, *The Jewish Mind* (1977), argues for and attempts to document Jewish superior intelligence. Had Storfer followed Armin Hermann's 1978 study of Nobel Prize winners, he would have found a number of the "Jewish"

A Problem Still

winners labeled as "German."[28] The difficulty in such catalogs is in how "the Jew" is defined. For Storfer it must be defined racially, for only then can a list of "Jews" cutting across the national designation of winners be compiled. Having shown Jewish intellectual preeminence in science, Storfer turns to "classical" music and lists performers from Vladimir Ashkenazy to Bruno Walter, and with a bow to American popular culture of an earlier era, throws in Irving Berlin and Benny Goodman for good measure. Here again, the standard of the "educated man," the *Bildungsbürger,* defines Jewish superior intelligence. The confusion between "talent" and "genius," which is standard in nineteenth-century analysis of catalogs of accomplishments, is repeated here with all the high-culture bias of the nineteenth-century savant. "The Beastie Boys," Jewish rap performers, or even innovative klezmer artists such as "The Klezmatics" need not apply for admission into the pantheon of talented Jews! "Brilliant chess masters," another standard model for Jewish intellectual superiority in the nineteenth century, is extended in Storfer's next category to include contract bridge players.[29] Here the "intelligence" of "Jewish" chess and bridge players is assumed because of their facility at their games, but the facility of "Jewish" boxers and baseball players at their games is seen as an absence of superior intelligence.

Jews, according to Storfer's catalog, do not have equivalent rank in painting, architecture, and the "more observational sciences" such as geology, botany, and zoology (323). Jewish intelligence is the intelligence of the word, not the eye. This distinction is a comment on the anxiety associated with the role attributed to the Jews in the creation of the "modern," as art and architecture mark for conservative thinkers in the late twentieth century the bounds of the modern. Without any doubt, the impressionistic and culturally loaded compilation of source books on Jewish genius in the "observational sciences" reveals them to be subjective. A contemporary study of Jewish achievement, for example, dismisses a standard biographical handbook on American art as a questionable source because none of its editors appear in *Who's Who in America.*[30] But in his reading of Zborowski and Herzog, Storfer takes the print record as a mimetic representation of a "real

18

world." For him, the accomplishments recorded in these "best of" lists illustrate the results of the inheritance of "left hemisphere" skills (324). He concludes that the Jewish brain has certain advantages of training. In 1899 Jewish savant Joseph Jacobs, whose work on Jewish intelligence is discussed in chapter 3, commented that "in races where progress depends upon brain rather than muscle the brain-box broadens out as a natural consequence."[31] It is not very far from nineteenth-century craniometric claims to Storfer's view about left-hemisphere development among Jews; indeed, the last half of his monograph deals with the question of brain anatomy and intelligence. He thus explains Jewish superior intelligence as the transmission of acquired physical characteristics of the brain over generations (339–522).

Storfer has now provided "statistical" detail about Jewish superior intelligence and a catalog of Jewish accomplishments, and has foreshadowed his argument as to how these qualities of mind become qualities of race. Yet this catalog does not completely fulfill his initial promise to show how Jewish superior intelligence is demonstrated in Jewish "proficiency in conducting and playing classical music, acting, selling, and practicing psychotherapy." Classical music (Bruno Walter) and psychotherapy (Sigmund Freud) are accounted for, but his examples for "acting" and "selling" seem to be missing. Acting, even that of Woody Allen, is part of the sphere of American popular culture. The actor, or at least the actress, has a much different role in nineteenth-century accounts of Jewish genius. And the "salesmen" have vanished here as they will vanish in most nineteenth-century accounts. Jewish stockbrokers, savings and loan owners, and bankers, given the climate of the late 1980s and early 1990s, could not appear. Michael Milliken and Albert Einstein in the same list of "smart Jews"—an impossible task for the tabulator of genius. Indeed, the anxiety about the central stereotype of the Jew in the late twentieth century, the economic stereotype, makes it virtually impossible to evoke the merchant in such a context.[32] The conflation of the seeming economic success of the Jew and the representation of Jewish superior intelligence harkens back to older myths of the relationship between virtue and capital, as does Mark Twain's comment in 1898 that the Jew's "contribution to the world's list of great names in literature, science, art,

A Problem Still

music, finance, medicine, and abstruse learning" is "way out of proportion to the weakness of his numbers." But Twain also attributed the hatred of the Jews to "the average Christian's inability to compete successfully with the average Jew in business."[33] The subject of business and the Jews is virtually taboo in contemporary evaluations of Jewish superior intelligence, as it raises the hoary question of Jews and white-collar crime. This question is obliquely raised by Andrew Hacker in an essay published in Steven Fraser's anthology of essays on *The Bell Curve*, in which he stresses "the high level of mental ability needed to perpetrate corporate crimes, ranging from verbal versatility to mathematical sophistication" while not relating this to any specific group discussed in *The Bell Curve* (F 103).

Such a list of accomplishments makes sense only if the ideological presumptions of Storfer's positioning of Jewish superior intelligence and his definition of it are explored. And Storfer makes this very easy for us. Having constructed a unilateral category of the Jew—even Sephardic Jews can be brought back into the fold of smart Jews with a minimal exposure to the "outstanding" form of Israeli life, the kibbutz—that is as much a myth as the ideal life in the shtetl (222–24), he ends his chapter on Jewish superior intelligence with a call for action. The human race can and must become smart Jews:

> What an optimistic scenario this Jewish model offers the human race! If the child development principles employed by the Jewish family can generate such a *multifold increase in the rate of productive genius,* then understanding and utilizing this knowledge for the betterment of all mankind could and should be viewed as a golden opportunity—not just an opportunity to develop a future population of highly intelligent people but, most importantly, an opportunity to use these heightened gifts of intellect to promote the kinds of achievements exemplified by the Jewish mission. (330)

Thus Storfer's chapter on "smart Jews" ends. But it is an ending that needs clarification even in Storfer's eyes. What is the "Jewish mission," as opposed to "the mission to the Jews" that historically was part of European discourse on the conversion of the Jews? He provides his truly dedicated readers with a footnote:

A Problem Still

In virtually every one of the so-called helping professions—medicine, psychology, the shaping of legal and ethical standards, the education of young minds, or the shaping of public opinion, the "people of the book" have made their presence keenly felt. It is almost as though (irrespective of whether the researcher/practitioner was a devout practitioner of the Hebraic faith) his or her efforts have been dedicated to the fulfillment of the "Jewish mission": "To help make the world a better place to live, in the hope that God will finally say 'You have done well my children,' and will cast down his countenance to shine upon the human race and reveal himself anew." (333)

Intelligence is virtue, and both reflect a divine plan. One must take pause here and consider: Is economist Miles J. Storfer, former chief economist of the Department of Social Services, Bureau of Program Forecasting and Economic Analysis, whatever his self-definition, himself possessed of Jewish superior intelligence by dint of his professional role in the "helping professions"?[34] In his superior intelligence, can he tell us all how to improve the species? All human beings can become like Jews—just swaddle your children and talk to them for thirty or forty generations until superior intelligence is so imprinted on your gene pool and the structure of your racial brain that you will never lose it. You will become virtuous, like the good Christian or a good economist, and prepare for the second coming of Christ, when He reveals Himself anew. Thus the biological model of adaptation reveals itself to be the Christian revision of the claim of "the chosen people." Historically, Christianity rewrites the covenant of God with the Jews to alter the claim that only those born within the Jewish covenant could be chosen and expands the covenant to include all peoples who are willing to hear the word of Christ. Storfer's message becomes a gesture of proselytizing in which all people can become intelligent, just like the Jews. The evocation of the priestly blessing evoked in the final quote is double-edged. It is the Christian notion of Christ, the (Jewish?) physician curing the sick as part of his mission to redeem mankind, that haunts this passage. And the smart economist is the surrogate of Christ—or at least of the priest—in this scenario, which

21

is not far from the claims of eugenics for the eventual perfection of the human species.

One does not have to quibble with the notion of whether lawyers are necessarily part of the "helping professions" to realize that the pattern of Jewish professional employment was historically tempered by restrictions on the professions Jews could enter and by Western traditions of family patterns of employment. Freud's choice of his profession as a physician was determined not by the representation of Jewish superior intelligence but by the options open to Jews even in as "open" a society as late-nineteenth-century Vienna.[35] As the son of a truck driver and the grandson of a junkman, my presence in a "Jewish profession" dedicated to the education of young minds was motivated primarily by a desire to move into the middle class, as my father's luckier Jewish contemporaries were able to move into white-collar jobs during the Depression by getting jobs in the post office. As we shall come to see, Storfer's text provides a sense of mission in these discussions of Jewish superior intelligence. But it is a mission not limited to the Jews—it only has value if it can be infinitely replicated.

According to the late Richard J. Herrnstein, a Jew, and his non-Jewish collaborator, Charles Murray, Jews are disproportionately smarter than non-Jews. Alan Ryan claims that "Herrnstein essentially wants the world in which clever Jewish kids or their equivalent make their way out of humble backgrounds and end up running Goldman Sachs or the Harvard physics department."[36] This self-image, according to Ryan, is played off against the assumption that the other end of the "bell curve" is predominately African-American. Miles Storfer postulates that "frequent intrauterine problems and less-favorable family configurations" account for the lower end of the bell curve (119). But this deficiency becomes imprinted on the African-American brain as surely as does the Jewish superior intelligence on the brain of the Jew.

One unspoken aspect of this contemporary American view is that if the Jew is smarter, he is also physically weaker. Again one can contrast the comment made by Joseph Jacobs at the turn of the century: "If they [the Jews] had been forced by persecution to become mainly blacksmiths, one would not have been surprised to find their biceps larger than those of other folk; and similarly, as they have been forced

A Problem Still

to live by their exercise of their brains, one should not be surprised to find the cubic capacity of their skulls larger than that of their neighbors."[37] This notion is linked to the historical assumption of the physical difference of the Jew and to the hidden notion that superior intelligence is a form of biological compensation. Franz Kafka's friend Felix Weltsch wrote in the Prague Zionist journal *Self-Defense* that the Jews must "shed our heavy stress on intellectual preeminence . . . and our excessive nervousness, a heritage of the ghetto. . . . We spend all too much of our time debating, and not enough time in play and gymnastics. . . . What makes a man a man is not his mouth, nor his mind, nor yet his morals, but discipline. . . . What we need is manliness."[38] This lack of manliness is compensated for by genius. The Jewish physician Martin Engländer commented in 1902 that "the inheritance and the quality of life [in the ghetto] evidenced two grotesque parallel facts: the skull size of the Jews is on average greater than that of the non-Jewish population; on the other hand, their chest circumference absolutely and relatively in relationship to body length is less than for non-Jews."[39] Engländer did not need to interpret these "facts" for his Jewish readership at the *fin de siècle,* as they could easily do it for themselves: thin-chested Jews may have "insufficient muscles and badly developed breathing apparatus," may "live with poor nutrition and conditions which harbor infection," and may therefore "have an enormous rate of tuberculosis," but they are smarter than non-Jews. Intelligence is the compensation for the physical weakness signified by small chest circumference and tuberculosis.

Big psyche rather than big biceps or chest: framing *The Bell Curve,* the myth of Jewish-American superior intelligence—and its antithesis, African-American muscular development—remains alive and real in contemporary discourse in a wide range of contexts. Here the problem of the masculinity of the male Jew and its relationship to his intelligence is raised as part of the discourse on Jewish superior intelligence. Or, in Paul Breines's terms, are smart Jews tough Jews?[40]

INTELLIGENCE, THE INTELLECTUAL, AND THE SCIENTIST

The problems attendant to the discussion of Jewish superior intelligence infiltrate the writing of the academic history of "the Jews" even

23

A Problem Still

where there seems to be no direct discussion of "intelligence." Thus there is a standard trope in the writing of the modern history of the Jews that speaks of the "Jewish intellectual" as if this phrase were somehow unproblematic. Is such a view a comment on inherent intellectual ability, social or public status (or image), or virtue? Or is it a mix of all? Are Jewish intellectuals a specific "case," as in Alexander Bloom's excellent study of the New York Jewish intelligentsia, *Prodigal Sons: The New York Intellectuals and Their World,*[41] or Gert Mattenklott's anthology of letters, *Jüdische Intelligenz in deutschen Briefen, 1619–1988* [Jewish intellectuals in German letters, 1619–1988],[42] or in the work of Michael Steinberg, who wrote in 1988 the standard essay, "Jewish Identity and Intellectuality in Fin-de-Siècle Austria: Suggestions for a Historical Discourse" in *New German Critique?*[43] Steinberg's work is but the most recent linkage between "Jews" and "intellectuals" that builds heavily on the work of George Mosse and his sense of the bourgeois educated man of letters [*Bildungsbürgertum*] as the essential self-definition of the secular Jew at the turn of the century. According to Mosse, the Jewish intellectual is the German Jew beyond Judaism, working out his or her role in society through acceptance of the leveling effect of the Enlightenment promise of equality, at least of the intellectuals.[44]

The core of the Jewish intellectual's comprehension of Jewish superior intelligence is that it is a function of the situation of the Jew — and thus anyone can become a Jew — but more important, the Jew can become anyone. For if Jewish superior intelligence is a quality that can eventually be found in all intellectuals, it is no longer a brand that differentiates the Jew. Is this not the underpinning of the claim by Weimar Jewish intellectuals and their heirs, such as Leo Strauss, for a universal aristocracy of the intelligent based on a shared experience, such as the reading of specific "great books"?[45] Such reading makes for moral action and virtuous people. Is this not the answer of the Jewish *Bildungsbürger* who sees in the texts that shaped his identity the ability not only to achieve insight and wisdom but to cancel his own particularity? Cannot everyone become a Jew and eliminate, in universalizing, the representation of a Jewish intellectual particularism, with its racial and negative overtones of inauthenticity and parasitism? Yet

A Problem Still

Strauss understood that institutions could not redeem the Jew. The Enlightenment project failed. Strauss's answer was to create a dialogue among superior minds, which for him included Spinoza and Maimonides, linking Jewish superior intelligence with other forms of intelligence, as in the works of Plato or Rousseau, that were accepted by the bourgeois intelligentsia of Europe. The "Dead White Males" of Strauss's new canon that measured Western intelligence were expanded to include the Jews as Jewish thinkers and as moral preceptors.

The work on "Jewish intellectuals" assumes some link between the "intellectuals" and "intelligence," between those who are defined by the rational (rather than feeling or will) and the faculty of rationality. This Cartesian assumption underlies the role ascribed to the intellectual in modern culture. For in a world of unequal mental talents, those most intelligent should dominate. Shouldn't they? Isn't intelligence also a sign of virtue? And a sign of power and, therefore, of masculinity? Even in the light of the close linguistic relationship between "intellectual" and "intelligent" since at least the seventeenth century, this cultural link is highly problematic. Indeed, as Dietz Bering has elegantly shown in his study of the conceptual history of the intellectual, the term is polluted from its origin during the Dreyfus Affair with complicated references to Jews and their intelligence.[46] The coinage of "Jewish intelligentsia" linked the Jews and their defenders as a collective and exemplified them by a false intelligence and the subsequent undermining of "French virtue."

Thus the question of Jewish superior intelligence is riddled with the rhetoric of nineteenth-century science as well as nineteenth-century racial politics. When seen from this perspective, the symbiotic relationship between "internal" and "external" perspectives must be understood. Those who see "the Jews" as a unitary category from "without" shape the category of Jewish difference. Those who are labeled as different and who must construct the notion of a Jewish superior intelligence from "within" labor under extraordinary handicaps. Those "without" must define themselves vis-à-vis inarticulated ideas of their own intelligence. Those "within" see their intellectual ability at stake. Such views split along precisely the lines we find in the discussion of Jewish superior intelligence in terms of the "insiders"

A Problem Still

and the "outsiders." But there are subtle distinctions that must also be made between these two perspectives. Virtually all the studies that examine Jewish superior intelligence are undertaken as part of the discourse of "science" (psychology, economics, genetics, sociology, etc.), and the definition of the "scientist" may well be part of the configuration of the image of Jewish superior intelligence. In modern science, virtue is tied to the image of the scientist and the relationship between that image and the contemporary understanding of the meaning of science. Is the scientist "virtuous"?

If the construction of Jewish superior intelligence is a projection of a particular identity, that identity is most probably the scientist as intellectual. On the one hand, the "problem of Jewish genius" (to use a nineteenth-century formulation) for the non-Jewish scientist may be a projection of the "intellectual's queerness" onto the Jew.[47] The culture of the nineteenth century, in the long series of "professor's novels" in Germany or the earliest science fiction novels of Jules Verne, saw the scientist's brilliance as a mark of social deviance. One can imagine Professor Otto Lindenbrock from Verne's *Journey to the Center of the Earth* (1864) as does Paul Delvaux in his great canvas, *The Awakening of the Forest* (1939). The professor, off to the corner of the huge canvas, studies a tiny geological specimen while the rest of the canvas is covered with dozens of nubile male and female nudes whom he studiously refuses to see. Being brilliant meant being unattached to the realities of the world in very specific ways—such as not being at the romantic center of the novel. Scientists are rarely the protagonists of sexual or romantic adventures in the nineteenth-century tradition of the academic novel. This demasculinization of the scientist marked the separateness of the scientist from the material world. Such a notion of the "queerness" of the scientist becomes a constituent part of the image of Jewish intelligence.

Yet if scientists were observers in a positivistic model of science, merely observing eyes who record but do not shape the data they uncover, they should have been untouched by the discussion of the role of the scientist as genius, as in the popular image of Pasteur or Koch. Instead they were affected by it. The cultural image of difference is projected by the scientist onto the image of the Jew as a locus of su-

A Problem Still

perior intelligence. Such Jews may be brilliant but their brilliance is in specific ways inherently flawed by their lack of masculinity.

On the other hand, the "queerness" of the scientist was answered by the claim that the scientist was not an intellectual at all—indeed, that the scientist was the least intellectual of all the academic disciplines. So Friedrich Nietzsche wrote in *The Joyful Science* (1887):

> *"Science" as a prejudice*—It follows from the laws of the order of rank that scholars, insofar as they belong to the intellectual middle class, can never catch sight of the really *great* problems and question marks; moreover, their courage and their eyes simply do not reach that far—and above all, their needs which led them to become scholars in the first place, their inmost assumptions and desires that things should be *such and such*, their fears and hopes all come to rest and are satisfied too soon.[48]

Scientists, because they are hampered by the rigid systematization of their world, are the least likely to have true intelligence. They are bound by the paradigms of their psyche and character to see the world in ways that might appear to be brilliant but reveal themselves to be pedantic. This becomes a major problem for the scientists of the nineteenth and early twentieth centuries as they attempt to deal with the meaning of their own intelligence by placing themselves in the broad middle of the bell curve, as "normal" and "virtuous."

Jewish scientists and thinkers must accept the range of meanings attached by a culture to the "intellectual superiority" of the "Jews." "Jewish" (however defined) scientists are simultaneously the object observed and the observer. Placing themselves in this role means that they must constantly reflect on the meaning of their own intelligence, as the institutional presumption of science is that only the "most intelligent" can become scientists. As with all "positive" stereotypes, such as the "noble savage," the construction of a unitary category of difference provides the inventors of the category with subtle means of controlling their own world. Attributing "intelligence" or "cleverness" to the Jews provides a model to explain the relative quality of the observer's intelligence or cleverness. Such a superiority comes to categorize the Jews' intellectual ability as deviant from the norm, as in a bell curve. The invention of the "smart Jew" has little or nothing to do with the real accomplishments or virtue (or lack of accomplishments or absence of virtue) of individual Jews (however defined) in the modern world. No "kernel of truth" in the reality of Jewish activities lies at the core of this "philo-Semitic" myth of generalized Jewish intellectual superiority.

The question is not, as Ian Hacking shows, whether there is a calibration between the thing measured and the instrument that measures.[49] It is not the problem of what psychologists call "construct validity," but rather the establishment of a relationship between two constructed entities: the "Jews" as a racial category and "intelligence." One can measure "intelligence" or "creativity" or "achievement" only after there is a cultural agreement as to what these categories encompass. Therefore there is always an exact calibration between the measure (or the instruments) and the thing measured, as the cultural construct ("intelligence") determines the measurement. Thus, as Hacking suggests, if "intelligence" were a measure of the inability to fulfill the norms of education, if the best students were the stupid students, there would be an accurate correlation, but there would be no consensus as to what was being measured. But a further qualification must be made, as the quality of what is measured can be so constructed as to create subcategories that qualify the thing measured. "Intelligence" can quickly become "craftiness" when this category is applied to the "Jews."

That Jewish scientists and others accept this image as an aspect of the construction of their own identity does not make the image any more valid. Indeed, the existence of this myth is a comment on the anxiety about status and accomplishment that haunts all human beings, which is part of what Karen Horney once described as the *Angst der Creatur,* the anxiety of being a human being. The projection of this anxiety into the world and into the category of "the Jew" is shaped by a Western (read: Christian) definition of the Jew as the inherent marker of difference. That this difference takes the form of "philo-Semitic" myths as well as "anti-Semitic" myths is of little surprise. For the positive images of the Jew as a unitary category provide the location and a control of specific, universal anxieties of inferiority.

A Problem Still

One further aspect of this model of control is that it appears to be fixed and stationary. And yet, as with all stereotypes, it is all-encompassing and ever-shifting. "Jewish intelligence" comes to encompass a wide range of topics. Thus Charles Murray, in his offhand remark at Aspen, also conflates two related, overlapping, and yet, in the literature of the time, quite distinct categories: intelligence (also called genius or cleverness) and talent (also called creativity or facility). In his remarks to a cellist—who may be creative or talented but not necessarily intelligent or clever—he responded to a question about "creativity," that is, about the production of "ancient literature" in Africa. In denying the existence of a "creative" literature he also comments on the intelligence of "the Black." Murray offers the offhand view to the Israeli that "you guys are off the charts"—but which charts? The IQ scale or the creativity scale? Conflating creativity and intelligence adds a greater complexity to the meanings associated with Jewish superior intelligence.

In this book on the construction of the image of Jewish superior intelligence, I examine how the notion of the mind of "Jewish intellectuals" (*jüdische Intellectuellen,* to use the formulation of the age) was constructed primarily by "scientists" from the mid–nineteenth century to today in light of the constantly renegotiated meaning of "intelligence."[50] The examination is also attuned to the association of Jewish superior intelligence with questions of virtue and morality. "Intelligence" becomes the public field on which the role and the purpose of the intellectual is contested. For no one can truly be an "intellectual" unless he or she is also intelligent, though the reverse is not necessarily the case. In defining the "Jewish intellectual," Western European and American culture, through "science," also undertakes to bound its own "intellectuality" and, therefore, its own "intelligence."

This is an ongoing trope. The current *fin-de-siècle* fascination of the academy with intellectuals and their intelligence mirrors in many ways the problem as stated a hundred years ago: who writes the books about the people who write the books? Yet the academic interest with the intelligentsia today is completely narcissistic. *The Bell Curve* may have as its goal the mapping of the origins of crime in Ameri-

A Problem Still

can society, but its major function is to plot Charles Murray onto the map of the conservative intellectual. In grasping the social construction of "the intellectual" and what enables people to be "intellectuals," that is, "intelligence," we desire to measure our own insight and abilities. The end result is clear—if we condemn others as socially deviant, we stand apart from them; if we idealize others as leaders, we identify with them. Whenever we, as members of the academy, comment on "intellectuals," we must be aware that this category must be understood as rigorously self-reflexive in a way that is rare in most other examinations of categories of difference and identity. Otherwise we fall into the trap of seeing ourselves as somehow more able to understand than those whom we create as the class to "be understood." In analyzing *The Bell Curve* and the scientific and popular discussions of Jewish superior intelligence, we must always understand the careful positioning of the authors as "intellectuals."

This book is a short look at the qualities ascribed to Jewish superior intelligence in light of arguments about Jewish difference. It is—I hope—a case study in how praise becomes blame. It is a study in the politics of scientific stereotyping in which the victim is often co-opted into believing that positive stereotypes are accurate comments on his nature. It is a study in "philo-Semitism" and its pitfalls. And it is also an attempt to examine the Jewish response and internalization of this image. Leon Wieseltier, in his very Jewish response to *The Bell Curve,* bemoans what would have happened if he had been born "differently," if his intelligence had predetermined him to be a tailor (like his mythic ancestors?) rather than an intellectual. He notes that "I am, after all an Ashkenasic Jew of European origins. More to the point, a retreat to tailoring is precisely what Murray would prescribe for a Jew who discovered, as the result of some new 'definitive' measurement, that he was a member of the cognitive underclass" (F 159). What Wieseltier does not imagine is that being a Jewish intellectual, believing oneself to be a member of the "cognitive elite," has its own problems in terms of being different from the norm. This difference is the topic of this book.

2

The Origins and Format
of the Image

FRANCIS GALTON AND JEWISH CHARACTER

THOSE WHO DEFINE themselves as non-Jewish took many different approaches to Jewish intellectual ability during the nineteenth century. All accept the notion that Jews are or are claimed to be, by one measure or another, intellectually superior to other racial groups. Like Miles Storfer, proponents of a quasi-theological approach see Jewish superior intelligence as a biological advantage of Jewish practice, specifically a beneficial result of the divinely inspired "hygienic" laws followed by the Jews. In 1874, the Louisiana physician Madison Marsh commented on the "fact" of the Jew's "high average physique . . . [as being] not less remarkable than the high average of his intelligence."[1] Marsh's comments are grounded in his understanding that any nation, as long as it adheres to the hygienic practices prescribed in the Bible, can become as inherently healthy and intelligent as the Jew. Health is a divine sign of virtue.

Such views linking "the Jews" as a unitary category with notions of "health" and "illness" are a commonplace in the medical literature of the time. Jews are either mad, ill, and immoral or brilliant, healthy, and virtuous. What appears to be a dichotomy is, in fact, a common trope that constructs the inherent and negative difference of the Jews from the standpoint of the "scientific" observer.[2] Implicit in this view is the contrast or identification between the "intelligence" of the intellectual observing the Jew and the Jew who is observed. It is vital to see how the observer is defined, for Marsh speaks as a physician/scientist whose authority rests on his "intellectual" ability to evaluate the "facts" that he has gathered to make his argument.

Marsh positions himself on the British end of the two great mid-nineteenth-century models of "genius." One model is that of the upper-middle-class British savant (and cousin of Charles Darwin) Francis Galton, who attempted in 1869 to tabulate "hereditary genius."[3] Galton's view is rooted in the notion of the inheritance of genius and grew out of his interest in the "mental peculiarities of different races." In the preface to his study, Galton acknowledges the pres-

33

ence of genius in Jews and Italians, "both of whom appear to be rich in families of high intellectual interest," but he feels that he cannot include them in his present study. Yet at least one poet "of Jewish parentage" was included in his list—Heinrich Heine (234). Heine's presence in this list of "hereditary genius" places Galton's initial bracketing of Jewish "families of high intellectual interest" into question. For in order to reflect the image of high art in the 1860s in Europe, Galton could not exclude Heine, the most widely read continental poet among the moderns. The association of "genius" with "high culture" is as important as the underlying definition, even in England, of superior intelligence as tied to the identification of the scientist with the educated bourgeoisie, the *Bildungsbürger*. Yet when Galton studies the "Jews" as a category, he finds "craftiness" rather than true genius.

In the mind of Francis Galton, genius is a virtue. Galton postulated for the first time the existence of a "bell curve," a "normal" distribution of genius that is bound to inheritance. He created this distribution in analogy to the "normal" distribution of height. In the latter case environmental factors can play a major role; in the former, the question of "genius" is complicated by Galton's definition of it as that quality measured by the appearance of individuals' biographies in standard reference books. He begins his categories of the deployment of genius with "the judges of England between 1660 and 1865" and notes that "a judgeship is a guarantee of its possessor being gifted with exceptional ability" (55). The social dimension of such appointments— a social dimension that also happens to run in British families—is submerged, and the sole criterion is the inherited wisdom of the judges passed down across generations. Galton continues to tabulate famed statesmen, peers, commanders, literary men, men of science, poets, musicians, painters, divines, and senior classics of Cambridge, but he concludes with oarsmen and wrestlers of the north country. Here the mix between ideas of intelligence and talent is clear; Galton also evidently sees inheritance of athletic ability as a form of "genius" because of its inheritability. But his examples of inheritance are drawn from the standard reference tools of his day.[4] Those in such lists reflect the "best" of the English race—the upper end of the bell curve.

The race that marks the lower end of the bell curve is the African. Galton observes that "the mistakes the Negroes made in their own matters were so childish, stupid and simpleton-like as frequently make me ashamed of my own species." His understanding of the lower end of the bell curve came about "during my travels in Africa" (395). Thus to perceive Galton's formulation of the relationship between measurement, intelligence, and the instruments of measurement, one should return to his initial understanding of the bell curve of intelligence and of the patterns of hereditary genius.

Galton was one of the first "scientist/explorers" in South Africa, and the journal of his 1852 trip catapulted him to fame as a geographer. But it was not the intelligence of the African that Galton attempted to measure during his sojourn in South Africa. He writes in his account of the trip

Mr. Hahn's household was large. There was an interpreter, and a sub-interpreter, and again others; but all most excellently well-behaved, and showing to great advantage the influence of their master. These servants were chiefly Hottentots, who had migrated with Mr. Hahn from Hottentot-land, and, like him, had picked up the language of the Damaras. The sub-interpreter was married to a charming person, not only a Hottentot in figure, but in that respect a Venus among Hottentots. I was perfectly aghast at her development, and made inquiries upon that delicate point as far as I dared among my missionary friends. The result is, that I believe Mrs. Petrus to be the lady who ranks second among all the Hottentots for the beautiful outline that her back affords, Jonker's wife ranking as the first; the latter, however, was slightly *passée,* while Mrs. Petrus was in full *embonpoint.* I profess to be a scientific man, and was exceedingly anxious to obtain accurate measurements of her shape; but there was great difficulty in doing this. I did not know a word of Hottentot, and could never therefore have explained to the lady what the object of my foot-rule could be; and I really dared not ask my worthy missionary host to interpret for me. I therefore felt in a dilemma as I gazed at her form, that gift of bounteous nature to this favoured race, which no mantua-maker, with all her crinoline and stuffing, can do otherwise but humbly imitate. The object of my admiration stood under a tree, and was turning herself about to all points of the compass, as ladies who wish to be admired usually do. Of a sudden my eye fell upon my sextant; the bright thought struck me, and I took a series of observations upon her figure in every direction, up and down, crossways, diagonally, and so forth, and I registered them carefully upon an outline drawing for fear of any mistake; this being done, I boldly pulled out my measuring tape, and having thus obtained both base and angles, I worked out the results by trigonometry and logarithms.[5]

The difference that captures Galton's attention is sexual difference: difference of the body, not of the mind. And he captures that difference by interposing the instruments of science. Thus, voyeurism becomes science and the intellectual position of the scientist/intellectual is shown to be dependent on his ability to use scientific instruments, like the sextant, to measure the female "object of admiration."

When Galton actually measures the Jews, a similar displacement occurs. It was not Jewish superior intelligence but the "Jewish physiognomy" that Galton tried to capture in composite photographs of "boys in the Jews' Free School, Bell Lane."[6] Galton photographed a number of pupils in this school and used a form of multiple exposure to create an image of the "essence" of the Jew—not just the Jew's physiognomy but the Jew's very nature. Such an interposition of the instruments of technology, as with his earlier use of the sextant, enabled him to reduce the Jew to the object of observation and to place the Jew in a specific and limited category: science as measurement through an intermediary to create a type. This methodology found acceptance, as he was invited to give two papers to the Anthropological Institute "on the race characteristics of the Jews."

Galton believed that he had captured the "typical features of the modern Jewish face." The use of the photograph rather than sketches as a means of recording this difference was actually suggested to him by Herbert Spencer. Galton's trip to the Bell Lane school confronted him with the "children of poor parents, dirty little fellows individually, but wonderfully beautiful, as I think, in these composites." There, and in the adjacent "Jewish Quarter," he saw the "cold, scanning gaze of man, woman, and child" as the sign of Jewish difference, of their potential pathology, and of their inherent nature: "There was no sign

of the Image

of diffidence in any of their looks, nor of surprise at the unwonted intrusion. I felt, rightly or wrongly, that every one of them was coolly appraising me at market value, without the slightest interest of any other kind."[7] It is in the Jews' gaze that the pathology of their soul, the true meaning of their superior intelligence, can be found. Using Galton's photographs, the anthropologist Hans F. K. Günther, whose anthropology of the Jews was a standard work of Nazi science during the 1930s and 1940s, attempted to describe the "sensual," "threatening," and "crafty" gaze of the Jew as the direct result of the physiology of the Jewish face and as reflecting the essence of the Jewish soul.[8] This is the reading of the "bell curve" when science applies its instruments to the physiognomy and, therefore, to the mind of the Jews. The "notable families" and their genius hinted at in the 1860s have become reduced to the average "crafty" Jew. And for Galton and Günther, the photograph is the instrument of choice because it is objective science. Galton makes no such claim for his selection of geniuses; he knows full well that his list of names is impressionistic.

The Jewish social scientist Joseph Jacobs, whose discussion of intelligence was heavily indebted to Galton, was taken aback by Galton's reading of the "bell curve" concerning Jewish genius. He reacted differently to Galton's finding of an absolute Jewishness of the gaze:

Cover up every part of composite A but the eyes, and yet I fancy any one familiar with Jews would say: "Those are Jewish eyes." I am less able to analyze this effect than the case of the nose. . . . I fail to see any of the cold calculation which Mr. Galton noticed in the boys at the school, at any rate in the composites A, B, and C. There is something more like the dreamer and thinker than the merchant in A. In fact, on my showing this to an eminent painter of my acquaintance, he exclaimed, "I imagine that is how Spinoza looked when a lad," a piece of artistic insight which is remarkably confirmed by the portraits of the philosopher, though the artist had never seen one. The cold, somewhat hard look in composite D, however, is more confirmatory of Mr. Galton's impression. It is noteworthy that this is seen in a composite of young fellows between seventeen and twenty, who have had to fight a hard battle of life even by that early age.[9]

37

The Origins and Format

For a Jewish social scientist such as Jacobs, the inexplicable nature of the Jewish gaze exists to mark the Jew. Unlike Galton, Jacobs seeks a social reason for the "hard and calculating" glance. Jacobs's example of that glance is one of the standard figures evoked in the discussions of Jewish superior intelligence during the nineteenth century, Benedikt Spinoza, who was supposed to reveal through his Jewish visage the craftiness of his race. In the anthropological literature of the age, the Jewish "race" could never be truly intelligent, only "crafty."[10]

Another source from the 1860s provides a contemporary corollary between the Jews' appearance, intelligence, and character. In the standard American phrenological text at midcentury, Samuel R. Wells's *New Physiognomy, or, Signs of Character: As Manifested through Temperament,* the Jew's appearance is the guide to his mercenary character.[11] Wells speaks of the fact that "the more cultivated and advanced the race, the finer the nose" (189). Yet the Jews' nose has not changed after millennia. It shows a "worldly shrewdness, insight into character, and ability to turn insight into profitable account" (196) and is a sign of "commercialism" (196). "The Jew has a larger head than the Arab, and at present undoubtedly stands at the head of the Semitic sub-races" because of his intelligence (445). His intellectual qualities are clear: "He is religious; he is fond of trade; he is thrifty; he is unconquerably true to his racial proclivities; he is persistent in everything he undertakes." He is also "prejudiced, bigoted, stern, stubborn, irascible, exacting, secretive, and unrelenting" (445). Such are the qualities Galton found in the eyes of the Jew.

Galton's views about genius are paralleled and in many ways preempted for the latter nineteenth century by the work of Italian Jewish forensic psychiatrist Cesare Lombroso, which is discussed in more detail in the next chapter. Lombroso also first addressed this question in the 1860s when he drew analogies between the products of genius and works made by the insane. If for the non-Jewish Galton genius is the positive, exceptional individual, for Lombroso it is deviance above the norm. Thus, by the 1860s the scientist/intellectual used "intelligence" to label his own difference. For Galton, "intelligence" marked the originality of the scientist as intellectual; for Lombroso, it signaled difference between the insight of the scientist, a category that cuts across all groups, and the degenerate—who in his system replaces the Jew.[12] One might add that by 1892, when Galton revised his work on genius, he had adapted Lombroso's view, seeing in the families of those with genius "often insanity or idiocy [that] has appeared among the near relatives of exceptionally able men." Here too he attempts to rescue the category of "genius," for it is only the "relative [who] would be 'crank,' if not insane"—not the genius![13] The genius may not be mad, but his family is! Here "family" can be read in an extended manner: for Lombroso, the genius is mad; for Galton, the family is the replacement for the race. The maddest families can have an odd genius or two, even among the Jews. But the Jews themselves constitute a negative force in human development. Indeed, Galton argues in the 1892 edition, based on remarks he made in his 1892 Presidential Address to the International Congress of Demography, that the exclusion of the Chinese and Jews "from the customary privileges of settlers in [three] continents" may have a salutary effect on the development of the human species analogous to eugenic selection of the "appropriate" individuals and the "abstention from marriage" by the weaker members of the human race (35).

For the Louisiana physician Madison Marsh, the certification of his own ability lies in his position in his society, that of the physician/scientist writing in a scientific journal. In addition, his society, the Reconstruction South, is consumed by the idea of race and focuses on a "scientific" definition of racial contours. In such societies, the question of the "superior" race is as important as that of the "inferior" race. Marsh's comment on the "high average . . . intelligence" of the Jews is a result of his view that the Jews, through their divinely revealed hygienic laws, provide a model by which all "Caucasian" peoples could achieve the same level of physical and mental ability. For Galton, the colonial model of the science of the observer, so clearly demonstrated in his trip to South Africa, provides an analogous difference. One further aspect is also clear: for Galton the scientific observation of the Jew is equivalent to that of the Woman. The "crafty" Jews who critically scanned him in the East End are reduced to the composite image of the male Jew in his photographs. The composite image thus created subsumes the females who also observed him into the image

The Origins and Format

of the male. Jewish genius is different enough to be understood as a quality of the most feminine of the races (according to contemporary commentators), the Jews.

Even the ideological opponents of Jewish ritual practices, such as Ernst von Schwartz (1905), agreed that "Moses was the great, wise reformer and hygienist."[14] If Moses was divinely inspired and the gifts provided to him and the Jews are accessible to all who desire to follow the Divine, Jewish intelligence is potentially the state of all "Caucasian" peoples. This position argues the universal acquisition of "Jewish intelligence" if the divinely revealed laws of God (here seen within the Christian reading of the Old Testament) are obeyed. The scientific observer has the intelligence and the insight to see this. In this field concerned with the intellectual and the intelligence of the Jew, the complexity of the construction of a Jewish mind can be found.

By the 1920s, assumptions about Jewish intelligence were keyed to a canon of "smart Jews." Spinoza and Moses had become touchstones for explaining the special nature of the Jew otherwise seen only as the perpetual outsider and deicide. Such a catalogue of Jewish achievement becomes part of the ironic interrogation that marks Leopold Bloom's and Stephen Dedalus's discussion about the Jews:

> Accepting the analogy implied in his guest's parable which examples of postexilic eminence did he adduce?
> Three seekers of the pure truth, Moses of Egypt, Moses Maimonides, author of *More Neubkim* (Guide of the Perplexed) and Moses Mendelssohn of such eminence that from Moses (of Egypt) to Moses (Mendelssohn) there arose none like Moses (Maimonides). . . .

> Were other anapocryphal illustrious sons of the law and children of a selected or rejected race mentioned?
> Felix Bartholdy Mendelssohn (composer), Baruch Spinoza (philosopher), Mendoza (pugilist), Ferdinand Lassalle (reformer, duellist).[15]

In Dublin, on that fateful day in June 1904, Bloom the Jew presents a justification of the Jews in their achievements. And this list includes not only the "creative" Jews (such as lawgivers, philosophers, and composers) but "manly" Jews (such as boxers and duellist/politicians). Given the doubts about Bloom's manliness in the context of this novel, this catalogue presents the ironic self-justification of the Jew as outsider that "he" really is an insider.

Such views have an unironic echo in the science of the day. The assumptions about Jewish superior intelligence are appropriated in the field concerned with the improvement of the species through the increase of intelligence. In 1929, Thurman B. Rice, one of the leading American academic eugenists, wrote,

RACE CULTURE AND RELIGION. It is a strange fact that many persons of a religious turn of mind are very doubtful of the propriety of many of the teachings of racial hygiene, and yet a great number of these same teachings are identified with the principles set forth in Holy Writ. The chosen people of Israel are the most spectacular and successful of all experiments in human race culture. The principle of keeping the race pure is nowhere better illustrated than in the history of the Jewish people; sex hygiene began with the Jews; race hygiene was almost a fetish with them.

The result is that the Jewish race in spite of centuries of persecution, still persists with a religion, language and tradition intact, and with a race consciousness and solidarity which are quite remarkable in the light of the jumbled national history that has been theirs. Although scattered in the four winds the Jews remain Jews; races rise and fall but Israel is immortal. In every line of progress the Jew stands at or near the head of the list and has done so for forty or more centuries. In science and medicine, in philosophy and literature, in music and art, in statesmanship, business and finance, investigation will show that a large percentage of the men at the very top are Jews. There is no better argument for the universal practice of the principles of eugenics than the marvelous success of the Jewish race—the only race to put a rational race hygiene to the test, and probably as a consequence, the only race of importance to have a history of progress extending over a period as long as a thousand years.[16]

Self-selection becomes the key to any understanding of the preeminence of Jewish superior intelligence. But it is a self-selection that now puts "Moses" in the place of Galton as the ideological founder of eugenics. Hegel's concern about the anomalous position of the Jew in history as a people that seems never to vanish like other historical peoples is transmuted into a proof for the racial resilience of the Jews through divinely inspired science. It is, of course, a resilience that can be copied by any "people."

ANATOLE LEROY-BEAULIEU AND

THE DEFENSE OF THE JEWS

Certainly the most widely read "philo-Semitic" *fin-de-siècle* analysis of the "genius" of the Jews, after Francis Galton's refusal to include the Jews in his study of hereditary genius, was undertaken by Anatole Leroy-Beaulieu, a French historian and member of the French Academy, in his 1893 study *Israel among the Nations: A Study of Jews and Antisemitism.*[17] Written immediately prior to the Dreyfus Affair, this volume proposed a complex analysis of Jewish intelligence on the eve of the first major political catastrophe of acculturated European Jewry. Leroy-Beaulieu's text frames the discussions of Jewish intelligence at the turn of the century. Not only does he summarize the common threads in European culture on the nature of Jewish intelligence, he also creates a "friend" whose voice represents the anti-Semitic rhetoric of his time. In this text the reader has an attempt to create a "scientific" discourse examining and "positively" explaining Jewish genius as well as a countervoice that denies or "negatively" explains these qualities. Thus Leroy-Beaulieu's text can serve as an outline for the debates and their rationales as it reveals in the construction of this apparent dichotomy the inner contradictions of both perspectives.

In the chapter "Jewish Genius," Leroy-Beaulieu follows his question of whether there is a specific Jewish psychology with an investigation of whether that psychology produces exceptional individuals. He explains what Thorstein Veblen in 1919 called "that massive endowment of spiritual and intellectual capacities [of which the Jews] have given evidence throughout their troubled history, and not at least during these concluding centuries of their exile."[18] The psychology of the Jew is the result of two thousand years of persecution, writes Leroy-

of the Image

Beaulieu, but the real question is "whether there is a Jewish genius or spirit, that is to say, whether in letters, science and politics the Jew is characterized by a national genius or a national spirit different from that of the nations among whom he lives" (226). Here the limits placed on the definition of "intelligence" or "genius" forms the basis for any discussion of the intellectual. For Leroy-Beaulieu, "genius" exists only in "letters, science and politics." For Veblen it exists in "science and scholarly pursuits."[19] These areas form a specific category that excludes the "material," which is traditionally associated with pre-emancipated Jewry. No "genius" can be associated with capital and its formation. Only the realm of the *philosophes* can be the province of the intellectual and "genius."

Yet the fields that Leroy-Beaulieu points to as showing the "highest ability" of the Jews are "music and philology." The rationale for the latter seems to be a cultural one. The Jew is "compelled to be a polyglot." But Leroy-Beaulieu also quotes an unnamed (anti-Semitic) friend, whose remarks echo through this chapter, that the "rules of [philology] were easily mastered by the Jew, quick at every sort of change" (234). It is the permanent mutability of the Jew that marks his abilities as a philologist. This mutability is a racial quality. Veblen in 1919 agrees that "a peculiarly fortunate intellectual endowment, native and hereditary" does exists among the Jews, but he does not accept that endowment as sufficient to explain the "intellectual pre-eminence" of Jews in the modern world.[20] For him, any denial of "special Jewish traits, of character and of capacity, . . . any refusal to recognize something which may be called a Jewish type of hereditary endowment would come to nothing much better than a borrowing of trouble."[21] Hidden within the recesses of Leroy-Beaulieu's chapter are echoes of this argument about inheritance and its risks.

For Leroy-Beaulieu, "Jewish Genius" can best be seen in music, which was the arena for the initial dismissal of Jewish superior intelligence as mere mimicry. In 1850, Richard Wagner, in his widely read essay "Jewishness in Music," turned to the question of the nature of the Jews' aesthetic sensibilities as a result of his personal conflict with the popular Franco-Jewish composer Giacomo Meyerbeer. (Meyerbeer's operas were simply more popular in Paris than were Wagner's,

43

a fact which Wagner understood in racial terms.) Wagner, in line with the general view of Christian Europe, denied the Jew any ability to create aesthetically valid works of art, such as musical compositions, by denying the Jew access to civilized discourse:

> By far more weighty, nay, of quite decisive weight for our inquiry, is the effect the Jew produces on us through his speech; and this is the essential point at which to sound the Jewish influence upon music. The Jew speaks the language of the nation in whose midst he dwells from generation to generation, but he speaks it always as an alien. As it lies beyond our present scope to occupy ourselves with the cause of this phenomenon, too, we may equally abstain from an arraignment of Christian Civilization for having kept the Jew in violent severance from it, as on the other hand, in touching the sequelae of that severance we can scarcely propose to make the Jews the answerable party. Our only object, here, is to throw light on the aesthetic character of the said results. In the first place, then, the general circumstances that the Jew talks the modern European languages merely as learnt, and not as mother tongues, must necessarily debar him from all capability of therein expressing himself idiomatically, independently, and conformably to his nature in any higher sense. A language, with its expression and its evolution, is not the work of scattered units, but of an historical community; only he who has unconsciously grown up within the bond of this community, takes also any share in its creation. But the Jew has stood outside the pale of any such community, stood solitarily with his Jehovah in a splintered, soilless stock, to which all self-sprung evolution must stay denied, just as even the peculiar (Hebraic) language of that stock has been preserved for him merely as a thing defunct. Now to make poetry in a foreign tongue has hitherto been impossible, even to geniuses of highest rank. Our whole European art and civilization, however, have remained to the Jew a foreign tongue; for, just as he has taken no part in the evolution of the one, so has he taken none in that of the other; but at most the homeless person has been a cold, nay more, a hostile onlooker. In this Speech,

this Art, the Jew can only mimic and mock—not truly make a poem of his words, an artwork of his doings.[22]

For Wagner it is a racial predisposition that makes the Jew never truly original in his contributions to music. Such views denying Jews creativity, even as they acknowledge Jewish cultural presence, are echoed in the work of the anti-Semites of the late nineteenth century, such as in Eugen Dühring's comment that "in their entire long history the Jews have never contributed anything to the sciences" or Houston Stewart Chamberlain's view that the Jews "evidence an absolute ignorance and cultural crudeness that has never made the smallest contribution to a single area of human knowledge or creativity."[23] The contrasting notion of a Jewish superior intelligence was supported by the contested image of the Jew as the most modern (and, therefore, most creative) of thinkers, as in the later views of Nietzsche. Nietzsche, in *Human, All too Human,* saw the Jews as having produced "the noblest human being (Christ), the purest sage (Spinoza), the mightiest book and the most efficacious moral code in the world." But it is also the "nation" that preserved the intellectual patrimony of the West against the onslaught of "Asia." "In the darkest periods of the Middle Ages, when the cloud banks of Asia had settled low over Europe, it was the Jewish freethinkers, scholars, and physicians who, under the harshest personal constraint, held firmly to the banner of enlightenment and intellectual independence and defended Europe against Asia."[24] Yet all these views postulated the Jews as devoid of virtue. For Wagner, Dühring, and Chamberlain, the Jews' immorality was a marker of their character; for Nietzsche it was a sign of their ability to transcend the common world.[25]

Leroy-Beaulieu sees the situation from a reversed perspective. Jews are superior musicians because of their ill treatment at the hands of the Christian world, not because of their inheritance; yet both inheritance and environment are indelibly stamped on their psyches. For Leroy-Beaulieu, music may have its roots in social conditions such as "their compulsory confinement behind the gates of the Ghetto" and their seeking "greater solace than ever in their national melodies" (236). But most likely their "predilection . . . for that one of our modern arts which appeals most searchingly to our inmost being" comes from "the spirit of combination." And this spirit, like the drive for excellence in philology, is a function of the biology of the Jew: "the nervousness which we have already noticed in them predisposes them to the most vibrating of all arts, that one which has most sway over the nerves" (236).

The nervousness of the Jews, according to Leroy-Beaulieu's earlier comments, is a result of two thousand years of persecution; yet, as with all such comments at the turn of the century, it is clear that a radical change in environment will have only a tenuous and partial effect on such long-term acquired characteristics. The anthropologist Ludwig Woltmann, one of the leading German followers of Arthur de Gobineau's definition of race at the turn of the century, commented in 1904 that the "substantially higher percentage of Jews in institutions of higher education cannot be accounted for by a superior ability, but can be explained by the 'family hothouse culture.'" There is no idea of virtue in this rereading of Jewish superior intelligence. Excessive intellectual effort is also one of the most important reasons for the physical collapse of the Jews, specifically the "degeneracy of the nervous systems."[26] Civic emancipation, only a century old, does not yet have the ability to reshape the modern Jew and end his nervousness. Indeed, modernity, with its stress on the intellectual, provides the key to the downfall of the Jew. "Jewish pseudo-intellectualism," following Woltmann, is a sign of the collapse of the race under the strain of the modern. This view is not far from the aura of "immoral Jewish music" as postulated by Wagner.

Leroy-Beaulieu, in seeming to make nervousness an environmental rather than a racial category, also sees it as the wellspring of a positive idea of intelligence and creativity. From this "nervousness" comes the Jew's "taste for versifying" (236), "scarcely to be expected in this commercial race" (237). And Leroy-Beaulieu, as with virtually all *fin-de-siècle* writers on Jewish intelligence including Galton, cites as his example Heinrich Heine, the touchstone in the late nineteenth century for Jewish "originality." Leroy-Beaulieu notes that German critics, such as William (Wilhelm) Scherer, dismiss Heine out of a sense of "race pride" and deny him "all originality and inventive faculty" (251). For the French scholar Leroy-Beaulieu the combination of Heine's

of the Image

"residence in France" and his "Jewish extraction" make him a genius. Leroy-Beaulieu also comments on the fact that each nation, when it looks at the Jews from a positive perspective, sees in them exactly those qualities that it prizes in itself.

Heine's irony "has a touch of the Satanic," however, as the Jew functions like the "deformed person": "We know how caustic is the wit of deformed persons; Judaism was regarded, for centuries, as a sort of deformity" (258). But Heine is also a convert; and Leroy-Beaulieu commented that the irony of the Jew is the weapon by which "the baptized Jew takes vengeance upon the God of the Christians and upon their social system, for the disgrace of compulsory baptism" (258). Thus Heine serves as the exemplary Jewish genius and intellectual/poet. He contains within his self-construction all aspects of the image of the Jew, from the erotic feminine to the diseased.[27] Or, in the *fin-de-siècle* bon-mot by a Viennese Christian Social politician, "literature is what one Jew plagiarizes from another."[28]

Genius in poetry is the result of nervousness; genius in the theater is the result of the "self-centered" nature of the Jew, whose mutability, seen as a racial quality, is "modeled by his sons and daughters with the muscles of their faces, and painted with the accents of their voices" (238). In the words of Leroy-Beaulieu's typical anti-Semite, the Jew possesses a "monkey- or squirrel-like agility" (246). Indeed, this is the view of Werner Sombart, the most important German sociologist of the turn of the century to comment on the nature of Jewish genius. For him the "intellectual attributes of the Jews," whether in the desert or in the banks of Europe, "have remained constant for thousands of years."[29] This is not necessarily a quality of race ("there is no certain connection between somatic attributes and intellectual capacities") but may well be a result of "the aid of tradition." Yet Sombart does not eliminate the possibility that "Jewish characteristics *may* spring from the blood." The qualities of the Jewish mind, of the "common mental constructions" that define the Jew, usually are understood in *fin-de-siècle* culture as negative and destructive.[30] Sombart stressed the economic hegemony of the Jews over the Christians from the Middle Ages to the early twentieth century. Economic control was the result of adaptation, and adaptation was a pathological quality. For Leroy-

47

The Origins and Format

Beaulieu, the "Jew's flexibility, his talent for imitation and his faculty of assimilation" is the result of the "trades which we have forced on him and the low esteem in which we have held him" (239). It is the low quality, the anti-intellectualism of capital, that has led the Jew to the nervousness and mimicry that provide the basis for his genius.

This mimicry is seen best in Jewish actresses, such as Sarah Bernhardt (1844–1923) and Rahel [Félix] (1820–58), and their innate ability to "distinguish themselves . . . in awe-inspiring tragedy" (239). In an aside on Sarah Bernhardt, Leroy-Beaulieu comments on the tortured relationship between emancipation and gender, between master and slave, in the contemporary French theater: "It was a strange revenge, won by art or genius, when an uneducated Jewess, picked up one morning in the street, gave to the royal creations of our classical poets their noblest embodiment" (239). But productive mimicry as a quality of genius has a hidden, pathological dimension. Earlier in his text, Leroy-Beaulieu also inadvertently comments on the feminization of the male Jew as the result of the pathologies of the Jew. The difference of the male Jew is visualized in terms of a gendered image of illness, specifically the image of the tubercular female, who is "beautiful" but dangerous and "diseased."

The Jew's "bodily infirmity" is marked by the Jew's "unmanly appearance." He is like but not identical to the tubercular woman, specifically the tubercular Jewish woman. His visage is like "those lean actresses, the *Rahels* and *Sarahs,* who spit blood, and seem to have but the spark of life left, and yet who, when they have stepped upon the stage, put forth indomitable strength and energy. Life, with them, has hidden springs" (150). Sarah Bernhardt and Rahel, the two best-known Jewish actresses on the nineteenth-century Parisian stage, both tubercular, are evoked to mark the essence of the normal physiognomy of the *male* Jew. Here the question of mimicry vanishes as the tubercular female actress comes to embody the image of the Jew.

But Leroy-Beaulieu's Jewish actress simply represents the essence of Jewish "sterility" and "parasitism" he hopes to counter.[31] This view ends with Adolf Hitler's comment three decades later in *Mein Kampf* that "the Jewish people, despite all apparent intellectual qualities, is without any true culture, and especially without any culture of its own. For what sham culture the Jew today possesses is the property of other peoples, and for the most part it is ruined in his hands."[32] The classical anti-Semitic view, represented in Leroy-Beaulieu's text by Richard Wagner's comments cited above, is that the Jews are an "inferior race" (247). Unable to produce anything "original," the Jew, in his "absence of creative power, of spontaneity and of originality . . . displays in this respect something of a woman's nature. The Semites are said to be a feminine race, possessing to a high degree the gift of receptivity, always lacking in virility and procreative power" (246–47).

This view is countered in Leroy-Beaulieu's discussion of Jewish genius as a masculine force, in which the Jew's relationship to capital is not solely a socially constructed one. For the Jew has "the bump of mathematics" and has great genius in "mathematics, physics, and the natural sciences" as well as medicine (239–40). It is the "talent for combination and calculation [that], for ages, has been inherent in this race" (240). This talent is seen by Leroy-Beaulieu as an inherent failing, as the Jew "is even more apt than any other race to exaggerate the value of mathematics and to abuse the inductive method" (240). His examples are Spinoza, Ricardo, and Marx!

The center of Leroy-Beaulieu's anxiety concerning the Jews is whether this genius in all of its "ascendancy" would "threaten to de-nationalize the modern nations" (226). For the transnational presence of Jewish genius in Europe would work against the established national boundaries if this genius were inherently different from the "genius" of the various nations among which the Jews lived. To examine this threat, Leroy-Beaulieu begins with a sketch of what he judged to be the "principal features" of Jewish genius. He departs from Ernest Renan's definition of the Jews as the people of the desert: "not an artistic, but a prophetic people," possessing an "inflexible Hebrew genius," that was "all of a piece, like the bare rocks that loom up far off in the desert" (227). Renan (1823–92) is Leroy-Beaulieu's authority but also his prime foil. Leroy-Beaulieu cites Renan's history of the Semitic languages (1858),[33] for example, when he wishes to stress the originality of Jewish genius, stating that "the eminently subjective character of Arabian and Hebrew poetry is due to another trait of the Semitic spirit, to its complete lack of creative imagination and to the consequent absence of fiction" (247). This view became a standard anti-Semitic view, as in the *fin-de-siècle* statement of Wagner's son-in-law Houston Stewart Chamberlain that the Jews "possess no imagination . . . All who have any claim at all to speak, testify unanimously that lack—or let us say poverty—of imagination is a fundamental trait of the Semite."[34]

But those were the Jews of the Bible; today's Jews "issued from the Ghetto and the *Talmud-Tora*" (227). These recently emancipated Jews already have "invaded the chairs of our universities, the stages of our theaters, and even the platforms of our political assemblies." Here again the new genius of the Jews finds the trinity of "letters, science and politics" central to their new self-redefinition. It is in these "professions, . . . which demand only intelligence and application," that the Jews have flourished. The alternative meaning of the selection of these professions is that they are signs of the avoidance of physical labor. This can be seen in Sombart's comment that "even in Talmud times Jews preferred those callings which necessitated a lesser expenditure of physical energy."[35] Jews cluster in greater numbers in "science, literature, and art" and seem to have "three or four, often indeed—as it would really appear—ten times, as much aptitude . . . as the ordinary Gentile" (231). It is this very success, according to Leroy-Beaulieu, that is the "chief cause of the anti-Semitic spirit" (230).

Leroy-Beaulieu develops the question whether, given that the genius of the Jew is not a superior evolutionary quality, Jewish genius is simply the breeding of a superior race showing the "benefits to be derived from the crossing of neighboring races" (233). One must note that superior "Jews" are often cited as "men of half-Jewish blood." This is the antithetical view of the *Mischling* found in the work of anti-Semitic writers such as Werner Sombart.[36] For Sombart, race mixing may create "genius," but it is of a negative and destructive shape.

And yet Leroy-Beaulieu employs a biological model: the qualities are transmittable and translatable. And it is this model that "rescues" the Jews. Leroy-Beaulieu comes to accept the fact that the "Jews . . . with respect to social tendencies were receptive and not originative" (248). He asks, because the Jew has no "distinctive genius and is only capable of imitating, of borrowing, of transmitting to some what it has received from others, how can this slim remnant of Judah, thinned by intermixture with a hundred peoples, endanger our national genius?" (249). The secret of Jewish genius is "the faculty of assimilating, at the same time, the special aptitudes of two peoples" (253). The Jew is open to assimilation; his "pores are not closed" as are those of the Germans and the French. Thus "the modern Jew responds more rapidly than ourselves to the influences of his environment and his time" (253). Modernism is the mark of Jewish identity, and only the Germans fear this. Leroy-Beaulieu observes, concerning the comparative intelligence of the Germans (but not the French) and the Jews, "I have heard Germans urge this intellectual precocity of the Jews as a reason for debarring their children from the schools and colleges attended by other children. 'The struggle,' they said, 'between the sons of the North, the pale Germans with their blond hair and sluggish intellects, and these sons of the Orient with their black eyes and alert minds, is an unequal one'" (171–72). Not only are these displaced "Orientals" different in their bodies and their psyches from the Germans, but in their gaze they are smarter than the Germans (but certainly not smarter than the French). And the modern is the key to the coming age of Jewish assimilation in France and to eventual French superiority in the world. Thus it is the "Frenchness" of Jewish superior intelligence that will prove its value in the future. This assimilation is a result of the selection of the Jews in the course of their history, even in the world of present-day France.

EARLY-TWENTIETH-CENTURY READINGS OF JEWISH SUPERIOR INTELLIGENCE

The view that Jewish superior intelligence has its roots in the persecution and winnowing of the Jews has a long and complex history in the English-speaking world. In the 1920s Ellsworth Huntington, a sociologist at Yale, argued that the rebellion against the Romans in the first century C.E. weeded out the violent and destructive Jews. What was left was Jewish superior intelligence but not necessarily a more moral people.[37]

Huntington's views were expressly based on assumptions about a Jewish race. After the Shoah, Cyril D. Darlington, professor of botany at Oxford and one of the last clear proponents of Galton's view of genius, argued for a historical selection of the Jews in Babylonian captivity—a division that separated the intelligent wheat (the leaders and priests) from the chaff. The genius of the Jews was thus isolated in exile where it was forced to be self-sufficient and did not have to defend itself against the inroads of poorer genetic stock of those left behind.[38] Such views of the wheat and the chaff follow a rather primitive reading of Spencerian evolution through the means of historical selection. Here "cleverness" as a means of survival marks the quality of Jewish superior intelligence. But both views epitomize an understanding of the origins of Jewish superior intelligence in the biological effects of the persecution of the Jews, a view that is a clear holdover from mid-nineteenth-century views. Does such "genius" have any true virtue?

The Jew is certainly seen as "over-intellectualized," and this over-intellectualization is one of the sources of his pathological state. As the Heidelberg sociologist Alfred Weber noted about the Jews at the turn of the century, "The longer a people undergoes the process of civilization, the more intellectualized it is—to speak in a specifically biological manner: its genetic substance is implanted with intellectual gemmules, so that it is born with the tendency to place all of the aspects of its essence in the conscious which already reflects its personal fate."[39] Weber's understanding of the biological underpinning of Jewish intelligence links it to the process of modernization.

Such a materialist reading of Jewish intelligence is a counterargument to the idea that the physical difference of the Jew as a racial quality defines Jewish nervousness and Jewish genius a priori. The work of Richard Weinberg, a physician at the University of Dorpat/Tartu (now in Estonia), stressed the neurological difference of the Jewish brain, which was seen as being at the source of Jewish intellectual and emotional pathology.[40] Weinberg also wrote a detailed study of Jewish brain weight in the standard Jewish demographic periodical of the turn of the century.[41] In this essay he "proceeds with compass and yardstick ever deeper in the racial body of the Jewish people." And what he finds is very much in line with his earlier work on the degeneracy of Jewish brains: the Jewish brain is lighter, that is, has a lower specific density, than the norm of non-Jewish brains, even though

of the Image

Weinberg finds that the Jewish head is approximately the same size. Combined with his earlier finding that the Jewish brain shows specific pathological anomalies, this leads to the conclusion that Jewish intelligence, as far as it exists, is a sign of psychopathology. Virtue is not found in these "Jewish" brains, but incipient criminality. This is very much in line with the general view established at midcentury by Lombroso, who saw "genius" as a specific form of madness. It is not incidental that Weinberg cites Lombroso on the measurement of the Jewish skull in this context. Here the Jewish scientist becomes the best witness for Jewish difference. Who would know better? Jewish nervousness, for the biological thinkers, is a reflection of the racial predisposition of the Jew and his biological limitations.

Biological arguments concerning adaptation were also made in the ethnological literature of the time, such as in the work of Hans F. K. Günther. For him, "the considerable average intelligence which distinguishes the Jewish people" was the result of the "selection among the Jews" to have offspring who "were able to adapt to the specific conditions of life among foreign peoples, who possessed those talents of empathy into a foreign psychology, prudent demeanor, adroit speech, [and] versatile calculation of all conditions of the environment."[42] Preselection for intelligence through millennia of anti-Semitism becomes one of the staples for the explanation of the "reality" of Jewish superior intelligence. Fritz Lenz, the dean of German eugenics during the Third Reich, held that natural selection meant that those Jews "whose bodily aspect was markedly exotic were less successful than those whose bodily type resembled that of their host."[43] The German Jews "greatly excel in intelligence and alertness" for much the same reason. But these "quick-witted" Jews rarely "fulfill the promise of their early years." Lenz sees this as the transmission of favorable traits for survival but not for true accomplishment.

Ernst Kretschmer, however, as early as his 1919 study of genius, dismisses Günther's notion of the relationship between genius and race.[44] For Kretschmer, "racial" categories are merely types—and while types may evidence more or less brilliance, there is no absolute relationship. In his study of genius, Kretschmer avoids any discussion of the Jews. His examples, paralleling Günther's earlier study of

53

the racial makeup of the Germans, are the various "races" that make up the German people. He argues that the origin of the individual, magnified through what he calls "secondary inbreeding," produces genius (101). Yet he also admits that there is always a "kernel of truth" to claims about genius, even, one would suppose, about claims regarding Jewish superior intelligence (79).

In the same year, Thorstein Veblen, writing in the U.S. journal *Political Science Quarterly,* desired to deny a biological underpinning for "Jewish genius," but his use of strictly biological images of racial mixing reveals the depth of the racialist notion of Jewish identity at the turn of the century. At the close of World War I, Veblen is much clearer in his acceptance of racial heredity as the underpinning of Jewish "intellectual pre-eminence" (220). Yet he too argues that the Jews themselves are a "nation of hybrids," here following the most prominent *fin-de-siècle* anti-Semitic theoretician, Houston Stewart Chamberlain. While Chamberlain sees race mixing as creating negative, impure races, Veblen argues that such race mixing introduces positive qualities. Veblen denies the existence of a Jewish type: "It would perplex any anthropologist to identify a single individual among them all who could safely be set down as embodying the Jewish racial type without abatement" (223). Yet Veblen, like Leroy-Beaulieu, rescues these hybrid offspring of the Jews by using the "single drop of ink" model to be found in the negative literature on racial mixing. A single drop of Jewish blood makes an individual a Jew: "Cross-breeding commonly results in a gain to the Jewish community rather than conversely; and the hybrid offspring is a child of Israel rather than of the gentiles" (223). For Veblen it is the Jews, even in their "hybrid attenuation," that produce "the vanguard, the pioneers, the uneasy guild of pathfinders and iconoclasts, in science, scholarship, and institutional change and growth" (224). But when the Jew is exposed to the "alien lines of gentile inquiry and becomes a naturalized, though hyphenate, citizen in the gentile republic of learning," true creativity arises. The young Jew caught between two worlds remains alienated from both. "His own heritage and outlook [is] untenable" but he must also remain "an alien . . . intellectually" (229–30). With the rise of Zionism, this creative genius must be diminished and the Jews, returning to the fold of

Judaism, will return to the mentality of Talmudic Judaism and lose the "character of free-swung skeptical initiative which their renegades have habitually infused into the pursuit of the modern sciences among the nations" (231). This view comes naturally to Veblen's bicultural argument, in which "hybrid vigor" and "marginality" are related concepts.

Two decades earlier Leroy-Beaulieu believed he had similarly answered the charges that the Jews had no original genius. He saw the Jews as being merely "parasites of arts and sciences" or possessing a genius that was "foreign and antagonistic to our race" (246). He defended the Jews as long as they remained marginal to the enterprise of the Enlightenment but not when they became totally French or totally European, which must run counter to their natural state. If Jews become too much like Christians or Aryans, they are inauthentic: "If the Jew differs from us, so much the better; he is the more likely to bring a little variety into the flat monotony of modern civilization. I am rather inclined to find fault with these sons of Shem—as I find fault with the Orientals who adopt our customs—for resembling and copying us too closely" (261). The Jews must remain separate in their genius and augment that of the European. Mimicry is fine as long as it is identifiable as such; mutability achieves certain ends, but not if the original type is completely effaced. Here too is a prefiguration of Veblen's view that the Jew must be a "hyphenate" to remain creative and virtuous.

Veblen, as an immigrant, sees the state of hyphenation as a virtue in itself. He is writing at a time when this was not only not universally accepted in the United States, but when inherited mental illness or "feeble-mindedness" was being used more and more frequently to exclude potential immigrants. Unlike Veblen, other American social scientists of the age drew different conclusions using a different methodological approach, the quantification of Jewish intelligence following World War I. With the Americanization of the Stanford-Binet test for intelligence by Lewis Terman before World War I, the question of Jewish intelligence came to be used as a sorting mechanism to exclude undesirable immigrants. Alfred Binet, who developed the intelligence test, wanted to show that the intellectual ability of "retarded" individuals could be enhanced by education. The test was a sorting mechanism that enabled the educable to be segregated from the ineducable.[45]

Beginning in 1913 Henry Herbert Goddard became convinced that a much greater proportion of immigrants to Ellis Island was "feeble-minded" than had earlier been determined. He thought the application of the Binet test would help exclude individuals who would become wards of the state. But he assumed that after a good nonmedical training, even lay technicians could sort out the "defective": "After a person has had considerable experience in this work, he almost gets a sense of what a feeble-minded is so that he can tell one afar off." Needless to say, in 1913 a great percentage of these new immigrants were "visible" Eastern European Jews.[46] Russian Jews, mainly Yiddish-speaking, were excluded for reasons of diminished intelligence. The exclusion rate for feeblemindedness increased 500 percent over the initial five years that the testing took place. Yet these tests were rarely seen as comments on Jewish superior intelligence: they located the lower end of the "bell curve" and rarely addressed the upper end.

The Canadian military psychologist Carl Brigham, later a professor at Princeton, published the study "American Intelligence" after the war in which he documented that immigrant Jews possessed lower intelligence. But Brigham had to counter the presumption of Jewish superior intelligence in order to "disprove the popular belief that the Jew is highly intelligent."[47] Even with the testing undertaken by Goddard and the radical increase in exclusion of immigrant Jews based on claims that they possessed a higher rate of mental defectives, the popular and scientific assumption was that Jews possessed a higher number of individuals of greater intelligence. Brigham argued that Jews as a group were more variable, that is, they had relatively more geniuses but a low mean of intelligence. The visibility of the Jew as a genius provides anecdotal evidence: "The able Jew is popularly recognized not only because of his ability, but because he is able and a Jew." It is the surprise at Jewish genius that makes it visible—a parallel argument with other anti-Semitic critics who deny any "genius" to the Jews.

Almost as if to counter the initial psychometric evaluations of Jewish intelligence, a number of pedagogical studies, all of which corrected for language facility, illustrated Jewish intellectual superiority. In 1920 Katharine Murdoch compared five hundred Italian and five hundred Jewish boys in New York City public schools and determined that the Jews were equivalent to nonimmigrant "whites" when the ability to use English was corrected for.[48] Murdoch defined "intelligence" as "the power to deal with certain situations which required the correct use of words and symbols" (150). This definition was echoed in the work of Seago and Koldin, who stressed in their comparative study that "the Jews are superior in mental capacity" to the Italians and that this "superiority is most marked in use and comprehension of language and in abstract verbal ability." They saw no difference "when sex, grade, and age are kept constant."[49] In 1924, May Bere stressed that Jews were more able at tests that measured "abstractedness" and "verbalness."[50] Even Lewis M. Terman, perhaps the best-known empirical student of "genius," found that "data on racial origin indicate that, in comparison with the general population of the cities concerned our gifted children show a 100% excess of Jewish blood."[51] Terman figured that 10.5 percent of the children in his sample were Jewish as against 5 percent of the overall population in the cities he examined. By 1937, Seth Arsenian, in a massive comparative study of Jews and Italians in New York City, showed that Jews had a substantially higher level of intelligence. His explanation was rooted in the closer relation between Yiddish and English and the urban origin of Jewish immigrants as opposed to the rural origin of Italian immigrants. Arsenian noted no difference between boys and girls in either group.[52]

These studies in educational psychology were intended to prove that groups of new immigrants could benefit from the educational system of the United States. The comparative studies of Jews and Italians were answers, as much as Herrnstein and Murray's *The Bell Curve,* to the question of the relationship between the permanent underclass and criminality. Here one must note that when contemporary commentators such as Martin Peretz compare Jewish physicians with Italian restaurateurs, the group excluded from comparison is the African American (F 152). In the studies done in the 1920s and 1930s prior to the northern migration of African Americans from the South, these comparisons are simply not made, because the question is which non-

The Origins and Format

English-speaking group would be most successful. Language comes to function as a racial marker in this context.

Would the Jews remain separate or would they have the intellectual capacity to enter into the mainstream of American life? Was their intelligence sufficient? The studies cited seemed to argue that this was the case, and yet it was precisely because of such studies that quotas were created in the 1920s to limit the access of Jews into the university system. Certainly Jews seemed to have the ability to compete in this new educational system, whether because of their urban culture or genetic background, but was their intelligence of the correct quality to enter into the gentility of the American educational system? That came to be the real question, and quotas seemed to be the appropriate response.

Pedagogical studies such as Murdoch, Bere, and Terman provided an answer to Brigham (and by extension to Goddard) and reflected the debates about language and intelligence. Indeed, both Goddard and Brigham later amended their views about Jewish intellectual inferiority. Each measured the Jews as a group against other immigrant groups or against African Americans. In each case Jewish superior intelligence came to be seen as a function of the comparative examination of the Jew; the observer and his or her group was always held outside the object studied. With this debate about testing, the case is closed. Miles Storfer in 1990 can begin (at least chronologically) his study of Jewish superior intelligence with Terman's study of California schoolchildren and continue to studies in the late 1980s that test various categories of "Jews," from Israelis to Long Island Jews. Because Terman's children remained under study through the close of the twentieth century, Storfer can hook his argument into the studies of the Terman pool and come up with further proof of Jewish superior intelligence. Of course, each category of the "Jew" and each test is constructed to provide very specific reflections of the meaning of Jewish superior intelligence. Storfer's conclusion from the Terman test, for example, is that Terman underestimated the superior genetic stock of the Jews (because he recorded only twice as many Jewish geniuses as their proportion in the population) since he ignored those "Jews" who did not have both parents and all four grandparents as

Jewish (320). The idea of Jewish superior intelligence is postulated here on a model of inheritability that also underlies the other tests of Jews cited by Storfer following Terman's study in the 1920s. But in Storfer's reading, this inheritability can be transferred to other groups. It is not Jewish cultural mutability and integration as advocated by Leroy-Beaulieu but the mutability of all human beings toward the pattern illustrated by the Jew that can be the saving grace of humankind.

When intelligence as measured by IQ tests is understood as measuring a fixed quality, there is real anxiety that the meritocracy promised by the intelligence test—that the best and the brightest regardless of class or race will be advanced—can be achieved because of suspicion about the validity of the tests. At that point, intelligence testing becomes attributed to the corrosive impact of "Jewish" science. In Great Britain after World War II, intelligence testing came to be a leveler in society. The tests allowed the students with the best academic potential, rather than those from specific classes, into the public schools, and the revolutionary potential of IQ testing was seen as a "Jewish" invention. The Cambridge psychologist Edward Welbourne confronted a student who claimed to have an interest in IQ tests with the statement, "Huh. Devices invented by Jews for the advancement of Jews."[53] Welbourne assumes that the quality measured is limited and not transferable: Jewish intelligence is proven by Jewish testing, and intelligence cannot be developed independently of the innate potential of a race. It is ironic that precisely the same tests were used a few generations earlier to exclude Jews from entry into American society.

3
Jewish Scientific Responses to the Image at the Turn of the Century and Beyond

JEWISH SUPERIOR INTELLIGENCE AND ITS RELATIONSHIP TO MODELS OF PATHOLOGY

THE COMMENTS BY the Louisiana physician Madison Marsh that were quoted in the opening paragraph of chapter 2 were part of a published exchange of letters between him and a Jewish physician living in Cincinnati, Ephraim M. Epstein.[1] In his initial answer to Marsh, Epstein claimed that Jews were ill just as often as anyone else and that their hygienic precautions were no more efficient in extending their lives than the attempts of non-Jewish physicians to extend the lives of their non-Jewish patients. Epstein, however, did not comment on the question of Jewish superior intelligence in his rebuttal of Marsh's comments on the supposed health of the Jewish body.

Born in the Austro-Hungarian Empire and having practiced medicine in Central Europe, Epstein found himself on the U.S. frontier in the 1870s. There he began to undertake a series of Jewish activities, including translations from Hebrew. One of these translations was a booklet by a professor of Semitics at the University of St. Petersburg, Daniel Abramovich Khvol'son, whose writings on Jewish historical and philological topics were some of the most influential during the nineteenth century.[2] Khvol'son's pamphlet, cast in a classic ethnopsychological model, is an attempt to answer the racist ideology of the 1870s. The model Khvol'son adapted was developed at midcentury by two Jewish savants, Heyman Steinthal and Moritz Lazarus, to provide a model for national characteristics that would be somewhat more mutable than the model of racial biology. Their model showed how a group's psyche was shaped by its geographic context. Khvol'son's comments on the "Semitic nations" would have reinforced Marsh's observations on Jewish superior intelligence and the Jews' concomitant virtue as citizens in the post-Enlightenment world.

In response to the ethnopsychologists, Khvol'son conceives the "inborn character of the individual" as the central formative force of nature that can be shaped but is not determined by "religion, climate,

etc." (10). There are, according to his system, inferior cohorts of individuals whose character would produce inferior products (such as religion) even though superior individuals would appear among them.
For the "lowest" rung of humanity, he uses the Hottentots, "with a
nation of Hottentots, neither Alfred nor Peter the Great could have
achieved for their states a historic importance. The best of wheat cannot thrive in a sandy soil" (12).³ He uses the Jews to represent the
other end of the *scala naturae,* the scale of perfection (if not the bell
curve) of eighteenth-century biological science. Francis Galton, as we
saw in chapter 2, places the materiality of the Jew and the Hottentot
under the instruments of science in order to create the distance he
needs for himself as an intellectual/scientist. Khvol'son separates the
two into superior and inferior abilities and notes that the Jews' "worst
enemies, from Haman down to the celebrated composer Wagner, accord to them high intellectual talents. Nay, more these talents constitute the fortune and misfortune of this nation; fortune, because
the intellectual talents are the highest blessings of life; misfortune,
because they create envy and hatred; the blockhead is never envied,
never hated" (21). Thus anti-Semitism is the result of Jewish superior
intelligence and this intelligence places the Jews at the farthest remove
from the group hunted down and persecuted because of their physical difference, the Hottentot.

Khvol'son's definition of the "intellect" of the "Semite" differentiates it from that of the Aryan, whose intellect has "that fullness and
variety of ideas." The Semite "possesses a sound, practically one might
say almost mathematical intellect, a talent of easy and quick comprehension, and an acuteness, which often degenerates into subtleties"
(24). There are "comparatively fewer great men of prominent mental
gifts, so called geniuses" among the Semites than the Aryans, "but
the great mass of the former is more talented than that of the latter,
so that we find fewer geniuses, but relatively more talented individuals" (25). Jews are, therefore, smarter as a group (the concept of Jewish superior intelligence) without manifesting genius as a sign of the
particular: the Jews as a group nurture superiority yet possess few examples of the truly extraordinary mind.

Even the canon of "smart Jews" that always accompanies such
comments in discussions of Jewish superior intelligence is qualified.

to the Image

Again, Heinrich Heine is present in virtually all such nineteenth-century tabulations. (Joseph Jacobs commented in 1919 that "Heinrich Heine only shows, in higher degree and more modern form, the same incisive wit that animates Judah al-Harizi or Immanuel of Rome.")[4] Yet for Khvol'son, Heine's genius is not of the highest caliber. Jews write more "subjective than objective poetry" and are poor dramatists: "The great lyric writer Heinrich Heine was a poor dramatist, and the only drama which Berthold Auerbach wrote, has no great merits as such" (39). This is because the Jew is able to depict "his own feelings and affections" as in poetry, but, because he is so "sharply pronounced a character," he cannot represent those of another figure. Jewish narcissism makes the Jew a good lyric poet but a poor dramatist. Here one can cite a footnote from Epstein's translation. Khvol'son had noted that the Jews do not have a true dramatic sensibility and that the contemporary reading of the *Song of Songs* as a drama is faulty. Epstein, "true to [his] Semitic origin," dares to differ and intends to show through his translation that the Jews can write drama and are therefore not inherently narcissistic (39 n.). This debate over the poetic products of the Jews reflects the nature of Jewish character and the quality ascribed to Jewish superior intelligence. The collective, "the Jews," represents in Khvol'son's reading the source of superiority even though exemplary Jews attacked by commentators such as Wagner may never truly be "geniuses."

Such "subjectivity" is labeled as Jewish "enthusiasm" by Adolf Jellinek, rabbi in Vienna, in his ethnological study of the Jews from the 1860s.[5] Jellinek sees this quality as inherently feminine, labeling the Jews as the feminine among nations and stressing the Jews' "fantasy" as one of the primary qualities shared with the Woman (90). "The Woman is happy when she pleases a man and the Jew when he is praised by the non-Jew. This unique fantasy combined with the ancient heart and the quick, mutable spirit also influences artistic creativity of the Woman as well as the Jew. Their language is full of a richness of images, in poetry they are more productive in the lyric than in the epic or the dramatic arenas, and only the future will determine if their capabilities in the plastic arts will raise itself above that of an ordinary talent!" (95). Such views frame the idea of creativity and femininity that are found in Jewish as well as non-Jewish texts. Leroy-Beaulieu's image of the sick Jew, however, is contrasted with the healthy notion of enthusiasm and creativity in the work of Jewish savants such as Khvol'son and Jellinek. Jewish creativity and intelligence are signs of civic virtue in these works, and this is what makes the emancipated Jew a good citizen in the new "Enlightened" state. Whether in St. Petersburg or in Vienna, the contribution the Jew can make to the civic society in which she or he dwells marks the Jew as a desirable citizen.

Most interesting in the Jewish internalization of the complex and contradictory idea of a "Jewish intelligence" is that no *fin-de-siècle* self-defined Jewish intellectual simply abandons this idea of the inherent superiority of the collective and the unquestioned attribution of any specific Jew to the community of the genius. If the Jew has value in this world it is because of Jewish intelligence; Jewish civic virtue is measured by Jewish intelligence and creativity. Thus every writer on the topic assumes that there is a Jewish intellectual superiority but reads this in very different ways in regard to specific individuals, often including himself or herself. It is of little surprise that *fin-de-siècle* Jews—no matter how they understood their Jewishness or Judaism—came to internalize the question of Jewish superior intelligence, it being their sign of belonging to the society in which they dwelt. In principle, Jews could have simply rejected or totally internalized their special (negative or positive) intellectual status. But this would have meant placing their own position as intellectuals into question, for what is an intellectual without intelligence, no matter what qualities are ascribed to that intellect?

Jews' self-stigmatization as different, even as intellectuals, must also be taken into consideration. As mentioned in chapter 2, there had been seen a biological link between genius and madness as early as Italian Jewish forensic scientist Cesare Lombroso in the 1860s. In his first major work on the subject, *Genio e follia* (1864; *Genius and Madness*), Lombroso drew analogies between the products of genius and works made by the insane that he had seen during in his practice in the Turin psychiatric clinic.[6] Lombroso's book and his subsequent fame as the best-known medical champion of the concept of "degeneracy" as the central explanation of deviancy (defined to include acts from the socio-pathic and psychopathic to the creative), moved this question into the center of the concerns of modern clinical and asylum psychiatry. After Lombroso's work, the question was separated; one line led to the examination of the "great" in order to find the psychopathological origin of their genius; the other line led to the examination of the aesthetic products of the mentally ill to establish the nature of their creativity and discover the "creativity" in their illness.

By the 1880s, Lombroso directly addressed the relationship between race, insanity, and genius. Jews, following the accepted wisdom of the age, evidence a "curious" overabundance of "lunatics," "four or even six times . . . as [many as] the rest of the population." Lombroso was forced to separate this "fact" from its use: "This fatal privilege has not attracted the attention of the leaders of that anti-Semitic movement which is one of the shames of contemporary Germany. They would be less irritated at the success of this race if they had thought of all the sorrows that are the price of it, even at our epoch; for if the tragedies of the past were more bloody, the victims are not now less unhappy, struck at the source of their glory, and because of it deprived even of the consolation of being able, as formerly, to contribute to the most noble among the selections of species" (136). This is very much consistent with Wilhelm Wundt's view that "care and tragedy can influence nutrition by limiting the entrance of air and blood" and can thus affect the psyche.[7] Jews evidence greater levels of genius because of "the bloody selection of medieval persecutions, and owing also to the influence of temperate climate, the Jews of Europe have risen above those of Africa and the East, and have often surpassed the Aryans (133). (This argument about selection has its roots in Galton's views not about the Jews but about Protestants, as discussed later in this chapter.) At least one Jewish physician in Vienna, Arthur Schnitzler, writing in his father's medical journal in 1891, commented that Lombroso's information about the heightened risk of Jews for mental illness as the cost of the greater genius of the race is "of special interest for our times."[8]

Lombroso's statistical work relied on Joseph Jacobs, whose work is discussed later in this chapter.[9] But Lombroso could not see any connection between "this rhythmical caterwauling and the sublime notes of Meyerbeer and Mendelssohn (135). Can it be true that acculturated Western Jews whose liturgy is patterned on Protestant music owe their musical ability to Hebrew liturgical imprinting? While Jews have a much higher rate of men of genius, they have yet to produce "men like Newton, Darwin, and Michelangelo, . . . because they have not yet accomplished their ethnic evolution, as they show by the obstinacy with which they cling to their ancient beliefs" (136). The idea that Jews as a collective evidence brilliance but have yet to fulfill their potential lies at the heart of Lombroso's undertaking. As with Khvol'son, their potential lies in the production of genius within the model of the educated bourgeoisie, the *Bildungsbürger*. In the work of Lombroso, an Italian Jew, and for other Italian liberals of the latter nineteenth century, such as Paolo Mantegazza, the pure "genius" of the Jew was contaminated by the pathological: Jews' "religious" identity. Lombroso expresses this attitude when he stresses that the genius of the Jew in its positive appearance brings a new level of creativity into the Aryan race.[10] Genius here also mirrors the increase in the quality of the "host," a view that is consistent with the idea of the civic virtue of the Jews residing in the improvement of the peoples among whom they dwell.

The relationship between the idea of madness and the meaning of creativity was much discussed at the turn of the century. That Jews were active in the spheres of culture and science could not be contradicted—but was their activity to be understood as "creative"? The seemingly central role of Jews in culture was put into question by the argument that this type of art was superficial or perhaps even corrupting. Indeed, it was all too often argued that the "creativity" of the Jew was really a sign of his diseased, "mad" state. Thus Lombroso's evocation of Heinrich Heine reflected a central motif in the work of *fin-de-siècle* scientists, one already evoked in our discussion of Khvol'son, in which the ill Heine became the exemplary image of the diseased Jew. According to Lombroso, Heine's illness was not madness *per se*, but a disease of the spinal cord that "may have given a morbid character" to Heine's writing (152). Arthur Schnitzler, in his review of Lombroso, countered with the claim that Lombroso was misreading

to the Image

Heine's "hatred" for Germany as a sign of his pathology; what Heine desired, according to Schnitzler, was to be healed of his love for Germany.[11] The impossibility of being both a Jew and a German led, in Schnitzler's reading, to a true madness.

Confronted with the issue of degeneration and genius by his German followers, Lombroso was forced to restate his position in the 1890s. In *L'Antisemitismo e le scienze moderne* (1894; The Jews in the light of modern science), Lombroso accepts Leroy-Beaulieu's view of the generally positive quality of Jewish intelligence as well as his basic premise concerning its "cultural" origins. Yet he stresses the practical nature of Jewish genius rather than its "higher" quality, noting that the Jews have never produced a Dante or a Wagner. Jews are seen as the intellectual leaders of revolutionary change in Europe, a factor that grows out of their social position and intellectual ability. This biological rationale underlies his overall advocacy of the principle of biological and social integration of the Jews. Here, like Leroy-Beaulieu, Lombroso quotes the apocryphal saying of Bismarck that one must breed the German stallion with the Jewish mare. (Note the continued feminization of the "Jew" when the question of breeding/sexuality is raised.) Lombroso advocates a biological solution, the crossing of races, in order to improve both the Aryan and the Jew (42–50). The reason for this is the link the Parisian psychiatrist Jean-Martin Charcot had made, that along with a "greater talent among the Jews comes a greater amount of mental illness" (63). Lombroso attributes this to their "excessive endeavors and a residue of the persecutions they suffered" (64).

Prior to Lombroso's cultural-biological argument, there had been a series of studies of Jewish intelligence by Jewish savants outside central and southern Europe. One major study cited by Lombroso is the 1885 paper by the Australian-born Jew Joseph Jacobs, "the Comparative Distribution of Jewish Ability."[12] This was followed by his *Men of Distinction* (1916) and *Jewish Contributions to Civilization* (1919). Jacobs followed Francis Galton's 1869 attempt to tabulate "hereditary genius." Jacobs's view is strictly "eugenic" in that he is convinced that genius is inherited—genius here being defined as the inclusion of one's name in a biographical dictionary (xliv). In his initial work, after examining some thirty thousand biographical sketches, Jacobs comes up with a list of 169 "distinguished" Jews who represent the pinnacle of Jewish intelligence. In his list the first rank of geniuses is Disraeli, Heine, Lassalle, and Mendelssohn-Bartholody (xlv). These four names are substantially greater than what should be expected — about one and one-half names — based on the overall population of Jews in Europe at the time. In the second rank of genius, Jacobs finds twenty-five names (including Marx, Börne, and Ricardo) rather than the expected fourteen. But in the third rank the numbers suddenly reverse and a substantially lower number of Jews is to be found.

Jacobs calculates a 4 percent overall higher rate of Jewish ability than "should" be found in the general population. He finds a concentration in the fields of music, mathematics, metaphysics, philology, and finance. Jews tend to produce work that "strike[s] one as being predominantly abstract — a result, doubtless, of their long life in the cities and of their exclusion from Nature" (lvi). And he sees the reasons for abstraction in the urbanization of the Jews, their "addiction to commerce as distinguished from industry" (lv), the emphasis on their children's education, their bilingualism, and indeed, the successful overcoming of persecution (lv). But most importantly, "Jewish reason has never been in fetters, and finally the weaker members of each generation have been weeded out by persecution which tempted or forced them to embrace Christianity, and thus contemporary Jews are the survival of a long process of unnatural selection which has seemingly fitted them excellently for the struggle for intellectual existence" (lv). Here is a Jewish answer to the notion of the necessary improvement of the race. For Jacobs looks at Jewish intelligence as the end of a form of natural selection based on persecution: the failures of Jewish intellect have become Christians.

Jacobs ends with the question of whether his essay about Jewish intellectual capacity is biased because he is a Jew. He notes that a study of Swiss naturalists by a Swiss naturalist comes to the conclusion that Swiss biologists are the smartest cadre. He states that he has "guarded against it to the best of my power," but since his results do not "run counter to any common impression" he believes that his views are unbiased (lvi). He is a scientist here and not a Jew. And yet,

to the Image

in his posthumously published 1919 volume on Jewish contributions to civilization, Jacobs comments about the Jews: " 'Tis a little people, but it has done great things."[13] And central among these "great things" is their role in science or at least in its transmission (156–63).

In Britain in 1884, anthropologist Lucien Wolf gives a powerful answer to Jacobs's argument.[14] In a long essay in the *Fortnightly Review* Wolf, like Leroy-Beaulieu (who cites him) and Lombroso, argues against the rising anti-Semitic obsession with Jewish difference and inferiority by stressing the reasons for Jewish intellectual ability. Wolf begins with a long quote from Goldwin Smith, the former Regius Professor of History at Oxford who was one of the founding fathers of Cornell University and the first biological anti-Semite in Britain, and who sees, in addition to the "antagonism of race," that "Judaism is material optimism, with a preference to a chosen race. . . . Judaism is legalism, of which the Talmud is the most signal embodiment. . . . In the competition for the world's goods it is pretty clear that the legalist will have the advantage" (238). Smith had earlier stated that the "essence" of Disraeli "lies in his Jewish blood. . . . Certainly a century and a quarter of residence in England on the part of his ancestors and himself has left little trace on the mind and character.[15] Here Wolf stresses the question of the laws and the role of hygiene: Wolf, like Marsh, saw the law as something positive; his view embodies the first form of positivism, the high science of his day (239).

Wolf accepts the equation between race and religion and sees in this the "superior[ity], physically, mentally, and morally" of modern Jews. Through this system of laws, the "discipline of the artificial system by which this life has been regulated," the Jews have acquired this preeminence. They are thus "as a race really superior, physically, mentally, and morally, to the people among whom they dwell," and they evidence a "notorious intellectual superiority" that Wolf figures to be at least 40 percent greater than their "hosts" (240–41). "Brain power we know to be exceptionally developed among the Semitic races" (242) because of the Jews' compulsory education for their young children. But this quality has now been inherited: "the Jewish infant is already *born* with an exceptional capacity for resisting life-shortening influences" (244). Judaism is "strictly logical," and "the exceptional men-

71

Jewish Scientific Responses

tal power" is obtained through the "physical 'legalism' of Mosaism upon Jewish instincts by way of the Jewish mind" (251–52). Thus Jewish superior intelligence comes to be a factor of the training of the Jewish mind. It is transferable, but only over time, in light of the model of inheritance Wolf employs. Goldwin Smith's attack on Jewish superior intelligence as "mere legalism" comes to be the source for Jewish achievement. Wolf accepts the basis for Goldwin Smith's argument and simply reverses its outcome. But such simple reversals are rarely an effective rebuttal to anti-Semites who see their contentions supported.

MIXED RACE AND THE DECLINE
OF JEWISH INTELLIGENCE

If much of the argument about Jewish superior intelligence is about the role of such intelligence in the civil emancipation of the Jews, a closely related question is the intelligence of the offspring of Jews who marry into the non-Jewish world, the exemplary figures of Jewish acculturation. Mixed-race Jews do not appear in Lucien Wolf's argument, as he stressed that "racial separation is necessary for the perpetuation of [Jewish] teaching" (243). Wolf argued for "racial separation" because he understood Jewish superior intelligence as a factor of the culture of the Jews. Once intelligence is understood as the major biological "gift" Jews can provide for their "hosts," the argument about racial mixing and intelligence becomes more focused.

Racial separation rather than integration is the theme of Alfred Nossig's 1905 essay, in which the notion of "inheritance and adaptation" stands at the center of the attempt to explain the stagnation of the "Jewish racial character."[16] Yet the Jews show a remarkable "biological result of this idea," and the "eternal existence of the Jewish people is the result of the biological effect of their intellectual goal and their moral laws" (4). The Jews thus avoid the baneful influence of venereal disease and alcohol that preserves their capacity to transmit intelligence (4). But it is also through "incest" [*Inzucht*] that the Jews preserve their abilities: they avoid mixed marriages.

The question of *Mischling* (to use the technical nineteenth-century term for mixed-race Jews) becomes important to a number of Jewish

to the Image

thinkers of the turn of the century. One of the more interesting pamphlets in German to be written by an Eastern Jew, the anonymous 1883 *Wir Juden von einem Bukowiner Juden,* advocates the view that Jewish intellectual ability was the dowry Jews brought to the nations among whom they dwelt.[17] This view echoes Ernest Renan's comment that "the Jew was designed to serve as leaven in the progress of every country, rather than to form a separate nation on the globe."[18] These views correspond with the understanding of Jewish scholars that Jews increased the quality of the "host" people's culture. The problem Jewish savants find in the discussion of the offspring of mixed marriages is that these children are often characterized as only superficially brilliant, as in the words of German sociologist Werner Sombart: "The children of such marriages [between Jews and non-Jews] . . . even though they are so very beautiful and so very talented, seem to lack a psychological balance that is provided by pure racial stock. We find all too often intellectually or morally unbalanced individuals, who decay ethically or end in suicide or madness."[19] *Mischling* are neither brilliant nor virtuous.

In 1918, W. M. Feldman, a London physician, turned to the question of Jewish superior intelligence and the role of the child, especially the mixed-race child.[20] He concluded that "real" (i.e., smart) Jewish children show a "purity of descent" since "mixed marriages are comparatively infertile, and the bulk of such offspring leave the Jewish community" (98). This version of the myth of the infertility of mixed races, which rests on the animal model of the mule, eliminates the problem of inferior minds among those who could call themselves Jews. Genius, as Feldman notes, is the result of racial specificity linked to religious training, "the wonderfully good effects that an earnest study of the casuistry of the Talmud has in sharpening the intelligence and developing the faculties of subtle and abstract calculation." This is the reason that the Jew is successful.

Answering the idea of the inferiority of the mixed-race Jew underlies much of the later work of Christian von Ehrenfels, professor of philosophy in *fin-de-siècle* Prague, himself the offspring of a mixed marriage. For Ehrenfels, Jewish intelligence is the contribution of the Jews to the new race that will compete in tomorrow's world. In his widely read book on human sexuality, Ehrenfels writes of the competition between the "higher" and "lower" races and about the "great problem of our time": resolving the demand of race in light of the "liberal-humanistic fiction of the equality of all people."[21] He argues that the purpose of "natural sexual morals" (in his view a natural law) "is to conserve or improve the constitution of the tribe or people" (275). He sees the need for the "white, yellow, and black" races to remain "pure" and to avoid any sexual interbreeding. Jews are understood as not sharing a common biological inheritance with Aryans.

As with most of the racial scientists of his time, Ehrenfels justifies colonial expansion with the rationale that the "sexual mission" of some races could best be accomplished "if they place their generative powers in the service of others" (276). As the rhetoric of this statement seems to indicate, throughout Ehrenfels's discussion of race his prime example is the "Oriental": "These same directives are applicable to the Jewish problem, inasmuch as these are the result of differences in their constitution and not—as is actually generally the case—the result of resolvable differences in their social milieu" (356). The discussions about race are, in fact, encoded references to the Jewish question, for the Jews are understood as biologically different. Their strengths, like the strengths of each of the races, are preserved only when they remain within their own group. Intermixing leads to the corruption and the weakening of the race. Rather than intermixing with Aryans, the Jews, Ehrenfels implies, through their activity in Western culture, can "place their generative powers in the service of others."

Yet the racial theorist who advocated the purity of the race and the distinction between "healthy" and "civilized morality" in the "higher" and "lower" races was himself Jewish by descent even though raised as a Christian. Ehrenfels publicly acknowledged his own personal Jewish background and saw the rise of political anti-Semitism as a social anathema.[22] The real danger, Ehrenfels stated in a talk given in 1911, was the "Yellow Peril," the "hoards of Mongols" poised to confront the "Caucasian" race: "Among a hundred whites there stand two Jews. The German peasant has been awakened and armed with the holy weapons of his ancestors—not to struggle against 80 million Mongols but to confront two Jews! Is this not the height of folly!"[23]

to the Image

The Jews are a white race and, Ehrenfels stresses, close races, when they intermix, provide greater strengths for the resultant mix. Two decades earlier, in England, Joseph Jacobs condemned "Chinesism" as the "great danger that begins to loom before us as never before in the world's history." This leveling of quality, the "crush[ing of] individuality, and reduc[tion of] all its members to one dead level of mediocrity" would be the death of Jewish difference and Jewish superior intelligence.[24]

By 1911 Ehrenfels denies any substantial physiological difference between Aryans and Jews. Indeed, he sees the Jews as suffering from all the diseases and dangers of modern society: "They suffer more than we do from the present sexual and economic order."[25] A number of thinkers of the period assumed that the Jews were the worst example of the impact of civilization because of their weak nervous system. Franz Kafka mentions a response that Ehrenfels made to a presentation by Felix A. Theilhaber, a Jewish physician who lectured in Prague, on the "decline of Germany Jewry" to a public audience in January 1912.[26] Theilhaber had recapitulated the thesis of his controversial book: that urbanization, the struggle for profit, and mixed marriages and baptism were causing German Jewry to vanish—a social variant on the older biological argument that "mixed marriages between Jews and Aryans had a noticeably lower fecundity."[27] Ehrenfels's response, as Kafka noted, was a "comic scene" in which the philosopher (whose Jewish antecedents were well known) "smiling spoke in favor of mixed races." Here the role of the intelligent intellectual as spokesperson about his own intelligence is drawn into question.

Theilhaber is best known for his work on the decline of the Jews; yet in 1931, under the pressure of rising anti-Semitism, he published a defense of Jewish superior intelligence.[28] In this work, he states that his project is the refutation of the anti-Semitic trope of a lack of Jewish creativity. He attacks the notions that Jews are not a creative people in their own right and that their sole contribution in research fields consists of the organization and application of the genius of other peoples.

Theilhaber initially mounts a historical defense: in past centuries, Jews were denied access to the raw materials of constructive tech-

Jewish Scientific Responses

nological research. As a result, Jewish thinkers before emancipation tended to focus more on ethics than "civilizing endeavors," adopting a "spiritual-speculative" approach to the world: "Very different problems dominated the lives of the European peoples, who were separate from the Jews by the walls of the Ghetto" (8). While non-Jewish Europeans were thoroughly engrossed in developing techniques of warfare, the Jews, in their isolation, were not forced to conform their thinking to the political and economic needs of the states in which they lived. The Jewish thinker therefore tends to be little affected by external influences of any sort. Thus Jewish scientists (such as Albert Einstein) are freed from the ordinary limits on creativity imposed by the professional background of their parents. They do not come from the world of factories but from the more speculative world, which explains the abstract nature of Jewish thought (8). For Theilhaber, Jewish superior intelligence runs in cycles driven as much by the press of history as by the inherent "logic of the race" (13). There is also a psychological element to his argument that relies on the need of the Jew "to rise above his world" (13). Even so, the Jews' inheritance seems to be essentially a spiritual one. Theilhaber presents case studies, profiles of Jewish leaders in the fields of medicine, chemistry, physics, psychiatry. Freud, for example, is taken as a case study of the ethnopsychology of the Jew—of how Talmudic argument translates itself into the "sharpness of the psychoanalytic method" (33). The speculative areas of medicine are seen to be especially close to the Jewish psyche.

Theilhaber's defense of Jewish genius is a statement that such geniuses exist and are not superficial in their contribution to the world. His answer combines the arguments of a historical trajectory for Jewish genius with an answer to the charges of "Jewish pseudo-intelligence." For, as we have seen, Jewish superior intelligence is attributed to pathology and thus is seen as inherently superficial. Jews were neurasthenic or hysteric and evidenced the signs and symptoms of these debilitating diseases in the language that they employed. Their aesthetic creations were therefore inherently flawed, as they reflected diseased minds.

Jewish scientists, such as Arthur Ruppin, the founder of the "sociology of the Jews," constantly found it necessary to counter the view
that Jewish genius was lacking in Western culture: "It is incorrect to
accuse the Jews of having talent but producing no geniuses. Genius
is sown thinly among all peoples. . . . Certainly the number of highly
gifted individuals among the Jews will increase as soon as the Jews
are able to leave the merchant class in larger numbers, for it is clear
that the education to acquisitiveness certainly hinders the creative
gift." [29] In the work of Ruppin, the striving for education stands at the
very center. Ruppin authored the first major sociological study of the
Jews in 1904 (revised in 1911) that prefigured the work of educational
psychologists such as Goddard. He wanted to examine not a loose
canon of accepted "geniuses" following the Lombrosian model, but
the grades of "Jewish and Christian" schoolchildren in specific subjects. His desire was thwarted by the Prussian ministry of education,
who refused to give him access to this material. Ruppin was eventually able to obtain the detailed account of the grades in a private girls'
school in Berlin for the Easter term of 1904. [30] Ruppin found that in
the lower grades, Christian and Jewish children "show the same behavior and productivity," but in the middle grades, and especially in
the upper classes, non-Jewish students do substantially better. He concludes that Jewish female students have "less interest" and that this
should be taken into consideration when judging the comparative
ability of Jews and Christians.

But Ruppin is not above adapting his views concerning the appropriate means of evaluating Jewish intelligence. [31] In a long review of
Ignaz Zollschan's 1910 study of the Jews as a race, which is discussed
in chapter 4, Ruppin combats the view of Renan, Dühring, and Chamberlain concerning the racial inferiority of the Jews (91). He cites the
"cultural accomplishments" of the Jews but accepts the idea that there
are "talents but no geniuses" among contemporary Jews. He states
that geniuses are few in any age and proceeds to tabulate a list that
begins with Spinoza and ranges from Disraeli, Heine, Lassalle, and

Jewish Scientific Responses

Mendelssohn-Bartholdy to Josef Israel. He sees the appearance of Jewish genius as resulting from the Jews' leaving the world of commerce and notes that "the Jews in West and Middle Europe are at least as rich in intelligence if not richer than any other people" (91).

In his standard study of the Jews, Ruppin's views are somewhat more complex.[32] He associates "intellectual ability" with the "struggle of life" (used in English!). The Jew has superior ability because he is not bound to a single direction in life and is able to shift his goals with the pressures of society and time (49). But the Jews are also always obsessed with education [*Bildungsdrang*] and they are able to translate their religious obsession with education into secular interest (113–32). Ruppin quotes Josef Kohler (*Deutsche Montagszeitung,* 11 December 1910) to the effect that "the Jews have fewer geniuses but an overabundance of talent" (215–16). The Jews also have a mercantile ability. Ruppin stresses that the qualities that make the good merchant are also those of brilliant "academics, politicians, engineers and officers": "quick wittedness, logical thought, correct evaluation of the possible, talent for organization, quick response" (216). And he adds in a footnote that the claim that Jews have few geniuses is as unfounded as the distinction between genius and talent. He claims that the very small number of Jews in Europe (2 percent of the total population) did not produce any genius of the first rank (such as Napoleon, Beethoven, Goethe, or Darwin); this, however, was a sign not of the absence of genius but of the small number of Jews. And yet Ruppin does provide a complicated biological argument for the intellectual preeminence of Western (Ashkenasic) Jews as opposed to Sephardic and Arab Jews.[33] For the "rich Jews of the ghetto sought out for their daughters not a rich match but one very able in the study of Talmud. And thus the high breeding of the race" (218). Ruppin labels this *Intellectualismus.* But *Intellectualismus* can be a danger, for in the contemporary world, those who were labeled as "intellectuals" [*Intelligenz*] tend to be heavily represented among those who left the faith and were baptized: in Vienna fully one quarter of Jews baptized belonged to the *Intelligenz* (190). In the discourse on Jewish superior intelligence of the time, belonging to the intelligentsia may signal a rejection of one's Jewish identity and a flight into mixed-race relationships with all their attendant dangers.

to the Image

In the turn-of-the-century American setting, Ruppin's view on Jewish intelligence is countered by Maurice Fishberg. Fishberg, a physician, is concerned with the "inherent thirst for knowledge of the Jew."[34] According to his Lamarckian view of adaptation and change, the Jew "lives more on brain than brawn" (540). Jews in Eastern Europe live in urban areas and provide a disproportionate number of students at the university. When these Jews come to the United States they continue this tendency, which accounts for the higher proportion of Jews compared with non-Jews in American urban universities. This will vanish, Fishberg believes, when these Jews become acculturated and supply a regular number to the "mechanical professions," the working class (546). In order to see the Jews as unremarkable intellectually, Fishberg rebuts Weinberg's brain studies. Jews are alleged to have "great cerebral capacity," (56) which is perceived as "the danger [that] the Jew with his greater cerebral power may be to his non-Jewish neighbor, who has not been endowed with as much brain tissue in his cranial cavity" (56). While Fishberg concentrates on the tenuous relationship between brain size and intelligence, he notes that the existing studies (including Weinberg) stress the small skull capacity and the lighter brain weight of the Jew. This would indicate *lower,* not higher, intelligence. Fishberg eventually dismisses these studies, noting their slim database and questionable conclusions, but he also sees that the "social and economic" conditions of the Jews "account for the excessive proportion of neurotics and psychopathics among them" (59). Fishberg begins his argument with a discussion of Jewish intellectual ability and ends it with a discussion of psychopathology, for these are linked in this literature. He desires to dismiss the former as a chimera while seeing the latter as a function of two thousand years of Jewish persecution (to use the nineteenth-century formula). It is the Jews' response to their persecution and their "early physiological maturity" to which Elisha M. Friedman attributes the intellectual superiority of the Jews.[35]

The anxiety about the meaning of Jewish superior intelligence haunts the American scene at the beginning of the century. The German-Jewish founder of American Anthropology, Columbia University anthropologist Franz Boas, in his groundbreaking *The Mind of*

Jewish Scientific Responses

Primitive Man (1911), simply dismissed the relationship between "cultural achievement" and "mental ability" as a fallacy, noting that "the variations in cultural development can as well be explained by a consideration of the general course of historical events without recourse to the theory of material differences of mental faculty in different races."[36] No racial typology is necessary to explain achievement. Boas was not speaking about Jewish superior intelligence but rather about the seemingly "primitive" level of achievement among the so-called lower races and the claims of British and other European scientists about the higher level of cultural achievements (including science) among the "white" races in Europe. It is clear that Boas carefully removes the Jews from this discussion and attempts to counter Francis Galton's representation of the "primitive mind" of the African by refuting the relationship between "achievement" and "genius." Boas conflates achievement and genius on the one hand with the search for the relationship between physiognomy and genius (or cranial capacity and genius) on the other as a spurious attempt to prove racial superiority (23). Boas never mentions the Jews in this study, focusing rather on the other end of Galton's bell curve. He is careful to limit all discussion of "achievement" as a measure of racial value and to show how it mirrors the equally false assumption "that the white race represents physically the highest type of man" (23). "Achievement" and "physicality" are linked by Boas as false signs of superiority, ones that should be claimed neither by the Aryans nor by the Jews.

Maurice Fishberg's study of the Jews and his dismissal of Jewish intellectual ability as a chimera comes at precisely the moment of a shift between the biological or anecdotal views of Jewish intelligence to the empirical studies of H. H. Goddard. In 1927 Irma Loeb Cohen, a graduate student of Goddard's at Ohio State University, presented a master's thesis entitled "The Intelligence of Jews as Compared with Non-Jews."[37] Hers was not the first such empirical study: indeed, she lists ten prior studies, including that of Brigham. But Cohen's study is of interest because it was written under Goddard's supervision. In his introduction to Cohen's thesis, Goddard accepts the perception of Jewish intellectual superiority as a group. His proof is the constant persecution of the Jews, "for we are seldom jealous of our inferiors"

to the Image

(vi). Goddard notes that the author of the present study is "a Jew of far above average intelligence, . . . [who] desire[s] to contribute something to the question, 'How does the Jew rank in intelligence as compared with other people?'" (vi).

Cohen tests the intelligence of the Jews as a race. This biological component is outlined in her opening chapter: "That the difference is not one of religion can be proved by the fact that the mere acceptance or non-acceptance of a creed does not make a Jew. A Jew who denies his religion can thereby not deny his 'Jewishness' and a non-Jew who accepts the Jewish religion does not become a Jew" (7). The author argues against Fishberg's view, dismissing it as "too broad for serious scientific consideration, and many of his statements are not in accord with definite statistical data" (5–6). Tied to Jewish intelligence is the Jews' "tenacious application to their studies. Indeed, one of the chief criticisms hurled at the Jewish student in college by his classmates is that he gives himself over too much to his studies" (19).

The study uses a standardized test to evaluate the comparative intelligence of a group of 193 Jewish freshmen (128 men and 65 women) and 193 non-Jewish freshmen (135 men and 58 women) at Ohio State in the fall of 1925. Eliminated were foreign-born students and older students and all but 'white' students ("since the Jewish students were all white" [8]). But also eliminated are all students who "we might suspect for any reason to be Jewish" (8). The covert Jews (like the *Mischling*) have to be removed from this category since their invisibility would contaminate her "pure" categories. The test covered arithmetic, opposites, analogies, number completion, and reading. The evaluation of the test was by both "race" and gender. Cohen found that the most superior group was that of Jewish women, who were more superior to Jewish men than the Jewish men were to non-Jewish men (16). Non-Jewish women were the lowest in all the scores.

To this the evaluator added a note on "students on probation," that is, students who were on academic warning because of their poor grades. "We find that the more intelligent Jewish student is more frequently on probation than the more intelligent non-Jewish student" (19). Virtue (defined as playing by the rules) seems not at all connected to intelligence in this study. Jewish men show a relatively lower rank of probation than did Jewish women, though both were more frequently on probation than non-Jewish students (18).

The author concludes that while the overrepresentation of Jews in higher education may bias the study (7 percent of all students in the winter quarter of 1926 at Ohio State were Jewish, while Jews numbered only 3 percent of the total population of the state), purposefulness cannot be the answer; while more Jewish men had decided on their careers, most Jewish women ("The most superior of the groups"!) had not (35). Cohen leaves us with a series of questions, central of which are "If the Jew is highly intelligent, and really superior to the non-Jew, or to other races, nationalities, groups, etc. what factors of heredity and environment have been responsible for this superiority? Is this superiority a general one, or only evinced in connection with scholastic work or work having language knowledge and abstract reasoning?" (40).

The idea of a gendered Jewish superior intelligence is clearly biased by the gender of the observer. Storfer in the 1990s stresses Jewish male superiority in all categories of intelligence; fifty years earlier, in a study Storfer ignores, Irma Loeb Cohen argued precisely the opposite. If the question of gender is as central as it seems, the differences may well be attributable to the author's perspectives.

JEWISH SUPERIOR INTELLIGENCE AFTER THE SHOAH

Although intelligence testing came to be questioned more and more during the American civil rights movement in the 1960s, the myth of Jewish superior intelligence did not fade away. The work of the intelligence testers returned to the older Galtonian method, an inventory of the presence of Jewish superior intelligence in the high culture and in the intellectual life of the day. Because "genius" as measured in intelligence tests said absolutely nothing about accomplishment, the model used to establish "the Jews" as superior in post-Shoah American culture was to examine the record of Jewish accomplishments. The abstract reduction to statistics did not measure the positive or negative impact that "real" (named) Jews—whatever their background or identity—had on high culture. This impact came to be understood as the basis for a "scientific" evaluation of the meaning of Jewish superior intelligence. Only the examination of reference works, of lists of "great men," could prove this impact. If intelligence testers through the 1940s reflected the sense of Jewish marginality, by the 1950s the sense of anxiety gave way to using the discussion of Jewish superior intelligence to prove Jewish rootedness in American culture. The image of Jewish superior intelligence went from being a sign of liminality to being one of centrality.

Certainly the most extensive reading of the phenomenon of Jewish intellectual achievement, one to which I am certainly indebted for its extensive collection of materials (if not the argument of my study), was Raphael Patai's *The Jewish Mind*.[38] With all Patai's historical documentation of the myths woven around the idea of Jewish superior intelligence, he still ascribes to the view that Jews are smarter than everyone else because of genetic selection. He writes that "it is quite probable that such a historic process of Jewish genetic selection for intelligence (as measured by excellence in Talmudic studies) actually did take place. . . . it was an added factor in the modification of the Jewish gene pool in the direction of higher intelligence; added, that is, to the effect of persecution which also favored the survival of those mentally better endowed" (306). Although Patai's summary of the complex readings of Jewish superior intelligence was published in 1977, his arguments in favor of "selection" seem to give no weight to the change in the semantic field of the word "selection." For after 1941, or at least after 1945, "selection" had broadened its meaning to include the "selection" of those who would live or die in Auschwitz and the other death camps.

The poisoned idea of "selection" needs to be cleansed by referring back to a "science" that has its roots in the pre-Shoah period. The complex reading of intelligence as one of the roots for rationalizing the Shoah under the Nazis is repressed. One can easily refer to the case of Gottfried Benn, the German poet who in 1933 castigated all those who refused to acknowledge the truths of National Socialsm. Benn, an "intellectual" by his own or anyone else's measure before 1933, viewed "the intellectuals" who refused to see the truth of National Socialism as the enemy.[39] And "intellectuals" quickly became the Nazi code word for the Jews as it had been in France during the Dreyfus Affair. Thus at the book burning in Berlin on 10 May 1993, Joseph Goebbels was able to announce the end of "an age of exaggerated Jewish intellectualism."[40] Picking up a thread in Nazi rhetoric mirrored in *Mein Kampf*, Benn placed himself in a new class, no longer the bourgeoisie or left "intellectual" but the embodiment of true "intelligence" able to recognize the validity of National Socialism. In his work, Benn damned "the intellectuals," following the Nazi model of excoriating "the liberal intelligentsia," but left a hole for himself as a "fascist intellectual." At the close, his opponents, the intellectuals, were shown to be simply not smart enough to understand the truths of the new system. But he had limited his discussion of those who would fall into the category of intellectual—for the Jews are simply excluded from his (and Hitler's) sense of intelligence.

Thus when a Jewish "intellectual" such as Patai reinscribes the idea of selection in 1977, he is providing a strange post-Shoah reading that parallels Cyril D. Darlington's views from the 1920s. Perhaps one could argue in the 1920s that ancient murders left the "best and the brightest" alive to form a new, intelligent Jewish nation; but even then, this argument was an act of supreme ignorance given the pattern of the murders of Jews throughout recorded history. Patai stresses the survival of the best if not the fittest Jews, at the moment when writers on the Shoah from Elie Wiesel to Primo Levi were stressing the complete randomness of death in the camps. According to Levi, writing immediately after the Shoah, "in the Lager it is useless to think, because events happen for the most part in an unforeseeable manner; and it is harmful, because it keeps alive a sensitivity which is a source of pain, and which some providential natural law dulls when suffering passes a certain limit."[41] Not the smartest survived the camps, not the blessed of God, not the pure of heart—it was precisely the randomness of death (and the resultant random gene pool, to follow Patai's logic) that the myriad of commentators on the Shoah were stressing by the 1970s. Indeed, Raul Hilberg argued quite the opposite: the intellectuals were among the first to be murdered because they were willing to accept the German rationalization for the "collection" of the Jews and their "deportation."[42] One can add that certain leaders of

to the Image

Orthodoxy in central Europe refused to allow their followers to move to Palestine for ideological reasons when they would have been able to do so. Selection in the sense of murder certainly took place; whether selection in the sense of an improvement of the genetic pool took place is not only doubtful but actually obscene. Whatever did happen during the Shoah, there certainly was no selection for intelligence!

No sense of virtue can be ascribed to the survivors of the Shoah. Indeed, surviving branded many of the post-Shoah writers with a sense of their own loss of any virtue through the very act of surviving. But writers such as Patai "provide virtue," "make sense," and "give meaning" to the persecutions of the Jews by stressing how persecution makes one smarter (or stronger or more moral). The novelist Cynthia Ozick has commented, concerning those who would deny the reality of the Shoah, that "We think of the imagination as a *making* force, as that which puts something in place of nothing. The 'revisionists' employ imagination to put nothing in place of something. Who would have dreamed that a new sort of inventive cleverness would arise with the power to undo history? Who would have dreamed that somebody would come and say it never happened? The Swiftian fancifulness of it—that those who delight in its having happened are the very ones who say it never happened!"[43] Indeed, a similar gesture is made by those who read genetic purpose into "selection."

As with virtually all the "Jewish" readings of Jewish superior intelligence, it is evident that Raphael Patai's reading is part of a genealogy of myth rooted in non-Jewish theories. Patai's reading rests in part on his acceptance of Ernest van den Haag's 1969 conservative (and self-labeled "non-Jewish") reading of "Jewish intellectual superiority."[44]

The "historic process of Jewish genetic selection for intelligence" that Patai evokes was the preference for rabbis and scholars as marriage partners in the romanticized Jewish past. The model was that of Eastern European Jewry based on Zborowski and Herzog—one that ignored the ubiquitous tradition of the inherited leadership of rabbinical sects in this culture. It is a "scientific" formulation of the views espoused by individuals such as Jewish mathematician Norbert Wiener and Marxist mathematical geneticist J. B. S. Haldane, which American Jewish sociologist Lewis S. Feuer calls the "Wiener/Haldane" thesis.[45] According to Wiener, "The biological habits of the Christians tended to breed out of the race whatever hereditary qualities make for learning whereas the biological habits of the Jew tended to breed these qualities in."[46] This "thesis" has as its corollary that Christians could "breed in" these qualities again.

Ernest van den Haag restated this view, suggesting that Jewish males of higher intelligence were encouraged to reproduce, and "literally for millennia, the brightest had the best chance to marry and produce children, and their children had the best chance to survive infancy" (14). This argument goes one step further than Arthur Ruppin's view concerning the desire of rich Jewish men to have smart (but not necessarily rich) husbands for their daughters. Smart individuals reproducing bright and healthy children is again a form of control. Infant morbidity and mortality may be a factor of nutrition or exposure to contagious illness but is rarely a factor of the intelligence of the parents. Such views come to color the reading of Jewish superior intelligence even as the topic of Jewish humor. In at least one recent source, such jokes are the result of a Jewish selection for intelligence.[47]

But there is another side to this coin. Van den Haag argued that Christians sacrificed their "good" genes by making their priests celibate; the Jews rewarded smart rabbis with the best wives and the most support for the families. Christian genes for intelligence were diminished and genes for Jewish superior intelligence were reinforced: "The church offered the only career in which intellectual ability was rewarded, regardless of the origin of its bearer. . . . But the priesthood exacted a price: celibacy. Which meant that the most intelligent portion of the population did not have offspring; their genes were siphoned off, generation after generation, into the church, and not returned to the world's, or even the church's, genetic supply" (15). Is Catholic inferior intelligence the reverse of Jewish superior intelligence? It is a possible explanation for the history of Catholic anti-Semitism and the persecution of the Jews, for only stupid people, so such an argument could run, would do such things. Feuer, a sociologist, noted a further error in this logic, pointing to a long history of anxiety about misalliances among Jewish families.[48] Few rich parents sought out poor scholars; they sought equivalent marriages either with wealthy

Jews or with the scions of established rabbinical families. The range of marriage structures among Jews in Europe was also altered by the Enlightenment and by the rise of the women's movement in central Europe in the late nineteenth century. Only the reduction of all "Jewish" experience to a single model of genetic transmission enabled van den Haag's argument to work.

Van den Haag's rationale concerning Jewish superior intelligence explained only those communities that saw themselves as "spared" the murderous assault of the Shoah. Only communities such as the American Jewish community (here read as the direct offspring of Eastern European Jewry) preserved the positive genetic result of breeding for intelligence. Such a construction of the American Jewish experience and the uniformity of the American Jewish community provided a positive reading that was quite different from the alternative model, as represented in the fiction of Philip Roth during the 1970s (which is discussed in chapter 6). That model saw the survival of the Jews in the United States as accidental and, indeed, as the cause of a sense of guilt among American Jews. Survival, especially the survival of an intact Jewish community, is given a new meaning in theories of genetic selection. Survival is read as the preservation of the genetic result of Eastern European Jewish breeding practices in the cultural, political, and intellectual achievements of American Jewry. The survival of American Jewry comes to be the acknowledgment that the traditions of Eastern European Jewry, as represented in the work of Zborowski and Herzog, continue in spite of the Shoah. It is not accidental that to make this argument of genetic selection, all of "modern" science, the science of race leading to the Shoah, is bracketed, and the new "scientists" return to a Galtonian model of selection.

The return to the Galtonian model was heralded by a rereading of one of Galton's central contentions about the diminished intelligence of Catholic Europe:

The long period of the dark ages under which Europe has lain is due, I believe in a very considerable degree to the celibacy enjoined by religious orders on their votaries. Whenever a man or a woman was possessed of a gentle nature that fitted him or her to deeds of charity, to meditation, to literature or to art, the social condition of the time was such that they had no refuge elsewhere than in the bosom of the Church. But the Church chose to preach and exact celibacy. . . . She acted precisely as if she had aimed at selecting the rudest portion of the community to be, alone, the parents of future generations.[49]

Here Galton attacks the diminished intelligence of Christian Europe before the Reformation, which again permitted the priests to marry. Such views were also to be read as critiques of the barbarism and vice of Catholic Europe as seen through the eyes of the Reformation. This view is also reread in Charles Darwin's comments on the decline of the Spanish empire. He attributed this decline to the entry of "men of a gentle nature, those given to meditation or culture of mind" to "the bosom of a church which demanded celibacy." The "deteriorating influence on each successive generation" was "incalculable."[50] Like Galton, Darwin implies a positive and virtuous "Northern" as opposed to a degenerate "Southern" historical development. Contemporary discussions emphasize the decay of Catholic power and the concomitant growth of Protestant or northern European power as well as the development of Jewish superior intelligence as an answer to this "Catholic" degeneration.

In Jewish rereadings of this argument, the Jews come to hold the place of the figures of power, the "liberal" Protestants, in British nineteenth-century science. The Catholics remain as the exemplum of the mismanagement of their genetic "bank." Such an argument is of course the traditional, post-Haskalah gesture of acculturated European Jews in England and in Germany: the powerful over-identification of Jewry and Judaism with Protestantism. The confusion of these two models places the Jews in the intellectual power of those who encourage their "best and their brightest" to reproduce. This confusion is reflected in Galton's comment about the Jews in the 1890s who had left their appropriate places (such as Eastern Europe) and were competing with the British throughout the globe for resources and the space to reproduce.

The power of this argument even in 1994 can be seen in the following anonymous exchange among a group of academics over the

Internet concerning the Jews and *The Bell Curve*.[51] A Jewish academic commented,

> As hateful as the idea of race and intelligence is at a superficial level there is an interesting but by no means conclusive parallel from the Middle Ages. It was derived from a discussion of some length from the Jewish Genealogical Bulletin Board when the subject arose having to do with Yichus books. A little background for those not familiar with this strange and wonderful piece of Jewish history.

> Over the last 20 years a remarkable transformation has taken place among Jews doing their family histories. Prior to 20 years ago Jews that I knew did not do genealogy. It was considered an un-Jewish thing. Lenny Bruce would have called it, along with lime jello, goyish. Whenever I would ask my mother to speak of her family in Poland she would invariably say, "Go away! Who knows what the maiden name of my great grandmother was?" But the apparent disinterest in genealogical study was an exception in Jewish history. Genealogy has always been a most important aspect of Jewish life, particularly among the scholarly. At birth a new Yichus book would be begun for a son since that was his overture into Jewish society. Who were this young man's ancestors?

> How was a young man to get an acceptable or appropriate bride without a knowledge of his genealogy, his Yichus? And, as it turned out, good Yichus was better than money in arranging suitable marriages. Thus, the first thing a prospective father-in-law looked at when considering a marriage of his daughter to some young man was his Yichus book. Who was this boy? Was he going to permit his daughter to have children by a person who could not demonstrate smarts in his family? NO!

> And now to my point, somewhat belatedly after that belabored intro:

> For at least 700–900 years smart young men with good Yichus got the best brides. Their good genes were interbred back into society. One could almost say that Jews were breeding the smart ones. At the same time, the best minds of the Christian world—

the VERY best minds—went into the Church where their gene pool was lost. One could almost say that Christians were keeping their best minds out of the gene pool. If that happens for between 7 to 9 centuries, it has to have some effect on the relative intelligence of the two populations, assuming that intellect is transmittable through genetics.

So as racist as it sounds for *The Bell Curve* to assert that blacks are intellectually inferior to whites as measured by whatever measurement exists, one has to wonder about the elimination from the gene pool of the best minds of Afro-American society, if indeed that is happening.

Of course the parallels are by no means exact. The time periods for the narrowing of the gene pool for Afro-Americans is not the same as that to which I referred with respect to the epoch of the Yichus book.

A non-Jewish academic replied:

One crucial problem with your analysis—interesting as it was —is that you assert that the "best minds" of Christians went into the Church. Ecrasez l'infâme! I doubt that very much based on my Christian ancestry! Many went into universities, many into government and administration, etc.

Thus maybe we Christians are not as stupid as your analysis suggests. I hope so for both our sakes!

A third argument was then offered:

But there's another explanation for the bell curve phenomenon that has nothing to do with genetics. There are associated with IQ the large variables of drive and motivation, which are not biological but cultural and social determinants. The discrepancies for Jews on the bell curve may have everything to do with the fact that Jews are relatively recent immigrants. Immigrants tend to have high motivation, the sons and daughters of immigrants are also highly likely to display that high motivation, and their children in turn may also display that motivation. This can have a substantial impact on intellectual ability and intelligence testing.

to the Image

The real test for IQ is if in several generations' time the discrepancies for Jews still exist. I doubt that this would be the case.

Blacks when compared to whites have a different history that is more likely to pull IQ down due to social and cultural factors associated with racism and poverty, not biological variables. Educational and intellectual motivation may well be less because of a different set of values and motivations associated with their existential experience.

The debate about the meaning of inheritance as a function of the isolation or separation of the Jews evokes an anxious sense of the role that the "victim" plays in establishing his or her own position as a smart or not-so-smart Jew. The van den Haag argument stresses that Jewish isolation and social pariahdom had a positive biological outcome—it enabled Jews to maintain their superior intelligence because they were not accountable to forms of social and cultural pressure that "deformed" the intelligence of the Christian cohort. The non-Jewish academic answered by noting that one should not create a univocal category of "Christian" but should accept the category of "the Jew" as generated in the initial position. The third voice argues not from the standpoint of the beneficent value of isolation but rather the gradual elimination of differences, here not the racial or cultural difference of the Jew but rather the difference of the new immigrant who is being acculturated into society and losing his or her edge of superior intelligence.

The relationship between the "Eastern European" model evolved by van den Haag, a model that is argued to have a much longer tradition, and the "American" model of the intellectual melting pot illustrates the tension within a group, university teachers, that sees itself as "intellectual." The first argument evokes a specter of Jewish superior intelligence that transcends the immigrant experience; the second, a desire to include oneself in a favorable gene pool to prove intellectual ability; and the third, "after me, the deluge," the view that after the total integration of the Jews into the American body politic, Jewish superior intelligence will be eliminated. All these views accept an idea of Jewish superior intelligence as a given, staking their position as

91

Jewish Scientific Responses

intellectuals around this "reality." These are all elaborations of the van den Haag/Galton thesis that breeding affects "intelligence" over time.

This relationship to the van den Haag thesis, which cited the Galtonian model for explaining the origins of genius, is picked up again in the 1990s in a parallel text by Nathaniel Weyl, a Jewish social scientist writing on Jewish superior intelligence. Here too the pitfall of imagining a "pure" selection after the Shoah, a selection that reflected the virtue of the survivors, is clear. During the 1960s Weyl, a conservative writer and economist and author of works relating to the communist threat and racial, ethnic, and class analyses of political and intellectual elites, authored a major study of Jewish achievement.[52] Looking at "creativity" in 1966, Weyl argued that "the Jewish intellectual eminence can be regarded as the end-result of seventeen centuries of selective breeding for scholars."[53] (Weyl is acknowledged in van den Haag's preface as one of the inspirations for the latter's work.) In 1986 Weyl and Marvin Weitz stated that "Ashkenazi brainpower" is "a sort of natural selection" that led to a "survival of the fittest" phenomenon among Ashkenazi Jewry, winnowing out the less physically and intellectually successful. They argued, however, that the evident Jewish mental superiority still must be documented by "real" empirical evidence.[54] In 1989 Weyl provided this empirical evidence in his study *Geography of American Achievement*. Building on the work of Richard Herrnstein concerning the decay of the intellectual elite and the "multiplication of a class of permanent indigents" (7), Weyl evolved a further model for Jewish achievement (the American reading of Jewish superior intelligence) using the "Jewish" names recorded in reference works as his source.

Weyl's work on Jewish superior intelligence survyes the biological arguments that attempt to identify and explain Jewish superior intelligence. His material is the repeated occurrence of names that are tagged as "Jewish" in standard reference tools. Given the sophisticated history of Jewish naming in the modern period, as studied by Dietz Bering, it is clear that the "Jewishness" of names or its absence is a poor indicator of the presence of Jews.[55] But the model used is in fact that of Galton, the tabulation of a "Jewish" presence within categories labeled as the site of intelligence. The categories must be "long-last-

92

ing or permanent" and must "tend to spread across the entire range of achievement" (2). Here the relative nature of Jewish superior intelligence as noted in Storfer, with Jews being better at verbal and poorer at mathematical skills, must be leveled, for it is the ubiquitousness of Jewish superior intelligence that Weyl needs to have as his guide in order to exclude African Americans from the possibility of "achievement." This he buries in a note. Unlike Galton, he excludes sports from the world of accomplishments, for in sports "this rule of uniformity does not apply" (8, n.1). African-American achievement in this one area is excluded, even though Weyl argues that he is not basing his findings on "genetic equality or inequality," but will examine "hereditarian as well as environmentalist arguments" (2).

Jewish superior intelligence for Weyl seems also to be slipping. Now there are more "Asian Indians" in both *American Men and Women of Science* and *Frontier Science and Technology* than Jews (22). Here the argument that extends the category of Jewish superior intelligence to the Asian American is made with great emphasis. Science, especially medicine, had been the area of "intelligence" dominated by the Jews and Chinese in the United States, according to Weyl in 1978.[56] Jews were still well overrepresented in his tabulation in the 1980s. Jews are also in the lead in the world of finance, according to the number of citations in *Poor's Directory of Executives and Corporate Leaders* and the number of millionaires listed by *Forbes* (85). Weyl presents a biological argument for the "enigma of Jewish eminence," drawing on the work of those earlier theorists who postulated the positive effect of Jewish "winnowing" (135) over time from the Babylonian captivity through the Middle Ages. Thus he is able temporally to circumvent any question of the Shoah.

But Weyl still links the winnowing of the Jews to a bias in favor of having the best and the brightest reproduce, after the van den Haag hypothesis. He excludes *Mischling,* the children born of Jews and non-Jews, from the pool because they "were lost to the Jewish community" and stresses the "genetically quite homogenous" nature of the Jewish race (144). The Jews "breed for mind" (147), according to Weyl. He lists nine qualities of Jewish history that formed the Jewish superior intelligence: universal male education; preferential selection of scholars as husbands; high status of scholars; marriage as a requirement for men; nuclear-family-centered society; celibacy among Christian clerics; rich Jews' ability to circumvent the social limitation on Jewish abilities to reproduce; Eastern European Jews' continuation of this tradition into the modern era; and the absence of such processes in the "Jewries of Asia and Africa" (156–57). (Not quite a Dave Letterman top-ten list, but close enough!) But in all of this, "intelligence" remains a single, closely defined biological quality tied to success in worldly things—quite the opposite of the myth of the Eastern European religious Jew beyond worldly concerns. In this view, repeated by Zborowski and Herzog, the wife's work enables the scholar to study. But it is also evident that in every case, the male Jew is seen as the carrier of Jewish superior intelligence. Jewish women are placed on the periphery of this development.

Weyl's view is an American Jewish view after the Shoah. It is the exact opposite of the view of what was believed to be happening among American Jews during the 1960s and 1970s: the rejection of conservative religious qualities by liberal American Jewry with its heavily Eastern European roots as shown by the high rate of intermarriage, the sense of guilt from having survived the "selection" of the Shoah, the movement of its children into creative as well as professional fields of endeavor, and these children's often clear rejection of the "success" model of their parents. Weyl's emphasis on "achievement" rather than "genius" among the Jews would have looked very different when, in the 1920s and 1930s, the Jews in areas such as boxing and basketball were becoming dominant. Weyl's argument is essentially eugenic and Lamarckian in its notion that acquired characteristics, such as learning a specific mode of textual interpretation, can be handed down for generations. It also relies on a model that can, with little shift, be applied to the entire population. Weyl's reading of Jewish superior intelligence is in line with the model of denial in the work of post-Shoah writers on this topic. Through stressing continuity, Weyl and the others manage to mask the Shoah and transmute it as part of a meaningful and positive history for the Jews of Europe. This type of selective misreading of Jewish superior intelligence, now understood as Jewish achievement, rests on a desire to reread history in order to provide a space for Jewish intellectuals, such as Weyl, in a safe, American context.

Such a manipulation of the idea of Jewish superior intelligence is visible in Kevin MacDonald's recent book *A People That Shall Dwell Alone: Judaism as a Group Evolutionary Strategy* (and its projected sequel on the sociobiology of anti-Semitism).[57] MacDonald generally follows Weyl's "eugenic" argument, though he calls his own approach an "evolutionary" one (180). His publishers are less subtle and sell his book under the advertisement "Jewish Eugenics." Whatever the label, his work also relies on the model of eugenic selection with its roots in Galton's idea of "hereditary genius." He sees "Judaism" not merely as religious practice but, in light of the nineteenth-century model of Moses as the first hygienist, as a "group strategy that is fairly (but not completely) closed to penetration from gentile gene pools" (ix). It is not completely clear whether this strategy was initially a conscious model. MacDonald places "biological drives" in the place of the Divinity in his model of how the history of the Jews developed. What was initially articulated within the laws of Judaism for biological reasons has now become an "unconscious" mode of selection made by "the Jewish gene."

The Jews are, for MacDonald, the only group to "avoid the powerful tendencies toward cultural and genetic assimilation" (ix). Thus there seems to be a negative centripetal force in the genetic pool that drives closed, homogenous groups into mixing and thus, given the positive valence placed on "purity" in MacDonald's argument, into corruption. The Jews have maintained biological separation through a "variety of cultural practices" such as "religious practices and beliefs, language and mannerisms, physical appearance, customs, occupations, and physically separated areas of residence which were administered by Jews according to Jewish civil and criminal law" (ix). This list of "cultural practices" is an odd one and needs further interpretation. That language and "mannerism" might well be understood as cultural one can accept; even the idea of a set of practices, such as infant male circumcision, that defines the Jews who continue to practice them is probably true. But how "physical appearance" can be seen as a voluntary act, except in the question of costume, is puzzling. Do

Jews culturally select their supposedly Jewish features? Is the Jewish nose elective? Indeed, MacDonald places a positive valence on selection from within rather than measuring selection from without. The ghetto, for example, seems to have arisen from the desire to separate Jewish living spaces because Jews were becoming integrated into Venetian society, not because they were separate.

Among the various strategies that MacDonald sees as fostering this "group evolutionary strategy" is the tendency for Jews to favor their own kind through the use of charity (chapter 6) and in economic dealings (chapter 7). But at the very core of MacDonald's argument is the question of Jewish superior intelligence. Like Weyl, he stresses the selection model—he sees selection as a result of catastrophes in which the survivors, such as those of the Babylonian captivity, formed a genetic elite, and he sees "the Talmudic academy . . . as an arena of natural selection for intelligence" (181). He also advocates a "gentile selection hypothesis" in which because of "the hostile gentile environment, there were strong pressures that favored the resourceful, intelligent, and wealthy members of the Jewish community" (192). One need not repeat how bizarre such an argument is in American scholarship after the Shoah. It presumes an uninterrupted, historically pure practice of Jewish life that can be simply and directly traced back to the Biblical origins of the Jews. The historical discontinuities, especially the Shoah, are simply removed from consideration as part of a history of the Jews. This type of sociobiological revisionism, which reinterprets the Shoah as the means to a reinforcement of Jewish separation, is odd. For MacDonald "the Nazi holocaust" leads toward "a tendency to stress a unique Jewish identity, rather than to assimilate" (49). This instrumental use of the Shoah runs throughout his book. It shows a strange sense of "meaning" attributed to the extreme violence of the Shoah, reading the "selection" that occurred as an act that furthers the quality of the Jewish genetic pool.

MacDonald records in great detail those features of the Jewish family that are seen as furthering Jewish superior intelligence. His basis for this is the "virtually common knowledge" that Jewish parents are more supportive of the intellectual lives of their children (193). Evidently, not knowing Miles Storfer's work, MacDonald, like the earlier post-Shoah investigators, relies on Zborowski and Herzog as the model for the ideal Jewish family with its emphasis on education and seemingly visceral dismissal of the uneducated (185). This Western Jewish experience grows out of the Eastern Jewish educational practices that abhorred secular learning and its methods. For MacDonald the ideal physical type of this intellectual child, remembering Franzos's comments, is "pale, emaciated, aflame with inner light" (207). This quote, which MacDonald takes from Zborowski and Herzog, points toward precisely the body type seen as destructive to Jewish superior intelligence by earlier generations of Jewish commentators and is even the point of jokes in the 1920s: Werner Finck, one of the leading non-Jewish cabaret artists in Berlin during the 1920s, commented, when a heckler yelled "Jew Boy" at him: "You are mistaken, I only look that intelligent."[58] Or to read this in the American context, Herbert Lindenberger, professor of comparative literature at Stanford University, writes that his uncle, a plastic surgeon, offered him a nose job in the 1950s, stating that Herbert's nose would be "bad for your career the way it is." Lindenberger replies, "In my particular field people usually took you for bright if they also took you for Jewish."[59] Such post-Enlightenment fantasies of the visible body of the Jew becoming invisible yet retaining its intellectual difference is extended in MacDonald's argument. Jewish superior intelligence does not stand alone: Jews also, according to MacDonald, have higher rates of certain mental illnesses, especially affective disorders (211). Mental illness and Jewish superior intelligence seem linked in the recent literature discussing the relationship between bipolar disorders and creativity. Here it is one further attribute of the "Jewish" gene pool.

MacDonald recasts all the hoary myths about Jewish psychological difference and its presumed link to Jewish superior intelligence in contemporary sociobiological garb.[60] They become signs of Jewish virtue and the rationale for Jewish achievement, following the readings of Weyl and the eugenists. But his is also an inherently American sociobiological approach to the question of Jewish superior intelligence. For all the qualities read by MacDonald as signs of superiority in their historical context are qualities perceived as positive in American society. They are signs of success and virtue as well as of intelligence.

Jewish Scientific Responses

And these qualities are repeatable, if only other groups will undertake the same pattern of selection as the Jews. Here the risk-factors must also be taken into account, but the overall advantage of Jewish intelligence is so great as to compensate for other genetic anomalies.

By the early 1990s the claim of Jewish superior intelligence was also the butt of ironic comment among American Jews. Hillel Goldberg, editor of the *Intermountain Jewish News* in Denver, can write that "We Jews possess superior intelligence. It has been known through the ages. No one is like us for deftness of symbolic patterning and sheer feats of memory."[61] His object of derision is the proliferation of acronyms in American Jewish culture. But this claim, no matter how ironically stated, comes to be an American Jewish claim by the 1990s. The culture bias in the studies of Jewish superior intelligence by American Jews or Jews living in America (such as Patai, Weyl, and, by association, MacDonald) can be judged from the relatively plaintive work by Bill Rubinstein, professor of social and economic history at Deakin University in Australia and the leading historian of Jewish life in Australia.[62] After rehearsing a wide range of explanations for Jewish superior intelligence, from child-rearing practices to Jewish self-esteem, to explain why "the Jewish 'bell-curve' of intellectual ability is further to the 'right' than those of other ethnic groups," Rubenstein returns to the Galton/van den Haag thesis: "This may be because rabbis, the intellectual elite in pre-Enlightenment societies, always married and had large families while Christian clergy were celibate (in northern Europe of course, only prior to the Reformation)" (12). He then proceeds to list Jewish geniuses from music, science, and other realms of culture. Rubinstein comments on the absence of Jewish superior intelligence in Israel, which, given this catalog approach, is seen to have produced virtually no geniuses in the realm of culture, with the one exception of S. A. Agnon. Israel, with its mass of Jews and its absence of Jewish superior intelligence, is only the prologue to his real complaint—the lack of Jewish intellectuals in Australian life. He can mention two: writer Pinchas Goldhar and architect Harry Seidler. For Rubinstein "there is something clearly missing—a spark of genuine greatness, an absence of originality, style and excellence in all but the rarest cases" (14). Unlike in America, Rubinstein comments,

to the Image

"there is much less in the way of engagement with secular intellectual or cultural life" Jews in Australia become "professionals (especially lawyers and doctors) or businessmen" rather than "academics, scientists, or intellectuals and artists" (14). At the antipodes, the view looks very different from that of Europe and the United States. Intellectual talent seems to be missing from the Jews; and the inclusion of Jews in the professions, so vital to the eugenic and sociobiological argument, marks the absence of Jewish superior intelligence.

4

Fin-de-siècle Vienna and the Jewish Response to the Image

THE SCIENCE OF RACE, IGNAZ ZOLLSCHAN, AND INTELLIGENCE

IF "POSITIVE" EVALUATIONS of Jewish intelligence by Jewish savants are ambivalent in regard to their own position as intellectuals, then the internalization of the criticism of the nature of Jewish intelligence among certain *fin-de-siècle* thinkers is equally complicated. One example of the negative formulation of this position is the self-doubt that Victor Adler, cofounder of the Austrian Socialist Party, evidenced in a letter he wrote to his political ally Karl Kautsky on 21 August 1886: "I do not have the calling for a quiet, scholarly occupation. I believe myself quite useful as a copier of the ideas of others. We Jews seem predestined to copy others' ideas."[1] This notion of a Jewish intellect that is condemned to be a "parasite" on the real intellectuals of the "host" culture is a commonplace in the anti-Semitic literature of the day. But Adler acts this out in rejecting any Jewish specificity within his complicated understanding of national identity and national language. The Jews are clever, according to Adler, but not smart. And it is only true intelligence that can be understood as a sign of civic virtue. This re-reading of Jewish superior intelligence frames the question in Vienna during the nineteenth and twentieth centuries.

The Viennese context seems to be especially rich in cases of self-doubt concerning Jewish intelligence as creative rather than parasitic. Seen as the most anti-Semitic city in Central Europe and the one in which the Jewish visibility in intellectual circles was very high, one would expect the complex reading of Jewish intelligence to have an intense and evident form. Robert Wistrich noted that "the main components of Austrian anti-Semitism, its multinational character, agitational techniques, and mass impact, were distinctly novel."[2] It was generally assumed in Vienna that there was a "Jewish mind" that transcended conversion or adaptation and that this mind was inherently unoriginal.[3] In the writings of a number of Viennese "Jewish" intellectuals at the turn of the century, such as Ignaz Zollschan, Theodor

Gomperz, Sigmund Freud, Otto Weininger, Fritz Wittels, Otto Rank, Hugo von Hofmannsthal, and Ludwig Wittgenstein, one can see a wide range of the complex internalization of questions of Jewish intelligence that are linked in striking and rather unusual ways. It is not that this was a specifically "Viennese" problem, but rather that, in a city in which the *Bildungsbürgertum*—the intellectual middle class— was defined by ideas of originality and creativity, this quality of mind came to be central in the self-definition of those labeled or self-labeled as Jews.

The tone is set in what is without a doubt the most important Viennese contribution by a Jew to the question of the racial identity of the Jews, a study by Ignaz Zollschan, which first appeared in Vienna in 1912.[4] Zollschan, a physician whose strong support of political Zionism made him an opponent of Nazi racial anthropology, redirects the Jewish question in two specific ways. He is interested first in determining the *racial value of the Jews,* whether the Jews make a fruitful cultural and economic contribution to the lands in which they live. Second, he questions whether it is possible to speak of a discrete Jewish race marked by particular qualities that predetermine their historical path. In both, the question of Jewish superior intelligence becomes one of the touchstones of his arguments. He also draws on anthropological and historical research in developing his views.

In order to address the anti-Semitic claim that Jews lack originality and productivity, Zollschan takes a comparative approach, asking whether these qualities can be recognized in all peoples except the Jews. Zollschan suggests that the anthropological basis erected to support most contemporary racial theory is an utter fabrication. Recognizing that the Germans seem to be in possession of all the qualities necessary to see themselves as superior, Zollschan deflates the idea that these qualities are inherent in the German people by establishing that the qualities of bravery, morality, rectitude, and truthfulness are not inherited from the Germanic tribes. The presence of any degree of these qualities in the Germanic tribes (and the German people through the ages) was the result of the utilitarian function of these qualities—the Germanic tribes could use these "virtues," as it were, as suited their needs. Moreover, Zollschan argues, at no time did the

Germans hold a monopoly on these positive qualities. The presence of these qualities in twentieth-century Germans is not inherent but has been acquired through hard cultural work, "in mühsamer Kultur-arbeit errungen" (177). Thus Jews too could achieve the status of "smart Germans" through their work in and contribution to the cause of *Bildung*.

But adding to the virtue of culture only works if the necessary bio-logical substratum is present. Zollschan's theory of intellect is bound up with his general racial theory in complicated ways. Intelligence is racially determined and not affected by environment: "Character, quality of genius and the quantity of genius is determined by race. While the character and the quality of genius may be determined and modified by the environment and eventually through free will, the *quantity of genius* is the single constant in all environments" (233, Zoll-schan's emphasis). Above all, one is born, not educated, to genius. Whereas "talent can be cultivated, genius arises with the power of a drive or instinct" (274). Germans as well as Jews have this innate intel-lectual ability, but this ability can and must be cultivated.

Central to Zollschan's view is the question of why a people may be predisposed toward a particular *mode of thought*. His answer is that this predisposition stems from an inherited mneme. He argues that the mneme that determine psychic instincts are not equally distrib-uted among various races (279). The Jews show a superior intelligence not only because of their inherent biological nature but also because they are a pure race and have not diluted their intellectual abilities. For Zollschan, the intellect is the rational antithesis of instinct ("intu-ition"). Genius is the result of intellect overcoming instinct, which actually succeeds only if one has a racial stock comprising the right mneme. Overcoming instincts is thus a process that differs in mixed and pure races: "Overcoming instincts is relatively easy in crossed races . . . for the great segments are so disparate that truly deep in-stincts that could be difficult to overcome are not present. Brilliant but not profound intelligence is often found here, but deeper insight is rarely found" (295). Pure races, on the other hand, show "brilliant intuition" and "creativity." Zollschan thus projects the image of the clever Jew onto the mixed-race individual: the *Mischling* becomes the locus of faulty Jewish intelligence. This fault is not the result of Jewish racial qualities but rather of the irresponsible (and thus un-Jewish) act of intermarriage or conversion. Zollschan's projection of fault onto a subgroup of Jews is a classic move on the part of Jewish scientists dealing with the charges of racial difference at the *fin de siècle*.

For Zollschan, pure races (Germans or Jews) are creative races; thus he spends the last two hundred pages of his study documenting the "creativity of the Jews." The centerpiece of this effort is neither a list of "great men" nor a calculation of the relative statistical preeminence of Jewish superior intelligence but rather a complex refutation of the charge of Jewish unoriginality and parasitism. This charge, first made in the "scientific" anti-Semitic literature by Eugen Dühring (who is cited by Zollschan), contends that Jews have made no independent contribution to civilization. According to this view, all Jewish contributors to culture are "exploiters, arrogant upstarts, and moral perverts" (369). This is, of course, another way of speaking about the modern, but it is the modern understood as Jewish and therefore as derivative. Because the virtue of originality marked "genius" even in late-nineteenth-century scientific thought, this charge of parasitism has the greatest resonance in Vienna, where the link between the original and the creative is absolute. It is this creativity that Zollschan's contemporaries in Vienna most doubted in themselves, and that becomes one of the means of understanding the self-doubt not only of the Jew but especially of the mixed-race writers at the turn of the century.

THEODOR GOMPERZ AND THE JEWISH GENIUS

We continue our quest for the meaning ascribed to Jewish superior intelligence by Jewish intellectuals in Vienna with Theodor Gomperz, one of the most widely respected members of the faculty of the University of Vienna. A classicist, he was one of Sigmund Freud's teachers and mentors, and his wife was one of Freud's patients for decades. His position was that of a "public" intellectual. In 1904, eight years before his death, he penned an unpublished, untitled essay on the "limits of Jewish intellectual ability."[5] For Gomperz the central question is why, given the Jewish "gift" for art and science, there are so few Jews of the "very top range" (384). Gomperz uses the phrase "Jewish intellectuals [*jüdische Intellectuellen*]" for this cadre.

Gomperz's argument uses a catalog to provide a short history of how Jewish intelligence failed to cope with the rise of modernity. For Gomperz, although Jews form a tiny minority who have been emancipated for only a very short time (384), they have managed to establish themselves well in a number of intellectual fields. Intelligence and acculturation are thus interchangeable categories. Yet after civil emancipation in the nineteenth century, Jews are of the first rank only in the realms of the reproductive arts—acting and musical performance. Here he evokes the canon: Sarah Bernhardt and Rahel, Joseph Joachim, and Arthur Rubinstein. Jews may be visible as performers, but they are not creative in Wagner's sense and do not contribute much to the production of literature or music. Here Mendelssohn-Bartholdy is cited as a true exception, but, like Adolf Jellinek in the 1860s, Gomperz notes the absence of a Jewish writer of tragedies, such as Heinrich von Kleist or Christian Friedrich Hebbel (386). After Goethe (and *Faust*), tragedy marks the high point of bourgeois cultural production. The novel—even Goethe's, and even after Hegel's reappraisal of the genre—remains for Jews in the nineteenth century an art form that is not "serious."[6] Yet poetry marks the Jews as gifted in the arts, if not on the highest level. Gomperz begins his catalog of poets with Heinrich Heine, who is disqualified as a "real" poet because of his destructive irony. Here Gomperz finds himself in good company among nineteenth- and early-twentieth-century Viennese Jews: Karl Kraus's similar view of Heine shows the anxiety about distinguishing between "real" art and "Jewish" art—qualified because of Heine's image as the arch-convert and because Heine's diseased body was seen as matching his caustic wit.[7]

Gomperz's catalog of Jewish superior intelligence moves through the realms of science with Herschel, Hertz, and Ehrlich and political economy with Ricardo and Marx; philology and medicine follow. Mathematics and chess show the intellectual "sharpness" of the Jews (388). All these examples show that Jews excel when "pure rationality" is needed, which accounts for their absence on the roll of great poets. Thus Jews have "to a high degree critical rationality, a sharpness of judgment, dazzling wit and spirit" that are missing in "the unconscious [*Unbewusste*], twilightlike, dreamlike, presentiment-full" mind of the Aryan (387). Thus "for certain types of excellence the Jewish mind is too brilliant/clear" (387). This clarity is the result of two thousand years of urban life devoted to trade and the pursuit of the "casuistry of the Talmud" (387), which also causes an extremely high degree of mutability mirrored in the acting of a Rahel or the poetry of a Heine.

If the superior intelligence of the Jews is the result of two millennia of urban life and persecution, the Jews also lack rootedness in the "soil of the *Volksthums*" (387). This isolation from the land, from agriculture and the raising of animals, gives Jews a fragmented relationship to nature and disqualifies their intelligence from the realm of true genius. As a result, the Jews have not been able to create a mythology of their own and, without such a mythology, have not been able to produce true poets (388). Here Gomperz reflects the views of Ernest Renan and the idea that the origin of Judaism (or indeed of monotheism) was not an original contribution of the Jews but rather a by-product of their cultural insularity. The diminished quality of the Jewish contribution to Western civilization can be measured by the absence of a Jewish mythology—to equal Wagner's!

In terms of the Galtonian claim of the inheritability of Jewish superior intelligence, Gomperz cites his own family's contribution, such as having had the first Jew admitted to the university in the eighteenth century and the first to become a member of the Royal Society of London (385). But Gomperz's reflection on his own family's ability places them in the realm of the not-quite-creative, the not-quite-genius. For all their movement toward insight is blighted by being limited to the "critical rationality, a sharpness of judgment." Theirs is a brilliance without mythology, a science without metaphysics. The fragment closes with a representation of Spinoza as "almost" a mystic and thus the closest Jew to approach Gomperz's ideal of Jewish superior intelligence. But Gomperz cannot leave the explanation of genius to the realm of the irrational and the mystical. He stresses, following the good liberal ideology of his day, that such "an outline of national or racial character cannot have universal applicability. It usually concerns 'more or less.' A human being is finally a human being and can evolve qualities foreign to the majority of his racial peers [*Volksgenossen*]" (389). Transformation is possible. Indeed, mutability is a quality of the Jew evolved in the two millennia that have led to the production of this inferior or at least partial form of Jewish superior intelligence.

Gomperz's essay tries to rescue Jewish creativity by introducing Spinoza as the classic figure of Jewish superior intelligence; but the essay fragments at this point. Clearly Gomperz, seeing himself as a public intellectual like Spinoza, attempts to restore his own position as an intellectual. His family is intellectual as well as intelligent; yet his strengths lie in the abstract and not the poetic. Indeed, as a historian of classical poetry, he is in the perfect position to stress the positive attributes of the Jew as critic. Yet historians and critics are not original; they depend on the existence of the objects they study, on the great works of literature they explicate. Gomperz is not Spinoza. Certainly, any individual may depart from the model of the smart Jew that Gomperz sees as dominating Jewish intellectual life and circles, yet the national type seems rather more than less true as reflected by Gomperz's own production.

Gomperz's essay on Jewish intelligence remained unpublished in his own day. His response was similar to Zollschan's answer concerning Jewish qualities and, like Zollschan's book, stressed the limited accomplishments of the Jews in relationship to their "host peoples." The power of the parasitic model remained even as the intellectuals who attempted to rebut it were forced to draw into question their own insight.

SIGMUND FREUD, CREATIVITY, AND INTELLIGENCE

Sigmund Freud, Gomperz's protégé, also sensed this lack of creative genius attributed to the Jews. The Jews had been seen as a type of "superior degenerate" whose superficial brilliance masked their inherited degenerate state: "The majority of degenerates are Semites, at least in terms of their ancestry. The Jews are at the stage of physical and mental degeneration."[8] The young Sigmund Freud, in the 1870s, could ironically evoke the limitations of the Jewish mind in a letter to his Jewish friend Emil Fluss: "How well I can imagine your feelings. To leave the native soil, dearly-beloved relatives,—the most beautiful surroundings—ruins close by—I must stop or I'll be as sad as you—and you yourself know best what you are leaving behind. . . . Oh Emil why are you a prosaic Jew? Journeymen imbued with Christian-Germanic fervor have composed beautiful lyrical poetry in similar circumstances."[9] The unoriginality of the Jewish mind is a reflection of the limitations assumed to be inherent in the Jew. But, as with the much later comments of Gomperz, it is in the field of the creative writer rather than the intellectual that Jewish insufficiency manifests itself in the most evident form. Jews are "prosaic"; Christians/Aryans are poetic. This is the difference between the merely smart and the truly creative.

Freud plays with this distinction between creativity and intelligence in one of the jokes he recorded from the mid-1890s in *Jokes and Their Relation to the Unconscious* (1905): "Itzig had been declared fit for service in the artillery. He was clearly an intelligent lad, but intractable and without any interest in service. One of his superior officers, who was friendly disposed to him, took him on one side and said to him: 'Itzig, you're no use to us. I'll give you a piece of advice: buy yourself a cannon and make yourself independent!' "[10] Here Jewish intelligence is reflected in the mercantile spirit and the desire not to be a good soldier. Here, too, Freud associates intelligence with its alternative, the inability of the Jewish male to become a "real" man, a soldier. For the Jew thinks too much, and thinks in a material, crass way.

Now we must try to imagine Freud confronted with this view in terms of his own creativity. Of all the topics he could have addressed about the nature of the psyche, why did "creativity" capture him? This choice seems as idiosyncratic a means of discussing the normal structure of the psyche as those of dreams, or jokes, or slips of the tongue. One answer is that each of these can be linked to debates within the racial science of the late nineteenth century.[11] Freud's view was, on the surface, quite different from Lombroso's. In his writings from the close of the nineteenth century through the onset of World War I, Freud saw "creativity" (as he saw dreams or slips of the tongue or neurotic symptoms) not as a set of formal processes or disease mechanisms in a subset of the population but as clues to the normal functioning of the unconscious in everyone. Where Lombroso saw the "mad" and their aesthetic productions as "throwbacks" to an earlier, more primitive state of development or as a sign of the diseased nature of the Jew, Freud saw all "creativity" as a sign of the universal, underlying forces that make all human beings human. He, too, saw creativity as pathological, as the result of deviation from "normal" psychological development, but as such, this pathology was a potential of all human beings, not merely a predestined subset. He studied the creative to understand the centrality of unconscious processes, especially the role of unconscious motivation in human action.

Freud, in his case studies of Leonardo da Vinci (1910) and Michelangelo (1914), as well as in his critical readings of the creative works of Wilhelm Jensen (1907) and the strange autobiography of the "psychotic" Dr. Daniel Schreber (1911), looked at "creative" work as a sign of the displacement of psychic (for Freud, sexual) energy into a different, seemingly unrelated undertaking.[12] He sees the "creative" impulse as a form of displacement or repression analogous to the symptoms of the neurotic. The symptoms of the neurotic parallel the experiences or fantasies that underlie the symptoms but do not directly represent the underlying conflict that gives rise to the symptoms. For Freud, these products (whether symptoms or works of art) always arise in the sphere of the sexual. The "creative" individual is by Freud's definition one who *must* sublimate his sexual drive into the realm of fantasy, and the truly creative individual represses all his latent instinctual drives. Like Gomperz's image of the Jew in Viennese society, the creative figure must deny his essence to become what he can become. What is repressed in these creative individuals is the atavistic sex drive. The reason for this sublimation, as in the case of the artists and authors noted above, is the socially unacceptable direction of the expression of their sexuality, from the homosexuality of Leonardo to the incestuous leanings of Jensen. These individuals represent sexuality on an earlier plane of development than the sexuality of the heterosexual.

In certain individuals, Freud argued, the active, social repression of these drives leads to the total sublimation of sexual curiosity and, thereby, to the creative process and the true work of art (SE 9:167–76). The "creative" object thus represents the fixed fantasies of the individual. The essential nature of the process of "creativity" is to mask the inherently objectionable (from the standpoint of society) nature of its origin. Works of art "conceal their personal origin and, by obeying the laws of beauty, bribe other people with a bonus of pleasure" (SE 23:187).[13] The overarching "laws of beauty," the techniques of the aesthetic, are the means by which the "creative" works. The universal mask, separate from the "creative" impulse, hides and manipulates, and shapes how the observer sees the work of art. "Creativity" is seen in terms of the "creator" who produces a product, which is implicitly a commodity, as value is inherently attached to it. The product is cast in a form that is universal, and it manipulates the reader or viewer through its evocation of some universal law (the aesthetic). The "creativity" of the artist consists of placing a repressed aspect of the artist's psyche into the realm of the aesthetic. As Josef Breuer—focusing on the ultimate "creative" figure for nineteenth-century German culture—said in the *Studies in Hysteria* (jointly authored with Freud in 1895): "Goethe did not feel he had dealt with an experience till he had discharged it in a creative artistic activity" (SE 2:207). Goethe is the true creative genius for such Jews as Freud and Breuer. He represents German depth—the antithesis of Jewish cleverness. They are not the only Jews in German *fin-de-siècle* culture to understand Goethe as the exemplary genius—as poet, intellectual, and as scientist.[14]

But it is the act of seeing—the observer's act of seeing and responding to the creative product of the artist—that defines "creativity" for Freud. To use one of his examples, we (the naive viewers) look at Leonardo's *Holy Family* and "see" the perfection and beauty of the work, but we also are instructed in its "meaning" by the psychoanalyst, who "sees" beneath the initial evocation of the aesthetic (which disguises the motivation of the author) and provides interpretations of the work and the psyche of the artist. The uninformed viewer's response is aesthetic; with the aid of the interpreter (Freud), we can understand the source of the artist's "creativity" and thus truly understand the "unseen" aspect of the work. Analogous to the psychoanalyst's explaining to the patient the typography of the dynamic unconscious, the critic explains to the viewer what he or she is observing. We thus learn to distrust the initial act of seeing and link the act of seeing, not with a visceral response, but with the act of knowing. Freud's focus seems to be solely on the motivation that underlies "creativity." He illustrates the discovery that the "creative" individual is "subject to the laws which govern both normal and pathological activity with equal cogency" (SE 11:63).

Yet Freud's hidden agenda is to undermine our sense that we can see the world directly. This is clearly seen in his popular essay, "Creative Writers and Day-Dreaming," which was presented as a lecture to a lay (i.e., nonmedical) audience in Vienna in 1907 (SE 9:143–53). Freud's overt intention is to present the parallels between "creativity" and childhood play. He thus defines "creativity" and the special status of the "creative" artist: "We laymen have always been intensely curious to know—like the Cardinal who put a similar question to Ariosto—from what sources that strange being, the creative writer, draws his material, and how he manages to make such an impression on us with it and to arouse in us emotions which, perhaps, we had not thought ourselves capable" (SE 9:143). Freud places himself as a "layman" in opposition to the "creative" individual who makes a world that seems complete and who uses that world to manipulate our ("lay" or "non-creative") emotions. But he is a very special "lay" observer, one who has the insight to understand the underlying meaning as well as the immediate effect of the "creative." Freud's initial analogy is to the play of the child. Play is rooted in childhood fantasies of being able to control at least the immediate world of toys in opposition to the real world, which is beyond the manipulation of the child.[15] Into this universe, in which uncontrollable realities are transmuted into manipulatable fantasies, the child escapes: "for many things which, if they were real, could give no enjoyment, can do so in the play of fantasy" (SE 9: 144). For Freud, "humor" is the ultimate example of how the healthy adult can escape back into this world of playfulness: "by equating his ostensibly serious occupations of to-day with his childhood games, he can throw off the too heavy burden imposed on him by life and win the high yield of pleasure afforded by *humor*" (SE 9:145, Freud's emphasis).

Fantasy is like dreaming. It uses everyday impressions that are related to earlier (infantile) experience to create "a situation relating to the future." Thus, the "creative" individual is like the playful child but is also like the neurotic in that the "creative" individual has the compulsion to tell (represent) his or her fantasies.[16] Freud writes that "there is a class of human beings upon whom, not a god, indeed, but a stern goddess—Necessity—has allotted the task of telling what they suffer and what things give them happiness. These are the victims of nervous illness, who are obliged to tell their fantasies" (SE 9:146). In paraphrasing Goethe's *Torquato Tasso* in this passage ("and when a man falls silent in his torment / A god granted me to tell how I suffer"), Freud elides the artist as figure (Tasso) and the artist as author (Goethe) with the "mad person" as figure (Tasso) and the healer of the "mad" (Freud). The artificial line that Freud drew between the "creative" individual as neurotic and himself (and his listeners) at the beginning of his essay is shown at its close to be a false dichotomy. The informed, psychoanalytically instructed observer "sees" below the surface. Freud joins the world of art as artifact and inspiration in his "creative" role as the psychoanalyst, but only in the most hidden and covert way.

In this 1907 essay the "creative" individual is also not gender-neutral. Young women have more erotic fantasies than young men, who have more fantasies of ambition. Both must learn to conceal and repress these drives, as they are unacceptable in polite society: "The well-brought-up young woman is only allowed a minimum of erotic desire, and the young man has to learn to suppress the excess of self-regard which he brings with him from the spoilt days of his childhood, so that he may find his place in a society which is full of other individuals making equally strong demands" (SE 9:147). Human sexuality, the wellspring of "creativity," is initially and more strongly present in the fantasy world of the female—and, as Adolf Jellinek had commented in Vienna some forty years earlier, in the fantasy world of the feminized Jew. And while these trends merge at some point early in life, the female's fantasies are more sexualized in their most primitive (i.e., earliest) form. Here too the quality of such fantasy is drawn into question. For the female's fantasy is more primitive, less valuable, and more superficial. In the rhetoric of the day, as we have seen, this damaged fantasy is also that of the feminized Jew. Because it is impossible

for Freud to place his "masculine" fantasy at risk, he constructs a bipolar image of "fantasy" and thus negates the creation of a subset of
difference for the male Jew, whose spoiled creativity haunts the *fin de
siècle*.

Freud, in this essay, thus provides a set of working hypotheses
about "creativity": first, that "creativity" has to do with the representation of internal stories in a highly affective and effective manner;
second, that "creativity" is parallel to the states of "childhood" and
"neurosis," in that it is an attempt to gain control over the real world
by creating a fantasy world over which one can have control (with
humor as the prime example of this control); and third, that there is a
difference, but also a similarity, between the fantasy life (and therefore
the "creativity") of men and of women. These hypotheses are framed
by a most ambiguous narrative voice, which claims that the "creative"
artist is different from the author of the text we are reading (as made
evident in the banality of the hypothetical novel Freud outlines in his
essay), yet which draws parallels between the author's experience and
that of the artist both in reality and in the work of art.

Freud is, however, not interested in the problem of "creativity" for
its own sake. He sees his explanation of the nature of "creativity" as
one of the central proofs for the validity of his science, psychoanalysis.
In the programmatic 1913 text, "The Claims of Psycho-Analysis to Scientific Interest," Freud outlines the theory of repression not only as
the key to understanding the production of the "beautiful" but also
as a substantial piece of evidence of the explanatory power (read: scientific validity) of his views. He stresses the power of the aesthetic
on the viewer but leaves the door open to further meaningful contributions to the understanding of the aesthetic through the science of
psychoanalysis:

> Most of the problems of artistic creation and appreciation await
> further study, which will throw the light of analytic knowledge
> on them and assign them their place in the complex structure
> presented by the compensation for human wishes. Art is a con-
> ventionally accepted reality in which, thanks to artistic illusion,
> symbols and substitutes are able to provoke real emotions. Thus
> art constitutes a region half-way between a reality which frus-

trates wishes and the wish-fulfilling world of the imagination—a region in which, as it were, primitive man's strivings for omnipotence are still in force. (SE 23:187–88)

Freud's reading of the work of art is clearly within the paradigm of late-nineteenth-century visual and literary art and, more importantly, is still bound by Lombroso's association of the "creative" and the "primitive." But it is not the "primitive" in the inhabitants of the asylum or of the prison, the throwback, but the "primitive" in every human being. Freud associates the "creative" with the universal and with a universal science, psychoanalysis.

The basic difficulty of Freud's argument is clear: if sexual repression is the key to "creativity," why are not all individuals who are sexually repressed "creative"? Creativity, like the feminine and Jewishness, becomes a nut that cannot truly be cracked.[17] After World War I, Freud himself became quite aware of this objection, as he later noted in his study, "Dostoevsky and Parricide" (1928): "Before the problem of the creative artist analysis must, alas, lay down its arms" (SE 21:177). Or, as he states in his "Autobiographical Study" (1925): "[Psychoanalysis] can do nothing towards elucidating the nature of the artistic gift, nor can it explain the means by which the artist works—artistic technique" (SE 20:70). But I would rather ask the question in reverse: Why are Freud's early categories of "creativity" constructed to make all human beings potentially "creative"? Why does Freud universalize the question of the "creative"? Why does he place "creativity" within those sexual drives and psychic phenomena that are, according to Freud, present in all human beings, not merely the "insane"? Why does the feminine seem to have the closest relationship to the wellspring of the "creative"? What do "sexuality," "creativity," and "madness" have to do with one another at the turn of the century? Why must Freud maintain that "creativity" is like "neurosis" in its inherent characteristic of repression? Is not the real problem the lack of "creativity" on the part of the scientist as intellectual?

The meaning of Freud's representation of the "creative," not as Lombroso's "throwback" or deviant but as a reflection of universal processes, can be understood in the context of Freud's role as a scientist and a Jew in *fin-de-siècle* Vienna. We can assume that the question of creativity had a special significance for Freud, especially during the period from 1903 to 1910, when Otto Weininger's views were most widely circulated and discussed in Vienna. Weininger's views were being read against the more general debates in psychiatry about the special status of Jewish genius.[18] Freud moved the question of the Jew's "madness" and the Jew's "creativity" onto another level of debate by making the special definition of these concepts and their relationship part of his proof for the universality of the human psyche. Freud's stress on the sexual etiology of all neurosis led to his view that creativity is analogous to neurosis in its repression of conflicted sexual identity. The *fin-de-siècle* subtext that links the creative, the psychopathological, and the sexual to the portrait of the psyche of the Jew is precisely what Freud was battling—covertly—in his work on the "creative."

Freud's response to this subtext was to separate the question of Jewish "madness" and Jewish "creativity" from the universal laws he saw as causing psychopathology. These laws are parallel to the laws that determine the "creative." It is not surprising that Freud would focus so much attention on refashioning Lombroso's categories of the "normal" and the "abnormal." Unlike the Italian Jew Lombroso, Freud (according to his own account) only first began to sense his "racial" difference when he began to study medicine. For him, science and race were linked, and separating the two would become a lifelong struggle.[19] Seen in this context, Weininger also offered Freud a major challenge in his view of "Jewish" medicine as a purely mechanistic, materialistic medicine, more chemistry than the art of healing. Jews are not "creative" in the realm of science, Weininger argued, but rather destructive.

Freud first struggles to show how everyone who is creative or dreams or is "mad" responds to universal rules of psychic organization. Freud's science of psychoanalysis, which evolves over the closing decade of the nineteenth century, is rooted in a materialistic paradigm but self-consciously attempts to move medicine toward an understanding of the dynamic processes of the psyche, the immaterial aspect of the human being. Freud abandons "chemistry" for "metapsychology." He is constrained to do this because of his certainty that human sexuality—associated with the obsessive hypersexuality of the Jews, the very source of their perverse "madness"—lies at the center of human experience. Freud positions himself, more and more successfully as his thought develops after World War I, in opposition to the positivistic clinical gaze of Jean-Martin Charcot and the materialistic brain mythology of Moriz Benedikt. His is not the "Jewish" medicine castigated by Weininger and has, therefore, at least the potential to claim a position as "creative." Yet Freud positions himself ambiguously, as we have seen in his 1907 essay on creativity. For in openly labeling himself as "creative," he would be labeling himself as a Jew and setting himself off from the universal role of the "layman" (to use his word) as observer. But he is not the "layman," he is the scientist-physician. And his science must be universal, not particular, in its claims for "creativity." The scientist-physician lays claim to the universal gaze, unencumbered by national or racial perspective—especially in the arena of sexology, where the accusation is that Jews, by their very nature, are predisposed to seeing the sexual everywhere.

Freud thus has the "creative" operate as a function of the force present in all human beings—sexuality. As we have seen, this force was used to label the Jew as different; for Freud, it becomes the source of all human endeavors, including the truly "creative." That this sexuality is present more in the feminine fantasy than in the masculine is a (reversed) mirror-image of Weininger's dismissal of Jews' sexually contaminated "creativity." In fact, Freud reverses the poles of Weininger's anti-Semitic discourse on "creativity," and while he does maintain the link between "madness" and "creativity," he sees these tendencies as a product of universal rather than racial psychology. What is striking in Freud's discussions of "creativity" from 1900 to 1919 is that he never cites any Jewish writer or painter—not his contemporary and neighbor, the playwright Arthur Schnitzler, or the best-known German artist of his day, the Impressionist Max Liebermann, or the classic examples of Jewish creativity, Spinoza and Heine—in his discussions of "creativity" and the nature of the "creative." "Creativity" is universal; Freud's examples are not. They self-consciously eliminate the "Jewish" component in European culture.[20]

In the course of his writing, Freud eventually comes to terms with the claims of a parasitic Jewish intelligence. In his paper on a case of female homosexuality (1920), one of Freud's last uses of the term "degenerate" appears in this context (SE 18:149). The authority of medicine is the condemning voice that Freud mockingly quotes to illustrate its own limits:

> Perhaps you would like to know in advance, having in mind our earlier talks, what attitude contemporary psychiatry adopts towards the problems of obsessional neurosis. But it is a meager chapter. Psychiatry gives names to the different obsessions but says nothing further about them. On the other hand it insists that those who suffer from these symptoms are 'degenerates.' This gives small satisfaction; in fact it is a judgment of value— a condemnation instead of an explanation. We are supposed to think that every possible sort of eccentricity may arise in degenerates. Well, it is true that we must regard those who develop such symptoms as somewhat different in their nature from other people. But we may ask: are they more 'degenerate' than other neurotics—than hysterical patients, for instance, or those who fall ill of psychoses? Once again, the characterization is evidently too general. Indeed, we may doubt whether there is any justification for it at all, when we learn that such symptoms occur too in distinguished people of particularly high capacities, capacities important for the world at large. It is true that, thanks to their own discretion and to the untruthfulness of their biographers, we learn little that is intimate about the great men who are our models; but it may nevertheless happen that one of them, like Émile Zola, may be a fanatic for the truth, and we then learn from him of the many strange obsessional habits to which he was a life-long victim. Psychiatry has found a way out by speaking of 'dégénérés supérieurs.' Very nice. But we have found from psychoanalysis that it is possible to get permanently rid of these strange obsessional symptoms, just as of other complaints and just as in people who are not degenerate. I myself have succeeded repeatedly in this. (SE 16:260)[21]

The locus of this voice of authority is problematic. Is it merely the French medical tradition, with its general acceptance in Germany, against which Freud is arguing, or is it an internalized element of Freud's own system of belief that he is striving to overcome? If it is the latter, the internalized voice of the biologist in a struggle with the psychoanalyst, other residual elements of this conflict should be found in Freud's work. The subject of Freud's comment, the "dégénérés supérieurs," is a category by which late-nineteenth-century psychiatry defined the nature of creativity and was also one of the explanations of Jewish creativity in cultural and scientific fields. In destroying the myth of the "dégénérés supérieurs," Freud was also protecting his own position as an innovative scientist from the accusation of being merely a clever but degenerate Jew. Ability such as Zola's, which Freud admired and wished to emulate, is not one of the stigmata of degeneration.

The questions of Jewish creativity and the nature of Jewish superior intelligence shift when Freud addresses the B'nai B'rith in Vienna in 1926 on the occasion of his seventieth birthday. Freud tries to explain to a Jewish audience what being Jewish means to him in his old age. Being Jewish, for Freud, is sharing "many obscure emotional forces, which were the more powerful the less they could be expressed in words, as well as a clear consciousness of inner identity, the safe privacy of a common mental construction" (SE 20:274). But this secret quality of Jewishness, which exists on both an unconscious and a conscious level, and that redounds throughout history as the ethnopsychological definition of the Jew, provides the rationale for Freud's ability to do science. "Because I was a Jew I found myself free from many prejudices which restricted others in the use of their intellect; and as a Jew I was prepared to join the Opposition and to do without agreement with the 'compact majority'" (SE 20:274). Freud's scientific ability, an ability that was furthered by the "circle of picked men of high character" he found in the Jewish fraternal organization, was rooted in his Jewishness. Not that psychoanalysis was a "Jewish science," as Pierre Janet was claimed to have commented, but rather that Freud's own intelligence and character, in its essential Jewishness, enabled him to create this new field of science. Being Jewish meant having a Jewish superior intelligence that was defined as being rational and unprejudiced and experienced in persecution. This intelligence is a marker of Jewish virtue in a world given to the desire to always be part of the "compact majority." Any people could experience such a transformation and benefit, but the Jews already had experienced the world this way, and their experience was now transmitted in "the safe privacy of a common mental construction." His contemporaries, such as Theodor Reik (who, along with Freud and Eduard Hintschmann, was one of the only first-generation psychoanalysts to be members of the Viennese B'nai B'rith), "were especially struck" by these very words as the appropriate central definition of the Jew.[22]

Freud's work on "madness" and "creativity" in this period, which was limited by the anti-Semitic fantasies of *fin-de-siècle* medicine and culture, responded to the problem evoked by Jewish superior intelligence with a gesture toward universalization. It was only with the political triumph of the German Nazis in 1933 that Freud openly praised the Jews as an inherently superior people: "When one thinks that ten or twelve percent of the Nobel Prize winners are Jews and when one thinks of their other great achievements in sciences and in the arts, one has every reason to think them superior."[23] In 1938, Freud, writing in a German émigré magazine, directly confronted the question of Jewish creativity. His answer to the rise of anti-Semitism is a paraphrase of a lost or invented essay, reputedly by a non-Jew, in which the contributions of the Jews to the Diaspora are evaluated: "Nor can we call them [the Jews] in any sense inferior. Since we have allowed them to co-operate in our cultural tasks, they have acquired merit by valuable contributions in all the spheres of science, art, and technology, and they have richly repaid our tolerance" (SE 23:292). "Science," such as psychoanalysis, and "art" both are "creative" and mark the positive presence of the Jew in European society.

In his final study, *Moses and Monotheism* (1937–38; 1939), Freud resolved to his own satisfaction how the Jews "acquired the characteristics which distinguish them," but "how they have been able to retain their individuality till the present day" remained a riddle (SE 32:136–37). Freud's solution does posit a specific Jewish intelligence as opposed to a non-Jewish physicality. For Freud, "the advance in intellectuality" of the Jews is the result of Jewish belief systems. In prohibiting images the Jews emphasized intellectuality [*Geistigkeit*], "forces, that is, which cannot be grasped by the senses (particularly by the sight)" (SE 33:114). The result of this emphasis on the intellect is to make the Jews inherently different:

> The pre-eminence given to intellectual labours throughout some two thousand years in the life of the Jewish people has, of course, had some effect. It has helped to check the brutality and the tendency to violence which are apt to appear where the development of muscular strength is the popular ideal. Harmony in the cultivation of intellectual and physical activity, such as was achieved by the Greek people, was denied to the Jews. In this dichotomy their decision was at least in favour of the worthier alternative. (SE 33:115)

The Jews are weaker (than the Germans?) but smarter. They do not share the vice of violence that haunts the "compact majority." Their intelligence is a mark of their virtue and their virtue is the absence of brutality. But the source of this virtue is their inherited intelligence. Jews are intelligent not solely because of their pariah status, as Freud intimated in his birthday speech to the B'nai B'rith a decade before, but because their pariah status is inherited across the generations. Although the Jews are not like the Greeks, who managed to combine both physicality and intellect, the Jews made the right choice, intellect (unlike the Germans?). Better smart than strong, for being strong leads to brutality and being smart leads to creativity. For, as Freud had commented in the original draft line of the paragraph quoted above, "In this dichotomy their decision was at least in favour of the alternative that was more significant culturally."

The creativity of the Jews is a sign of their ongoing contribution to European culture. Yet how they remain identifiable as Jews is a mystery even in 1938. Their creativity, the sign of the intellect, places them in direct contrast to the cruel brutality of the Germans and the Austrians. The ambiguity of "creativity" in the *fin de siècle* vanished in the harsh light of the Nazi realization of German culture's anti-Semitic fantasies. Against this terrible reality, Freud no longer spoke indirectly.

One *fin-de-siècle* Jewish writer in Vienna who was labeled as a "dégénéré supérieur" was Otto Weininger.[24] Jewish scientists such as Freud's friend Leopold Löwenfeld, the Munich neurologist, saw Weininger as a "mad" scientist. In his study of sexual drives published in 1911, Löwenfeld labeled Weininger a "doubtlessly highly gifted madman whose *Sex and Character* has achieved unearned attention."[25] Sigmund Freud's younger Viennese contemporary, Weininger had presented the dichotomy between the Jew and the Aryan in his revised dissertation, *Sex and Character* (1903). Weininger, a student of philosophy and biology at the University of Vienna, killed himself in 1903, shortly after publishing *Sex and Character,* in the house in Vienna in which Beethoven had died. Weininger was both a baptized Jew and a repressed homosexual.[26] His book became an immediate bestseller and established him as a serious contributor to the discourse about the relationship between race and gender at the beginning of the century.[27] This work of intensive self-hatred had an unprecedented influence on the scientific discourse about Jews and women at the turn of the century. Why? Although Weininger's suicide shortly after publication of the book helped to publicize his ideas, they were hardly new to his contemporaries. The appeal of Weininger's work was not innovation but summation. To the beginning of a century he help up a polemical mirror that many found to contain truths of their times.

Read by Freud in an early draft, *Sex and Character* was fundamental in shaping at least some of Freud's attitudes toward the nature of the body. Indeed, the book was the basis of the rupture of his friendship with Wilhelm Fliess, who accused Freud of having betrayed Fliess's idea of bisexuality to Weininger. This accusation of plagiarism, however, never evoked the image of the unoriginal Jew, and the argument between Freud and Weininger over "Jewishness" is never mentioned in the exchange of letters between Freud and Fliess in 1904. The question of the originality and creativity of the Jew, especially the Jewish scientist, is central to their exchange but unspoken in their letters.[28] Weininger's *Sex and Character* restates in a scientific (biological) context Arthur Schopenhauer's views on women and extends the category of the feminine to the Jew. It argues, within the rhetoric of contemporary science, the existence of a psychological scale that runs from the Jewish mind at one end to the Aryan at the other. The ends of this scale are parallel to the "feminine" and the "masculine."

Weininger stresses that categories such as "Jew" and "Woman" are psychological states always found in tension with "Christian" and "Male." Weininger, a converted Jew, sees himself as less "Jewish" than the arch-anti-Semite Richard Wagner, whom he labels as "having an accretion of Jewishness in his art" (305). Jewishness is a "common mental construction" and does "not refer to a nation or to a race, to a creed or to a scripture. When I speak of the Jew I mean neither an individual nor the whole body, but mankind in general, in so far as it has a share in the platonic idea of Judaism" (306). Weininger constructs the image of the Jew, like that of Woman, as inherently negative, as necessarily to be transcended.

For Weininger, Jews, like women, are "without a trace of genius" (316). In this they are like "the Negroes" among whom "a genius has scarcely ever appeared" (302). True geniuses are the anti-Semites who sense the Jew within themselves, like Herder, Goethe, Schopenhauer, and Wagner, and can overcome the Jewishness within. Weininger attacks Spinoza and Heine as the representative Jewish thinkers who are viewed by his contemporaries as "creative" geniuses. He finds them incapable of true genius: "The philosopher Spinoza, about whose purely Jewish descent there can be no doubt, is incomparably the greatest Jew of the last nine hundred years, much greater than the poet Heine (who indeed was destitute of any quality of true greatness)" (216). Though great, Spinoza lacks genius. What passes for genius in the Jew and Woman is but "exaggerated egotism" (317). Jewish creativity is seen as inherently superficial. Weininger dismisses Heine as "destitute of any quality of true greatness" and Spinoza as "show[ing] his Jewish character" in his idea of nature (316). The Jewish mind is that of a "slave and a determinist" because it rejects free will. The Jew, like Woman, is incapable of either "genius or the depth of stupidity of which mankind is capable" (316). They "pursue any object with equal zeal because they have no intrinsic standard of value" (317). Jews and women are without virtue.

and the Jewish Response

What characterizes Woman is her language: "The impulse to lie is stronger in woman, because, unlike that of man, her memory is not continuous, whilst her life is discrete, unconnected, discontinuous, swayed by the sensations and perceptions of the moment instead of dominating them" (146). Women's language is lies; Jews' language is *Mauscheln,* so distinctive that it marks the speaker as a Jew: "Just as the acuteness of Jews has nothing to do with the true power of differentiating, so his shyness about singing or even about speaking in clear positive tones has nothing to do with real reserve. It is a kind of inverted pride; having no true sense of his own worth, he fears being made ridiculous by his singing or his speech" (324).

Jews and women, for example, have no "true humor," for true humor must be transcendent; Jews "are witty only at [their] own expense and on sexual things" and are "devoid of humor and addicted to mockery" (318–19). Jews are inherently more preoccupied by the sexual but less potent than Aryans (311). Their obsession is rooted in the fact that sex breaks down boundaries between individuals. "The Jew who does not set out, like the humorist, from the transcendental, and does not move towards it, like the erotic, has no interest in depreciating what is called the actual world, and that never becomes for him the paraphernalia of a juggler or the nightmare of a mad-house" (319).

Continuing Weininger's argument, Jews are historically quite adaptable, as can be shown by their talent for the superficial areas of "creativity" such as journalism. But in their essence they are truly unchangeable. They lack deep-rooted and original ideas (320). The Jews are the essential unbelievers, not even believing in themselves (321). The Jew has no center. He is critical, not a critic. He is not merely a materialist—he doubts all and any truths. He is irreligious; indeed, his religion is not even a real religion but a reflection of the Jewish mind, which always demands multiple choices. It is not the historical treatment of the Jews that has made them what they are: "Outward circumstances do not mold a race in one direction, unless there is in the race the innate tendency to respond" (308). And the Jewishness of the Jew is immutable. The Jew is a "parasite" who is "a different creature in every host and yet remains himself" (320). The Jew is the disease in the body politic, a violation of the very premises of civic virtue.

This immutability of mind and spirit, this moral "madness," most clearly manifests itself in science, specifically in medicine. For the Jews there is no transcendentalism, everything is as material and common-place as possible. Their effort to understand everything robs the world of its mystery (314). Evolutionary theory ("the ridiculous notion that men are derived from monkeys" [314–15]), for example, is mere materialism. The development of nineteenth-century medicine from its focus on bacteriology in the 1880s to its focus on biochemistry at the turn of the century was a shift of interest from the "organic" to the "inert" by medical scientists. For Weininger, Jews are natural chemists, which explains why medicine has become biochemistry: "The present turn of medical science is largely due to the influence of the Jews, who in such numbers have embraced the medical profession. From the earliest times, until the dominance of the Jews, medicine was closely allied with religion. But now they make it a matter of drugs, a mere administration of chemicals. . . . The chemical interpretation of organisms sets these on a level with their own dead ashes" (315). This Weininger interprets as a "Jewification" of medicine, for the Jews focus on the dead, the inert.

For Weininger, the turn of the century is the age of feminization, a corruption of society (including medicine) by the Jews: "This is the age which is most Jewish and most feminine. . . . It is a time when art is content with daubs and seeks its inspiration in the sports of animals . . . a time without originality and yet with the most foolish craving for originality. The choice must be made between Judaism and Christianity, between business and culture, between male and female, between the race and the individual, between unworthiness and worth. . . . Mankind has the choice to make. There are only two poles, and there is no middle way" (329–30). Jewishness, like the feminine, is condemned to be "uncreative." This litany of hate places the Jew in an antithetical relationship to true "creativity" and as bearing a great risk for "madness." Weininger's position is hardly unique: it reflects the general view of anti-Semitic racial science about the special nature of the Jew. Thus "creativity" is linked to Jews, their "madness," and the ultimate source of their madness, their sexuality.

Weininger thus located "genius" and "madness" on the same Lombrosian scale. When Freud was forced to confront the question of the relationship between the feminine and the Jewish, in reading the published version of Weininger's work, it became clear that the discourse on femininity was a mask for the parallel discourse on race. Since there had been a long Viennese history of this analogy, beginning with Adolf Jellinek's more benign use some forty years prior to the publication of Weininger's book, Freud's grappling with the very notion of the "creative" and his own (Jewish) relationship to it became a means of defining his status as a scientist beyond the myth of Jewish superior intelligence. Yet, as with Weininger, there was no place truly beyond this myth. No matter how Jews in the world of science represented their own abilities, these abilities were always understood in relation to the powerful myth of their own intellectual difference.

PSYCHOANALYSIS AND JEWISH CREATIVITY IN VIENNA AND BEYOND

Although Freud's use of Weininger excluded any overt restatement or rejection of Weininger's views on Jewish creativity, these views haunted his own work. Fritz Wittels, later the first biographer of Freud, authored a study of the "baptized Jew" in 1904.[29] Wittels stressed that the Jew's desire for baptism was a neurosis, and he rejected conversion as a matter of convenience.[30] Conversion is the counterpart to intermarriage—both result in the creation of antitypes whose intelligence is marred by their mixed inheritance. The German Jewish novelist Ernst Lissauer commented that "baptism, following the bureaucratic rules that declare the Jewish faith as an obstacle to promotion, is merely joining the state church; it is an official, not a confessional, act."[31] For Wittels a "baptized Jew" was a congenital liar who showed a form of "ethical insanity." Or, as French historian Anatole Leroy-Beaulieu wrote in 1893, "the de-judaised Jews are, in too many cases, lacking in moral feeling."[32] They are thus exactly like their offspring, the mixed-race children. For the relationship between conversion and intermarriage is a given in this literature on Jewish superior intelligence. Wittels's work is in many ways a direct response to Otto Weininger. He cites Weininger (28) as proof of his own dictum about Jewish self-hatred and the problem of the lying Jew as the baptized Jew. Converts and mixed-race Jews are two sides of the same problem. And both are comments on "the problem of Jewish genius."

Wittels focuses on a specific reading of Jewish superior intelligence: the question of the *goût juif,* Jewish taste. During the nineteenth century, Jewish taste became a hallmark of inauthenticity. The parvenu copies the reality of the non-Jew and becomes merely a figure of mockery whose *goût juif* reveals mimicry and a lack of true creativity. Authentic taste is a quality of Aryan genius. For Wittels, *goût juif* is the most intense type of critical intelligence, "a mephistophelian orgy of destruction of everything that is aged, used, or traditional" (35). It is the modern mind; it is ironic and cuts through all pretense. This is for Wittels the *positive* side of Jewish superior intelligence, and it is this side that writers such as Houston Stewart Chamberlain overlook (36). For such critics, there is no Jewish genius. Wittels counters that there is genius among the Jews, but it can only be determined by "real" Jews "who have not lost their national, i.e., Hebrew culture" (36). Wittels notes that real genius is not merely the result of national identification (the Frenchman of little knowledge will rank Victor Hugo above Goethe) or international acclaim (the Jews have had to work in a much narrower circle of fame). For Wittels, Moses, Jesus, and Spinoza prove Jewish superior intelligence (37). The inclusion of Jesus as an example of Jewish superior intelligence becomes a trope among Jewish thinkers who understand themselves to be acculturated. Fritz Kahn, for example, comments that "Jewish genius is not creative or observing like Aryan genius. Its genius is not of the mind, the eye, or the hand, but is a genius of the heart."[33] And his proof for this is Jesus. For Kahn, as for Wittels, Jesus is the epitome of Jewish ethics and action—he places Jesus between Jeremiah and Spinoza in his list of Jewish martyrs who suffered for ethical standards (204). Jesus is thus proven to be an example of Jewish superior intelligence and, in the rhetoric of the time, of virtue.

But for Wittels Jewish superior intelligence is tied to the productivity and creativity of the artist. Heinrich Heine is mentioned as possessing *goût juif* for his creation of modern journalism and poetry, but having a negative genius in his pushing the Romantic ideal until it collapsed. Heine's acerbic wit, therefore, is a negative manifestation

and the Jewish Response

of Jewish taste, a sign of questionable virtue. For Wittels, Karl Marx and Ferdinand Lassalle represent *goût juif* in politics, as they do for Fritz Kahn. But the essential point is that the mark of Jewish superior intelligence is not to be found in the extraordinary figure—in Jesus or Marx. Rather he notes that the average intelligence of the Jew is much higher than the average intelligence of the Aryan. Jews are natural followers, for "an average cannot create, but can understand and reflect" (37). The higher average intelligence of the Jew places his or her role as follower at a premium. Wittels's example is Jewish women as followers: here he places the "Jewesses" Dorothea Mendelssohn, Henriette Herz, and Rahel.

In Wittels's reading of Heine as forcing the Romantics to their breaking point, *goût juif* became an aspect of the body of the Jew, as Jewish acerbic wit was used as a defensive or offensive weapon against the non-Jew. The Jews' supposed predilection for mockery became a leitmotif in the *fin de siècle,* one that was related to the very nature of the Jewish body. Wittels himself argued, concerning the hunchbacked Viennese critic Karl Kraus, that Kraus's sense of satirical wit rested on his deformity: "Mockery seems to be linked with physical deformity, and in that way to be suitable as a special domain of the Jews" as Freud showed "in the analysis of the phobia of a five-year-old boy [Little Hans] with its stress on castration and circumcision."[34] The "Kraus-neurosis" was supposedly the result of Kraus's deformity, but Wittels related this directly to the overall perception of the difference attributed to the body of the Jew. In Heine's case, turn-of-the-century interest focused on his debilitating and crippling illness, understood as tertiary syphilis, which marked his body and his poetry as corrupt and corrupting. Here *goût juif* was both an attribute of the Jew and a sign of his physical difference. And the most evident effect of these physical attributes, according to Wittels, is to be found in the nature of the Jew's language. It is the hidden language of the Jews, it is *Mauschen,* that is related to the perceived universal physical nature of male Jews. Jewish males mock others because of their own physical infirmity, because of their circumcised penises. Alfred Adler commented in 1909 about a patient of Fritz Wittels, who saw Wittels as a woman in a dream. The patient "had the impression that Wittels, too, is in some sense castrated (circumcised)." Adler noted, "thus his representation of him as a woman (in the transference) signifies also a degradation."[35] The Jewish psychoanalyst (Wittels) is unmanned again by being seen as simultaneously castrated and circumcised by another Jewish psychoanalyst (Adler). *Goût juif* becomes the mode by which the very body of the Jew is both defended and condemned.

"Corrosive wit" is the hallmark of *goût juif*. Otto Rank notes in his essay "The Essence of Judaism" (1905) that "where the religion [of the Jews] is insufficient to do this [to maintain psychic balance], Jews resort to wit; for they do not have their own 'culture.' "[36] Rank adapts and reverses Weininger's theory of the centeredness of the Christian. "Culture," for Rank, is an advanced state of sexual repression, and the Jews exist in a "primitive" and "natural" state in which this level of repression has not yet taken place. Humor becomes an atavistic sign of the sexuality of the Jews. It is also a sign of the primitive return to the stage before culture, which marks the *goût juif*.

All these variations on the idea of Jewish superior intelligence are rooted in an ethnopsychology in which the individual Jew retains the imprint of the historical tradition of the Jew, forming a sort of racial memory that passes for intelligence or creativity or taste. Karl Abraham articulated the wish-fantasies of the race in his study of *Dreams and Myths: A Study in Race Psychology* (1909).[37] Myths (which Jews are not supposed to have) are wish-fantasies, according to Abraham. These wish-fantasies are eventually repressed: "There comes a time when the race forgets its myths" (71). The farther along this form of repression is, the more creative the "grandiose complex" of the nation becomes; the more practical (i.e., the more superficial) such myths remain, the fewer fantasies a nation has and the less creative it is. And thus Abraham writes of the Jews, "A race proceeds otherwise when it is widely separated from the realization of the national grandiose complex. The example of the Jews is typical. They have preserved, through long periods of time, the wish fantasies from the childhood of the race. One thinks of the wish dream of the chosen people and of the promised land" (72). Here the sublimation of desire for the past, the impossibility of the realization of the fantasy, is seen as the core of Jewish superior intelligence or at least a greater Jewish creativity. In

and the Jewish Response

many ways it is an answer to Freud's grappling with the exclusion of
"race" from his early discussion of creativity. Abraham's text highlights
what was radically repressed in Freud's writing on creativity until he
addressed the question before a Jewish audience—after the question
of race had become one of public policy.

This quality ascribed to the Jews comes to be ascribed, in the course
of the early twentieth century, to psychoanalysts. They too have so
submerged their identities as Jews, their early myth-building, that
they represent a type of genius formation. In 1937, after the seizure of
power by the Nazis in Germany and the beginning of the politics of
race that led to the Shoah, Karl Menninger, the non-Jewish American
psychiatrist, noted that "if we had no further illustration than the character of Sigmund Freud, we should have a basis for suspecting some
connection between the Jew and psychological genius. It would carry
us too far to list all of the outstanding Jewish psychologists and psychiatrists, nor would it, in my own mind, be fitting to associate lesser
names with that of such a master as he."[38] Jews are "distinguished for
their scientific accomplishments in all fields of medicine." This is a standard trope concerning the nature of Jewish superior intelligence, but
it is here applied specially to psychoanalysis. Yet Menninger is careful
not to interpret his own views as compensatory. "Furthermore, as a
Gentile, I am apt—like all Gentiles—to overestimate the superiority
and attainments of the Jews (a psychological fact which no doubt con-
tributes in part to anti-Semitic reactions)." Rather, it is the nature of
the Jewish psyche, of Jewish superior intelligence, that makes the Jewish physician different. "Jews seem to have a special gift which makes
them more likely than the average person in those requirements that
make for skill, if not genius, in psychiatry, gifts which are peculiarly
related to their Jewish origin" (127). The origin of such an image lies,
for Menninger and his time, in the racial makeup of the Jew. "For
the present, our social heritage is such that the average Jew thinks
of himself as a biological entity and he is so regarded by the average Gentile" (129). But here too the question of race, as in all of the
discussion of Jewish difference, leads to a sense that Jewish superior
intelligence is not purely a blessing: "[The Jew] has too keen an insight into human nature for his own comfort" (131).

Freud as a Jew, the Jew as Freud—both wrestle with the burden of too great an insight into the mind of the Jew. Here Jewish superior intelligence is a burden, a mark of difference that enables the Jew to understand more deeply and with greater compassion. Here is the world in which Jesus is transmuted again—a "smart Jew"—to prove Jewish insight and compassion. Through such transmutations the external, cruel world of day-to-day life in Vienna vanishes and Jewish intelligence stops being suspect.

WRITERS OF MIXED RACE AND CREATIVITY: HUGO VON HOFMANNSTHAL AND LUDWIG WITTGENSTEIN

Central to Ignaz Zollschan's awareness of Jewish superior intelligence was the projection of the image of the clever Jew onto the *Mischling*, the mixed-race individual. Indeed, this distinction provided a field onto which projections of Jewish cleverness could be made by Jews who defined themselves as "pure" Jews. Such a definition was rooted in the perceived double betrayal through conversion and intermarriage. But what of those individuals—who belonged to the non-Jewish majority in terms of their religious self-definition—onto whom this idea of Jewish cleverness was projected? Steven Beller has noted that no one in Vienna "could escape the social stigma of being a Jew by conversion, or even by being only partly Jewish."[39] At the *fin de siècle,* converting and intermarrying were seen to produce specific qualities of mind. Even Anatole Leroy-Beaulieu considered irony the weapon by which "the baptized Jew takes vengeance upon the God of the Christians and upon their social system, for the disgrace of compulsory baptism."[40] This is, of course, tailored to the definition of the Jew as exemplified by the *fin-de-siècle* reading of Heine. The *Mischling* had a special status in the culture of the period, for the *Mischling* magnified the most egregious aspects of both "races." These children of Jews and non-Jews are racially Jews, but in heightened form, bearing all the stigmata of degeneration that exist in incestuous or inbred families. The mark of the decay of the Jew is present even (or especially) in the *Mischling:* "The children of such marriages [between Jews and non-Jews] . . . even though they are so very beautiful and so very talented, seem to lack a psychological balance that is provided by pure racial stock. We find all too often intellectually or morally unbalanced individuals, who decay ethically or end in suicide or madness."[41] There is no place one can hide; there is no means of becoming invisible. The *Mischling* is the end product of the process of Jewish degeneration that produces children who reveal the hidden racial difference of the Jews, their "blackness."[42] The Viennese critic Ottokar Stauf von der March observed, concerning the aesthetic production of the *fin de siècle,* that "the greatest number of the decadents are Semites, at least according to their descent, and Jewry today finds itself at the stage of a physical and psychic decadence."[43] This decay was manifest in the questionable virtue of the Jews as citizens in modern society, and their "blackness," as we have seen throughout the discussions of race in this context, is related to a diminished or damaged intelligence, to cleverness rather than Jewish superior intelligence.

Certainly a major literary representation of this trope is to be found in William Thackeray's *Vanity Fair,* which was as much a part of the German as of the Anglophone canon in the nineteenth century.[44] In the very first chapter, we are introduced to a Miss Schwartz, "the rich woolly-haired mulatto from St. Kitts," who goes "in downright hysterics" when Amelia Sedley and Becky Sharp leave school (8). She is depicted as neither very bright nor very talented. She retains her "primitive" love of ornament: "her favorite amber-coloured satin with turquoise bracelets, countless rings, flowers, feathers, and all sorts of tags and gimcracks, about as elegantly decorated as a she chimney-sweep on May-day" (200). This hysterical type is a *Mischling* in the German sense of the word, as her German name, "black," suggests. Yet her patrimony is not German but Jewish: "Her father was a German Jew—a slave-owner they say—connected with the Cannibal Islands in some way or another," who has died and left his children a large inheritance (194). In the novel she is anomalous, an exotic whose sexuality is written on her body. Even her wealth does not cancel this out. Thus George Osborne rejects a potentially lucrative match with her, exclaiming: "Marry that mulatto woman? . . . I don't like the colour, sir. Ask the black that sweeps opposite Fleet Market, sir. *I'm* not going to marry a Hottentot Venus" (204). The reference to the Hottentot Venus evokes the body of the African woman and her "primitive sexuality" and foreshadows Galton's trip to Africa a decade later. But this figure represents a literary reworking of *Mischling* atavism. It also evokes the German Jew's supposed willingness, even eagerness, to cross racial lines, because of his or her innate sexual difference.

In 1909 Max Warwar published a biting feuilleton on the front page of the Zionist periodical *Selbstwehr,* a periodical of which Kafka was a fervent reader and sometime correspondent. Warwar bemoans the "flight from the type," the anxiety of Jews about their own bodies as signs of their inherent difference.[45] "There are reportedly Jews," he writes, "who stand for hours before the mirror and like vain women observe their exterior with jealousy and distaste, complaining against nature that had so irrationally formed them in the light of the laws of their development. These Jews feel their profile as a brand of shame, and suffer, for they have not learned to experience what is there as beautiful." These male Jews are like women, but women who are constantly unhappy with what nature has provided them in the way of beauty. They are ashamed of their own "type." This "type," of course, according to the Zionist Warwar, is a pure type, but these Jews act as if their bodies represented a mixed type. Some try to escape their bodies through conversion, by "crawling to the cross," but the conversion fails, and they do not acquire any respect for their "external being" from the "other" through conversion. Conversion is no escape from race, as it is only the desire to appear like the "other," in Warwar's term, that motivates their false conversions. What they wish to escape is the "Jewish type," being a "true, black-haired Jew." It is blackness that marks the Jews as different in Prague. Blackness, for Warwar, is a sign of the pure type, a sign of inherent difference. These "black Jews," seen by Warwar in the singer's self-representation in the *Song of Songs,* can be beautiful: "For the soul even of the blackest of Jews can be as pure as gold." And it is indeed the blackness of the Jew that should be the erotic center of their attraction: "Perhaps it is this very fire that burns in the eyes of Jewish men and women, that extends an inescapable attraction to all that come close to it. And the blacker such a type is, the more demonic and darker the fires burn in the eyes, and the more intimate the magic that such a Jew can exude." Warwar sees, however, that this is precisely not the case in contemporary Prague, where sexual attraction to such a "type" is felt only by "Christians, Teutons, and Romans," not by Jews. And this attraction leads to crossing racial boundaries and the creation of mixed racial types. In this argument, Jews must remain true to their own "type," to their own body, and to their cultural difference as "Orientals." And Orientals are simply clever, not smart.

Two *fin-de-siècle* writers who provide some insight into the anxiety about mixed identity as the source of Jewish cleverness rather than Jewish superior intelligence are Hugo von Hofmannsthal, the poet, and Ludwig Wittgenstein, the philosopher. Both are upper-class Viennese, belonging to long-established Christian families. They exemplify the problems of internalization of the myth of a corrupt Jewish intelligence. Their anxiety is not simply the generalized sense of the corruption of the Jewish intellect. Rather, it comes from the belief that their own inability to be creative reflects the pollution of the productive Aryan spirit by the merely intelligent or reflective Jewish one. It is this fear—the fear of being the possessor neither of a Jewish superior intelligence nor of the creative drive of the Aryan—that underlines Zollschan's image of the *Mischling*. This double projection, a projection from the Jew and the anti-Semite, provides a quandary for the Jews of mixed race in Vienna.

Of all the creative figures of the *fin de siècle,* none is more complex and more secretive about his anxiety concerning his hidden, corrupting "Jewishness" than Hugo von Hofmannsthal. Hofmannsthal's account of his anxiety begins in 1893 when he is only 19.[46] He writes in his diary, "If my entire inner development and struggle was nothing more than the disturbance of inherited blood, the revolts of the Jewish droplets of blood (reflection) against the Germanic and Roman, and the reactions against these rebellions."[47] For Hofmannsthal, raised a Catholic and with only one Jewish grandparent, Jewishness is a state of mind, but a state of mind that blocks his self-definition as a poet. In this configuration, real poetry is embodied not by Heinrich Heine but rather by the symbolists, specifically Stefan George, with his strong sense of the limited role that Jews could take in the "real" world of the poetic. "Jews," he writes, "are certainly clever in propagating and translating values. But they do not experience them as elementary as do we. They are totally different people."[48] Could Hofmannsthal fit into this world? Only if he was able to keep his clever but superficial side under control. In 1899 he wrote about his future Jewish brother-in-law Fritz Schlesinger, "Nevertheless I see without any pleasure—alongside his nice, open, rather sensitive character—a specific tendency developing to reflection, to the "critical," "historical," "objective," empathetic, and appreciatively educated Jewish manner of thought, which is so bloodless for life and contains within it the potential to lose the ability to experience."[49] Hofmannsthal's anxiety is being "Talmudic," of falling from the grace of experience onto the ground of mind. According to Hofmannsthal—and of course, to George—Jews think differently, and do not, *cannot* think poetically.

The moral component of Jewish creative difference can be judged in the comments of another member of the George-Circle, the poet and translator Rudolf Borchardt, a "Jewish" writer whose grandparents had converted to Protestantism in Prussia long before his birth in 1877. Defamed by George as "*Mauschel*-Pindar" ("Pindar with a Jewish accent"), the poet became a key figure in the debate about "Jewish self-hatred" in the 1920s.[50] As early as 1915 Borchardt makes a careful distinction between materialist writers who are merely "craftsmen" and who "procure necessary psychic costumes" and real poets, "the moral person." Material writers are the "Jews" in Borchardt's system; only pure, creative, nonmaterialist authors are truly virtuous.[51] Thus the reading of creativity in these writers of "mixed race" is also read with virtue as the hallmark of true creativity.

But the Catholic, upper-class, conservative poet Hugo von Hofmannsthal, like Borchardt, was himself seen or at least heard to be a Jew, certainly as much as his brother-in-law, in the poetic circles of Vienna. Leopold von Adrian, Hofmannsthal's friend and, like him, the offspring of a mixed marriage, commented that when Hofmannsthal spoke, he did so with a strong Viennese accent, speaking through his nose. Yet "in certain moments of excitement, [he spoke in] the accent of the Jews, but I don't know why, the lowest of them, the kikes." In addition, Adrian described Hofmannsthal as being as "sensitive as a hysterical woman."[52] Hofmannsthal thus embodied the noncreative feminine, which was read by Adrian as the very wellspring of his own creativity. For Adrian wrote of his own position as a gay artist as the "sole and happiest result of the mixing of two advanced races."[53] Adrian's mother was the daughter of the Jewish composer Giacomo Meyerbeer. In viewing himself, Adrian simply reversed the poles of Hofmannsthal's argument, seeing his difference as the result of his inheritance. Hofmannsthal could not do this. He remained contaminated and locked into the notion that his mixed-race identity was his hidden flaw—the error of sterile rationality.

For Adrian, everything artistic, indeed everyone who made art in Vienna (with the exception of Hermann Bahr), was a Jew.[54] While Adrian heralds this, Hofmannsthal separates his own art, real art, from the locus of Jewish art. Being an artist in Vienna means, according to Adrian, being "Jewish." But that Jewish tendency is the "modern," which is the bugbear of Hofmannsthal's world and the antithesis of his own art. The modern is for Hofmannsthal to be found in "a specific intellectual Jewish milieu in Vienna," which is "a mollusk and parasite world" and the antithesis "of the society that is represented in my poetry—and this is the element at least of my and the Austrian world."[55] The modern is, of course, as antirational as is Hofmannsthal, but it is "destructive" rather than "constructive," in his poetical/political terms. If he accepts the projection of a Jewish cleverness that is the product of race-mixing, he projects this accusation of Jewish cleverness and lack of creativity onto the modern, which is in turn Jewish. Hofmannsthal's case is one in which the anxiety about identity remains a private matter, reflecting itself in complex ways in the formation of his art and his politics.

This secret stain of the Jewish is also found in another Viennese intellectual, whose comments bring us up to the very moment before the Shoah. In a review of my *Jewish Self-Hatred,* the Anglo-Jewish novelist Frederic Raphael suggested that Jewish writers' anxiety about language and Jewish intellectuals' claim to a new, universal language would have been well illustrated by Ludwig Wittgenstein's rejection of "private language."[56] This is true in a much more complex manner than even Raphael imagined. For Wittgenstein's doubts about his creativity as a thinker are linked to the Viennese model of a damaged and damaging Jewish intelligence.[57] Jewishness, according to a contemporary commentator, is more "an intellectual than a moral limitation" for Wittgenstein.[58] But for a philosopher, such a limitation would seem to be catastrophic. What good is a philosopher who is not "smart"? Yet Wittgenstein never understands writing philosophy as creative in the same light as his brother's playing the piano—his anxiety about his own intellectual creativity is deep. He writes these anxieties out in private, as does Hofmannsthal, but they are also reflected in his writing and in his idea of philosophy and the cold, spare, transparent language of the philosopher.

Here, too, the question raised earlier, the question of the *Mischling* and converts, must be raised. Wittgenstein's "Jewishness" is an attribute taken from his understanding of the contemporary Viennese stereotype of the clever Jew, for, even though he had three Jewish grandparents, he always presented himself as a Christian with one Jewish grandparent. Yet he always assumed that "they knew about me."[59] His philosophy may also be read as a radical attempt to rewrite such doubts into a philosophy of language that is itself beyond language. Wittgenstein's comments and aphorisms on Jewish superior intelligence were published posthumously and provided a rather rich palate for his understanding of Jewish cleverness.[60]

Reinforced, if not first articulated, by his formative reading of Otto Weininger's *Sex and Character,* Wittgenstein's sense of the limitations of Jewish intelligence was palpable.[61] For Wittgenstein, Weininger himself serves as a classic representative of Jewish superior intelligence, yet one who does not fit into the "normal" categories of Western thought: "In western civilization the Jew is always measured on scales which do not fit him. . . . So at one time they are overestimated, at another underestimated. Spengler is right in this connection not to classify Weininger with the philosophers [thinkers] of the West."[62] Jews are different from Western thinkers according to this view. And yet the "Western" tradition, as we have seen, is defined as a "pure" tradition. Weininger cannot be a "real" philosopher because, following the model of the intellectual *Mischling,* he has abandoned the rootedness of the Jew. His conversion is a sign of his mixed, and therefore different, intelligence.

and the Jewish Response

For Weininger "Jewishness" of mind, an attribute shared by a wide range of thinkers, is simply the counterweight to the Aryan spirit, a "pure" pole in opposition to "Aryan" thought. Yet for Weininger everyone was "mixed": everyone had some attributes of the Jew and the Aryan, and one was defined by one's dominant tendency. For Weininger, even Wagner represented the Jewish mindset, since he showed a predominantly "Jewish" cast. Wittgenstein's reading of this was clear. Thus Wittgenstein can write that "Rousseau's character has something Jewish about it" (20e 1931). This "something Jewish" is the quality of mind associated with the different and the pathological. And yet Wittgenstein's appropriation of this model is quite different.

Jewishness—even in Weininger—is always a lack, whether in non-Jews or in Jews: "What does Mendelssohn's music lack? A 'courageous' melody?" (35e 1939–40) Mendelssohn as the Jewish composer par excellence lacks rigidity, lacks strength, lacks courage and therefore is in no way sublime. "You get tragedy where the tree, instead of bending, breaks. Tragedy is something un-Jewish. Mendelssohn is, I suppose, the most untragic of composers" (1e 1929). Mendelssohn-Bartholdy comes to represent in music the essence of Jewish lack of creativity. It is not at all surprising that Wittgenstein evokes the standard litany of smart or talented Jews in this lament. And it is more interesting that, like Hofmannsthal, he clearly understands himself as sharing this lack.

Wittgenstein could comment as late as 1931 about Jewish thinkers (including himself) that

> Amongst Jews "genius" is found only in the holy man. Even the greatest of Jewish thinkers is no more than talented. (Myself for instance.)
>
> I think there is some truth in my idea that I really only think reproductively. I don't believe I have ever *invented* a line of thinking. I have always taken one over from someone. I have straight-away seized on it with enthusiasm for my work of clarification. That is how Boltzmann, Hertz, Schopenhauer, Frege, Russell, Kraus, Loos, Weininger, Spengler, Sraffa have influenced me. Can one take the case of Freud and Breuer as an example of Jewish reproductiveness?—What I invent are new *similes*. . . .

The Jew must see to it that, in a literal sense, "all things are as nothing to him." But this is particularly hard for him, since in a sense he has nothing that is peculiarly his. It is much harder to accept poverty willingly when you have to be poor than when you might be rich.

It might be said (right or wrongly) that the Jewish mind does not have the power to produce even the tiniest blade of grass; its way is rather to make a drawing of the flower or blade of grass that has grown in the soil of another's mind and to put it into a comprehensive picture. We aren't pointing to a fault when we say this and everything is all right as long as what is being done is quite clear. It is only when the nature of a Jewish work is confused with that of a non-Jewish work that there is any danger, especially when the author of the Jewish work falls into the confusion himself, as he so easily may. (Doesn't he look as proud as though he had produced the milk himself?)

It is typical for a Jewish mind to understand someone else's work better than he understands it himself. (18e–19e 1931)

The Jewish mind, including his own, has no true originality once it transgresses the rootedness of the Jewish genius, once it ceases to be pure within its own limitations. This is an answer to Weininger; Wittgenstein sees any "Jewish taint" as a diminution of the overall quality of the pure race.

Wittgenstein's relationship to the concept of genius is also tied to his own complex reappropriation of "wit," the damning quality of Heine's work that marks it as Jewish, as the marker of deep ambiguity. The appearance of language calls for an interpretation when wit marks an interpretation as nonsense. This is a "Jewish" argument according to the critics of Jewish superior intelligence.[63] Thus, not everyone is partially Jewish—following Weininger's argument, an argument that rescues his own "mixed" status—but anyone who is partially Jewish is tainted by limited creativity. For Wittgenstein the "holy man" in his original purity remains the model for Jewish superior intelligence. Here Wittgenstein stands very much within the tradition of Renan's reading of the limits on Jewish creativity, the limitations of the nomad wandering in the desert. Yet something is hidden below the surface: "The Jew is a desert region, but underneath its thin layer of rock lies the molten lava of spirit and intellect" (13e 1931). This core is obliterated in the almost-Jew, in the *Mischling* who can draw from the wellspring of neither Jewish identity nor Austrian culture. Jewish copies, mere inventions, can be easily distinguished from true German art, as Stefan George claims, by simply placing the copy next to the original. The Jew does not nurture art but merely mimicks it.

Again Wittgenstein places himself in the catalog of smart Jews. Here it is Sigmund Freud and Joseph Breuer who are "examples of Jewish reproductiveness."[64] They represent the Jewishness that is merely the invention of "new *similes.*" At the core of this portrayal lies the unoriginality of the Jew as copyist, of the inauthentic Jew: "I believe that my originality (if that is the right word) is an originality belonging to the soil rather than to the seed. (Perhaps I have no seed of my own.) Sow a seed in my soil and it will grow differently than it would in another soil. Freud's originality too was like this, I think. I have always believed—without knowing why—that the real germ of psychoanalysis came from Breuer, not Freud. Of course Breuer's seed-grain can only have been quite tiny. *Courage* is always original" (36e 1939–40). Breuer almost has courage, unlike Mendelssohn, because he is neither of mixed race nor a convert. And unlike Freud, he does not abandon his Jewish religious identity and come to advocate a radical atheism. Breuer's originality has to do with the inexpressible, the unknowable, even in Freud's terms: his Jewishness. As Freud stated in the 1934 preface to the Hebrew edition of *Totem and Taboo,*

No reader of [the Hebrew version] of this book will find it easy to put himself in the emotional position of an author who is ignorant of the language of holy writ, who is completely estranged from the religion of his fathers—as well as from every other religion—and who cannot take a share in nationalist ideals, but who has yet never repudiated his people, who feels that he is in his essential nature a Jew and who has no desire to alter that nature. If the question were put to him: "Since you have abandoned all these common characteristics of your countrymen, what is left to you that is Jewish?" he would reply: "A very great deal, and probably its very essence." He could not express that essence in

141

words; but some day, no doubt, it will become accessible to the
scientific mind. (SE 13)[65]

The Jew is unknowable in his essence, but Wittgenstein pursues the
roots of this unknowability in the intellectual status of the Jew.

According to Wittgenstein the Jewish essence is the result of the history of the Jews: "It has sometimes been said that the Jews' secretive
and cunning nature is a result of their long persecution. This is certainly untrue; on the other hand it is certain that they continue to exist
despite this persecution only because they have an inclination towards
such secretiveness. As we may say that this or that animal has escaped
extinction only because of its capacity or ability to conceal itself. Of
course I do not mean that as a reason for commending such a capacity,
not by any means" (22c 1931). The essence of the Jew, the unknowability or secretiveness even of the "pure" Jew, is different from that of
the Aryan. But even the essence of the Jew today has radically changed
from the holy man wandering in the desert. History has perverted
the Jew and made the Jew lie. He is therefore the bad philosopher.

Such a view echoes Wittgenstein's understanding that the Jew in
the world of the European spirit represents disease and corruption.
The Jews are "experienced as a sort of disease, and anomaly, and no
one wants to put a disease on the same level as normal life and no one
wants to speak of a disease as if it had the same rights as healthy bodily
processes (even painful ones). We may say: people can only regard this
tumor as a natural part of the body if their whole feeling for the body
changes (if the whole national feeling for the body changes). Otherwise the best they can *do is put up with* it. . . . There is a contradiction
in expecting someone both to retain his former aesthetic feeling for
the body and *also* to make the tumor welcome" (20e–21e 1931). The
image encapsulates Wittgenstein's anxiety about the Jew within—the
hidden, speaking Jew who will reveal himself once pen is set to paper,
once the spoken word is heard. But it is the anxiety of the *Mischling*
that haunts Wittgenstein's world. Jewish superior intelligence is the
mark not of success but of failure. It is the sign of the Viennese Jew
and even more so of the *Mischling*.

Vienna is where the problematic nature of Jewish response to the
meaning of Jewish superior intelligence can best be seen. The image of

the "smart Jew" at the end of the nineteenth and the beginning of the twentieth century is so poisoned and so contested that Jewish intellectuals—no matter how defined—come to understand themselves as "spoiled." The Zionists, such as Zollschan, project this onto the "mixed-race" Jews; the *Mischlinge* such as Hofmannsthal and Wittgenstein repress this charge, but it frames their self-understanding; the liberals, such as Gomperz, project this anxiety about the absence of creativity and virtue onto the historical Jews and eventually onto themselves; the skeptics, such as Freud and Abraham, wrestle with their own creativity as Jews; and the self-haters, such as Weininger, find plenty of proof for their self-abnegation. Vienna is thus a place where the negative reading of Jewish superior intelligence shapes the way Jews understand their own intellect. Certainly, there were reactions to this in Vienna: Herzl's reinterpretation of Jewish intellect as "Oriental" genius is one such movement. And yet the poison took root. In Vienna at the *fin de siècle,* the normal self-doubt every individual has about his or her abilities became tied to discourses about race.

5

Alban Berg, the Jews, and the Anxiety of Genius

THE DISCOURSE about race and intelligence in Vienna continues to haunt the representation of Jewish superior intelligence in high culture as the negative ramifications of a Jewish superior creativity echo through early-twentieth-century modernism. Having established the parameters of the problem in the past three chapters, in these two concluding chapters I undertake readings of a set of cultural artifacts—plays, novels, operas, films, and television shows—in which the idea of Jewish superior intelligence shapes or focuses the artifact, first in Vienna and then in the United States. These readings show how a tradition is continued and reread in terms of excavating and reshaping new cultural artifacts.

In this chapter, I take up the most widely respected "modern" opera, Alban Berg's *Wozzeck*. I examine three intertwined problems in the representation of intelligence and the body in nineteenth- and early-twentieth-century German culture: the role of medicine in shaping the plot and ideology of Georg Büchner's 1836 play *Woyzeck;* how qualities associated with the idea of Jewish superior intelligence in the nineteenth century helped shape the Jewish writer and editor Karl Emil Franzos's interest in rescuing Büchner's play and publishing it for the first time in 1878; and what Berg made out of this aspect of the play and its reception, so central to its reading, when he set it to music between 1914 and 1925.[1] This reading structures "intelligence" (and "virtue")—and its opposite, "irrationality" (and "vice")—in light of the meanings attributed to them by nineteenth- and early-twentieth-century German culture.

Georg Büchner (1813–37), the author of *Woyzeck,* was a German physician and an active revolutionary, a pairing that today, at least, would be seen as rather unusual. As a medical student in Giessen, Büchner circulated broadsheets calling for a radical change in the government and was involved in day-to-day revolutionary politics in Hesse as the cofounder of the "League for Human Rights."[2] Büchner was also caught between two models of understanding medicine:

as a scientific undertaking rooted in research versus a means of ameliorating suffering, a higher calling rooted in a complex romantic metaphysic. His original draft of a call for popular revolution, "The Hessian Reporter" (1834), employed a detailed statistical argument to support the necessity for revolution.[3] Such argument was already part of the beginnings of German scientific medical thought. Büchner's understanding of medicine is linked to his revolutionary philosophy as inscribed in *Woyzeck:* the very roots of the drama lie in the question of the protagonist's diminished capacity.

I begin, however, not with "smart Jews" but with "irrational Germans": with the "real" "mad" Woyzeck, that is, with the historical person and his trial, with an eye on the other trials that may have contributed to the plot, such as those of Daniel Schmolling and Johann Dieß (whose corpse Büchner probably dissected as a medical student). Johann Christian Woyzeck, an unemployed wigmaker, barber, and former soldier, killed his mistress, the widow of the surgeon Woost, on 21 June 1821. He was immediately arrested and admitted his guilt. Woyzeck's mental status was examined because of an appeal by his defense attorney, who hoped to document Woyzeck's diminished capacity and thereby mitigate his sentence. This mental status examination was undertaken by the well-known physician Johann Christian August Clarus, whose published report formed the basis for Büchner's play. Büchner's version of Clarus's account of the crime virtually reversed Clarus's findings. For Büchner, Woyzeck's madness was the direct result of the power structures that deformed and destroyed Woyzeck's life, and central to these power structures was the institution of the new scientific medicine.

In his published report, Clarus claimed that the new scientific medicine eliminated the impressionistic responses of coroner's juries and allowed the pure, objective truth of science to dominate.[4] Indeed, Clarus's report, which is representative of the high medical science of Büchner's day (and which Büchner found a source of true amusement), used every possible means of diagnosis from an analysis of the physiognomy of the murderer to his raised pulse when asked questions (504). The physiognomy of the murderer links Clarus's epistemology to that of the new science of "seeing" the insane.[5] It is an approach followed by his fellow physician Henke, whose evaluation of Woyzeck, undertaken on 12 September 1821, relies almost exclusively on an analysis of the "normal" physiognomy of the murderer (546). In the play, Büchner dismisses this approach as "beastiognomy" (32), arguing that a person's appearance does not reflect his or her inner state. Such views as Büchner's had been a quiet but persistent result of Enlightenment skepticism since the philosopher Georg Lichtenberg's dismissal of physiognomy because of its links to irrationality and "subjective" modes of interpretation.

For the core of his mental examination, Clarus relies on the standard notion of early-nineteenth-century psychiatry, whether the patient's "speech and answers" revealed that he was "bad" or "mad" (491). Clarus uses a form of what comes to be labeled, in Great Britain at midcentury, the M'Naghten rule—he claims that even though Woyzeck is morally ill, he is "sane" in medical terms because he can articulate the difference between "right" and "wrong," as shown by his admission of guilt. Later physicians who examined Woyzeck in prison, such as Carl Moritz Marc, argued that he was insane because he had hallucinations in prison and claimed to be the victim of a plot by Freemasons.[6] Büchner employed aspects of these later visions to question Woyzeck's sanity before and during the murder; it is clear to Büchner that Woyzeck had been driven mad by the social forces amassed against him. Rather than committing suicide in his madness as he does at the conclusion of Büchner's play, Johann Christian Woyzeck was executed by beheading on 27 August 1724.

The question of Woyzeck's irrationality stands at the very center of the play and Büchner's claim for a revolutionary reading of society. Was Woyzeck mad? If so, what drove him to madness? Certainly, one central aspect of the play is the social tension between the powers of the dominant social class in the drama (represented by the Drum Major, the Captain, and the Doctor) and the underclass. Woyzeck is exploited by the Drum Major who seduces his mistress, Marie; the Captain, who uses him for menial tasks and mocks him; and the Doctor, who turns him into a human guinea pig. But the force that is clearly depicted as the most destructive is the institution of medicine, an area that Büchner knew very well. Indeed, the essence "of Büchner [is] in the scene between the Doctor and Woyzeck," as a reviewer of the first performance of the drama commented.[7] Büchner's brother, the philosopher Ludwig Büchner, had acknowledged that "it was only the study of medicine that had led Georg into such 'wayward paths'" of revolutionary activity.[8] Thus medicine and the representation of the person driven to irrationality color the entire drama in specific ways.

Büchner even portrayed military life, with its sexual exploitation, its abuse of power, and its betrayal of the individual, as relatively benign or at least somewhat human and self-questioning compared with the world of medicine. Büchner's Drum Major is the embodiment of an unselfconscious sexuality, and his Captain represents an odd self-reflexive awareness of power. Only the Doctor sees Woyzeck simply as a means to his scientific ends. Peter Gay agrees that "Georg Büchner's callous military physician in *Woyzeck* saw patients as interesting guinea pigs."[9] Büchner seems to have used one of his former professors, the Giessner anatomist and physiologist Wilbrandt, to shape the figure of the Doctor. But Wilbrandt, whatever his attitude toward his craft, was part of a revolution taking shape at the university in Giessen that included Justus Liebig, who was about to set up Germany's first chemical laboratory in Giessen when Büchner was a student.[10] This new science of medicine that was appearing in Germany, which would produce startling results over the next three-quarters of a century, stressed "scientific" materiality rather than "romantic" spirit.

The Doctor uses Woyzeck as a human guinea pig to test his theories of diet. He has him eat peas for a year and measures the resulting increase in urea in his urine. Given Woyzeck's position in society, there seems to be no reason to treat him as a human being. The Doctor sees Woyzeck as an intermediary stage between man and beast:

Take note of this man [he says to his medical students]—for a quarter of a year he hasn't eaten anything but peas. Feel how uneven his pulse is. There—and the yes. . . . Apropos, Woyzeck, wiggle your ears for the gentlemen. I meant to show it to you before. He uses two muscles. . . . This, gentlemen, represents a transition to the donkey, frequently resulting from being brought up by women and from the use of the mother tongue. How much hair has your mother pulled out for a tender memory? It's gotten very thin in the last few days. Yes, the peas, gentlemen. (49)

For the Doctor, so it seems, Woyzeck is "degenerate half-human," which is Clarus's label in the published account of the case for those who revel in public executions (488). Büchner echoes this oblique reference in his account, using the "prehensile" muscle of the human ear as a sign of the degeneracy of the working classes, a sign of physical degeneracy that Karl Marx documents in much greater detail decades later in *Das Kapital*. But according to Marx, such degeneration is the result, not of the inheritance, but of the exploitation of the working classes, especially of children. (It is important to note that Büchner substantially antedates the first widely read accounts of degeneracy theory.) The Doctor sees Woyzeck's degeneracy as exacerbated by his context and yet rooted in his biological inheritance. For him Woyzeck's feminization and his lack of *Bildung* [education]—he can only speak German and not Latin—proves his primitive state and failure of virtue. Also of interest as a marker of degeneration is his loss of hair, which the Doctor sees as one of the signs of the efficacy of his dietary experiment.

Woyzeck is little better than the animal show in the first draft of the play, in which the horse, like Clever Hans, responds to the questions of the announcer: "Show your talent! . . . Is there in the learned *société* an ass? (*The horse shakes its head.*) . . . That is beastiognomy. Yes, that is no dumb animal, that's a person! A human being, a beastly human being, but still an animal, *une bête.* (*The horse behaves improperly.*) That's right, put *société* to shame" (59). The horse's improper act, presumably defecating on stage, introduces us to another public act of shame that will serve to characterize the signs and symptoms resulting from the Doctor's experiment. For the signs of civic virtue, the signs of being truly civilized, are as lacking in Woyzeck as in the horse—Woyzeck, like the horse, does not show shame and commits acts that are shameful. "Behaving improperly" is one of the two further signs of the efficacy of the Doctor's experiment on Woyzeck. Woyzeck is unable to hold his urine:

Alban Berg, the Jews,

DOCTOR: I saw it, Woyzeck. You pissed on the street, you pissed on the wall like dog. And you get two cents a day. Woyzeck, that's bad. The world's getting bad, very bad.

WOYZECK: But Doctor, the call of nature . . .

DOCTOR: The call of nature, the call of nature! Nature! Haven't I proved that the *musculus constrictor vesicae* is subject to the will? Nature! Woyzeck, man is free. In man alone is individuality exalted to freedom. Couldn't hold it in! (*Shakes his head, puts his hands behind his back, and paces back and forth.*) Did you eat your peas already, Woyzeck? I'm revolutionizing science, I'll blow it sky-high. Urea ten percent, ammonium chloride, hyperoxidic. Woyzeck, try pissing again. Go in there and try.

WOYZECK: I can't, Doctor.

DOCTOR (*with emotion*): But pissing on the wall! (38)

"Freedom," one of the concepts that marked the French Revolution, is here given a purely biological context. Woyzeck is "free" to control his bladder, but the intervention of science has made this impossible and has reduced him to below the level of the rational human being. Woyzeck has reverted to type. Büchner's initial draft of this scene makes the relationship between Woyzeck's urination and the Doctor's science even more explicit:

DOCTOR: I saw it, Woyzeck. You pissed on the street like a dog. For that I give you three cents and board every day? The world's getting bad, very bad, bad I say. Oh! Woyzeck, that's bad.

WOYZECK: But Doctor, when you can't help it?

DOCTOR: Can't help it, can't help it. Superstition, horrible superstition! Haven't I proved that the *musculus constrictor vesicae* is subject to the will? Woyzeck, man is free. In man individuality is exalted to freedom. Couldn't hold it in! That's cheating, Woyzeck. Did you eat your peas already, nothing but legumes, cruciferae—remember that. Then next week we'll start on the mutton. Don't you have to go to the toilet? Go ahead, I'm telling you to. I'm revolutionizing science. A revolution! According to yesterday's report: ten percent urea, and ammonium chloride . . . But I saw how you pissed on the wall! . . . But pissing against the wall! I saw it. (71)

and the Anxiety of Genius

The Doctor's experiment is not merely to feed Woyzeck peas and measure the contents of his urine, urine that Woyzeck cannot seem to hold, but also to change his diet to add mutton within the week.

Before we discuss the structure of the Doctor's experiment with Woyzeck, the second sign and symptom of Woyzeck's reaction to his monotonous diet of peas must be mentioned: his madness. Büchner introduces madness in a discussion of the difficulty that Woyzeck has in interpreting natural signs, through a comment by Woyzeck that the Doctor takes as a sign of Woyzeck's deteriorating mental state. The Doctor is delighted by this, as he seems to have expected it. Woyzeck comments on the hidden meaning of the circle of mushrooms, the fairy circle with all of its folkloric associations:

WOYZECK (*puts his finger to his nose*): The toadstools, Doctor. There—that's where it is. Have you seen how they grow in patterns? If only someone could read that.

DOCTOR: Woyzeck, you've got a marvelous *aberratio mentalis partialis,* second species, beautifully developed. Woyzeck, you're getting a raise. Second species: fixed idea with a generally rational condition. You're doing everything as usual? Shaving your captain?

WOYZECK: Yes, sir.

DOCTOR: Eating your peas? (39)

The first draft makes the madness of the exchange (as seen by the audience and the Doctor) more evident:

WOYZECK (*stands rigidly*): Have you seen the rings of toadstools on the ground yet? Long line, crooked circles, figures. That's where it is! There! If only someone could read that. When the sun's standing high and bright at noon and the world seems to be going up in flames. Don't you hear anything? I think then when the world talks, you see, the long lines, and it's like someone talking with a terrible voice.

DOCTOR: Woyzeck! You're going to the insane asylum. You've got a beautiful fixed idea, a marvelous *alienation mentis.* Look at me. Now what are you supposed to do? Eat your peas . . . (74)

Woyzeck suffers from a specific, localized madness, a madness limited to one of his faculties. Although he can follow the Captain's orders as well as those of the Doctor, he is mad, which is Büchner's—if not Clarus's—point.

For Büchner, Woyzeck has been driven mad by the society in which he dwells and the science that controls him. But if Woyzeck is mad only in one of his faculties (or not mad at all) as the various doctors, real and fictive, claim, there is a moment in Büchner's play that tests Woyzeck's competence, a moment in which Büchner illustrates the difference between knowing right from wrong (i.e., being "sane" in the legal sense) and being driven mad by society. This moment is the scene in which Woyzeck purchases the knife he will eventually use to kill Marie. When Woyzeck buys the knife, the murder is premeditated and his madness is not evident. He goes to the shop of a Jew, who sells him the knife for two pennies. Woyzeck cannot afford a gun, but he is quite "rational" in his choice of a knife: "That can cut more than just bread" (46). Now the Jew's last line in this short scene is striking. Woyzeck has paid the two cents asked for without haggling, and the Jew shakes his head in disbelief: "There! Like it was nothing. But it's money! The dog" (46). Does this scene show Woyzeck's conscious planned intent? Does Woyzeck know the difference between right and wrong? And what about the Jew? Is his love of money "natural" or is it "learned"? Is he "morally mad" because he defines the entire world in terms of its material value? Does this scene place the Jew among the victimizers such as the Doctor or among the victims of materialism such as Woyzeck? Is the Jew an analogous figure to Woyzeck or an example of the forces that exploit the working class?

These questions about the role of the Jew cannot be answered in reference to this scene with the knife. But in a draft scene, Marie, Woyzeck's mistress in the drama, comments to her friend Margaret, who is quite aware that Marie's eyes are on the Drum Major, "Why don't you take your eyes to the Jew and have them polished—maybe they'll shine enough to sell as two buttons" (68). The Jew's materialism, in reducing the woman's eyes to a commodity, is indeed here parallel to that of the Doctor who deals with humans as body parts. Never spelled out in Büchner's text, which was written during the first generation of the political emancipation of the Jews in Büchner's Hesse, this view constitutes a commonplace of that era concerning Jews and the material world. Its most evident statement is in Karl Marx's notorious 1844 essay "On the Jewish Question." But such a view of the Jew does leave us with a series of questions about what constitutes "free will" in Büchner's world. Here the forces that shape the definition of madness are the forces of the world. The Jew is amazed by Woyzeck's lack of response to the "natural" order of haggling (according to Marx the natural language of the Jew).[11] The Jew is, like the Doctor, part of the system and reflects the limitations that exploitation imposes. For Büchner, Woyzeck's madness is evident in this scene only if the Jew's world-view is taken as the baseline of the normal—and that would itself be mad.

Büchner does not free the Doctor from the madness the Doctor attributes to Woyzeck's desire to understand the meaning of the mushrooms' magic circles. For the Doctor has found a visual pattern that makes sense of the world: the visual semiotics of medical science, which analyzes illness based on the visual association of signs and symptoms. This the Doctor does with Woyzeck's signs and symptoms and with many of the people he sees as he walks through the village. Büchner has his Doctor serve as a satire on the rampant use of physiognomy (or "beastiognomy") in contemporary medicine. The interpretation of that which is seen, of the signs and symptoms of illness, as Clarus stated in his evaluation of Woyzeck, becomes a sign of the new scientific positivism. For Büchner, the Doctor's repeated use of this technique disqualifies him as a caring physician. The Doctor looks at the Captain and says, "Bloated, fat, thick neck, apoplectic constitution. Yes, Captain, you might be stricken by an *apoplexia cerebralis*" (40). On the street he sees a woman walking whom he immediately reduces to a classroom specimen: "She'll be dead in four weeks, via a *coronar congestionis*. She's in her seventh month—I've had twenty patients like that already. . . . In four weeks the stupid beast. She'll make an interesting preparation" (75). Like Clarus taking Woyzeck's pulse and the Doctor experimenting with Woyzeck's diet, the interpretation of signs and symptoms is not simply early-nineteenth-century medical quackery. The semiotics of disease, from Hippocrates to the present, plays an important role in distinguishing the source and form of an illness in the Western tradition. And the central problem of Büchner's anger at "scientific" medicine is that even though he views it as madness, "scientific" medicine becomes the most important contribution of German science to the improvement of the health and welfare of individuals.

The parodies of medicine in Büchner's drama point to the destructive and divisive nature of the medical world-view. Büchner's attack on the science of medicine is cast in a rather interesting light once one realizes that his parodied Doctor is seeking the cause of a disease that was described about the time Büchner's father, Ernst, was in medical school. This disease was first chronicled in the medical literature by François Thiérry, who published an account of a new disease found in Spain in 1755. Its symptoms were marked as ugly alteration of the skin, a loss of hair, and, to quote a contemporary account, "a maniacal melancholia," or to use our contemporary labels, depression, irritability, anxiety, confusion, disorientation, delusions, and hallucinations. Another symptom was pronounced diarrhea. The disease received its popular name only when cases were found in Italy later in the eighteenth century: pellagra.[12] A niacin deficiency disease (or the inability to convert tryptophan to niacin), pellagra was understood as early as Thiérry as a disease of poverty caused by eating cornmeal as a staple food with little protein from meat or milk. Théophile Roussel, writing in 1845, said the "predisposing cause" for the disease was too little animal substances, and indeed, protein deficiency is the basis for the disease. Büchner's Doctor attempts to evoke pellagra with many of its attendant symptoms, such as loss of hair, madness, and persistent, constant urination (instead of diarrhea) by feeding Woyzeck a diet of peas. But peas, as Büchner could not have known, contain protein (if incomplete protein) as well as vitamins A and C. The mutton that was to be added to Woyzeck's diet would indeed have served as a "cure" for this phantom "pellagra," but the Doctor's regimen of peas would have not caused it. It was not until the 1920s that Joseph Goldberger induced scrotal dermatitis, a symptom of pellagra, in convicts by having them eat only corn, showing that pellagra was a vitamin deficiency disease that could be avoided and treated through adequate diet.[13]

and the Anxiety of Genius

Büchner's attack on the new scientific medicine is based on the charge that it is uncaring and destructive. Yet the experiment Büchner's "mad" Doctor undertook was quite in line with the medical research practices of Büchner's day. One might add that the materialism of Büchner's medical world led to the laboratory science of the mid- and late nineteenth century with its spectacular breakthroughs in the treatment of a wide range of diseases, including the typhus from which Büchner was to die. If his scientific writing is any guide, Büchner was firmly in the camp of the materialists. He wrote about the nervous systems of fish and of human beings and attempted to understand how the complex neurological structures of the individual determined the limitations of action and response. The "science" of the Doctor's medicine is very much in line with the science of Büchner's training and, indeed, of his reading of the meaning of the body in his essays on nerves and their functions. Yet he dismisses this medicine as an exploitative social institution only concerned with self-aggrandizement. Büchner's Doctor is the antithesis of Francis Bacon's *buccinator novi temporis* — the trumpeter of the new era — he is a scientific buccaneer, living off the rewards of a scientific revolution that benefits him but not his "victims." In *Woyzeck,* the Doctor does not care for his patients but rather sees them as subjects for scientific inquiry. Büchner rejects this reduction of the complexity of the human being to chemicals, fats, and mechanical drives. In doing so, he also rejects the clear improvements in the treatment of people suffering from catastrophic ailments, treatments whose potential was evident even at the beginning of the nineteenth century.

INTERMEZZO: KARL EMIL FRANZOS

Georg Büchner's *Woyzeck* was never published by its author. The young physician died in 1837 of typhus — the doctors, including his colleagues at the medical school in Zurich, were of little help — and the paucity of his published texts places him in the tiniest footnotes in the emerging literary histories of the new Germany. Indeed, he comes to be known as the "most obscure of all German writers."[14] A volume of Büchner's "posthumous works" was published by his brother

Ludwig in 1850, and this brother comes to be *the* Büchner for the rest of the century. The radically different reputations of the two brothers maintained itself until at least 1915, when Rainer Maria Rilke wrote that Georg was the "dead brother of the better-known Ludwig Büchner."[15] Georg thus comes to be read through the lens of his brother's reputation and image.

Ludwig Büchner, also a physician, became the icon of radical materialism at the close of the nineteenth century. His early work, especially *Force and Matter* (1855), one of the flagship books of German materialism, earned him a dismissal from the faculty of the University of Tübingen in 1852 as too radical and antireligious. Although he was the executor of his brother's literary estate, his role in late-nineteenth-century intellectual life was precisely as a radical rereader of social relationships in light of their material basis. One of the leading nineteenth-century monists, Büchner was also a political liberal, as can especially be seen in his reading of the meaning of anti-Semitism at the turn of the century. Ludwig Büchner thought that the Jews were neither better nor worse than other peoples, but that capitalism had forced them into exploitative professions. If Jews did not take up these professions, he states, non-Jews would (and often did). Yet he also condemns the Jews for maintaining their "odd and ancient ritual practices" as well as their self-imposed "separation from society." The Jews do, however, possess superior intelligence. Büchner saw the Jew's *Klugheit* [cleverness] as learned response to their environment and claimed that they had always been a people with desire for risky undertakings and the "drive for creativity."[16] Büchner's assimilationist model dominated German liberalism at the turn of the century. It argues that Jewish difference, especially Jews' preeminence in the realm of culture, was part of their nature and was sharpened by their persecution. Such a view was strongly supported by the first editor of *Woyzeck*, Karl Emil Franzos (1848–1904).[17]

Georg Büchner's only published work, *Dantons Tod*, had been discovered in 1867 by Franzos, a young Eastern European Jewish intellectual living in the Bucovina, in the outer reaches of the Austro-Hungarian Empire. Although Franzos published some forty essays on Büchner in his lifetime, his initial publications came in the 1870s at the very beginning of the expansion of German anti-Semitism. Franzos, himself the son of a German-speaking, highly acculturated Jewish physician, was the author of *Aus Halb-Asien* (1876; From half-Asia) and, most importantly, *Die Juden von Barnow* (1877; *The Jews of Barnow*). These works were banned by the Austrian government as revolutionary depictions of the poverty and ignorance of their eastern provinces. Franzos advocated the complete acculturation of the Eastern Jews into a German-speaking Western society.

Central to Franzos's texts about Eastern Jews written while he was excavating Büchner's *Woyzeck* is his understanding of Jewish superior intelligence within the parameters of the Viennese model (as described in chapter 4). For Franzos brought with him from the outer reaches of the Austro-Hungarian Empire to Vienna and Berlin the typical attitude of acculturated Eastern Jews—an attitude that was the antithesis of Zborowski and Herzog's some eighty years later. Franzos was, as a contemporary critic notes, more a Jewish German than a German Jew.[18] Whether in Vienna, his first stop in the West, or in Berlin, Franzos defined himself within the strict limits of German culture in terms of the ideal of *Bildung*. For Franzos, "creativity" underlined the destructive and pernicious effects of Jewish culture on Jewish superior intelligence and created a false intelligence that was marked on the body. His intelligent Jew was indeed Woyzeck—the individual whose body and mind are destroyed by the social institutions that control him.

Such arguments can be found throughout Franzos's writing. In the continuation of his "ethnographic" writing in the 1880s, Franzos presented a study of child prodigies in the ghetto in mock-ethnographic form.[19] The most elaborate of these studies serves as the centerpiece of his representation of Jewish superior intelligence. Franzos begins with Moriz Frankel, a mathematical genius who was able even as a small child to do complicated sums in his head. Frankel's parents exploited his gift, turning him into a sideshow attraction for financial gain, until the child outgrew his prodigy status and vanished from public view. Franzos began writing about young Frankel in 1879 while he was also writing about Büchner. He sees Frankel as typical of the difficult transition of Jewish superior intelligence from the "orthodox, talmudic tradition" to the "denationalized Jew" of the West (29). The world of mathematics is at least secular, even if the mindset that exploits the child's gift is "talmudic."

The centerpiece of Franzos's study of Jewish superior intelligence is his visit with a number of local skeptics to the home of a four-year-old prodigy, Ruben Grüner, in "Barnow," his pseudonymous town in Galicia. By two, this "ugly and pale" (31) child knew all of his prayers in Hebrew and had even learned to read the language. At almost five he is a wonder, at least in Barnow. He is seen by the "educated" in the town as a "sad figure, the living proof of what horrible training [*Dressur*] can do to a gifted child at the costs of his health and length of life" (33). The child is produced for the skeptical visitors and shows off his abilities: he has memorized the Torah and the commentaries and can answer complicated questions such as why God listened to Balaam's curse. Franzos shows Grüner's intelligence to be rote learning and his "rationality" to be merely the repetition of existing knowledge. The child appears "deathly pale and tortured" to the narrator, who fears he will not survive to the next summer. That winter the child dies of a high fever (47). For Franzos, the result of the talmudic training of Grüner's mind is his physical death. But his spirit had been long dead. Franzos speculates that the "incomparable material," the Jewish superior intelligence of these children, would have been better used in Berlin or Vienna—and to a greater reward (48)!

Franzos's third child prodigy is a young man with a "pale, sharply profiled face" who aspires to become a magician. He watches the "miracle rabbis" and learns all their tricks by a "simple feat of memory" (57). Here the association between rote learning and the absence of virtue is overt—for the child-magician's stated intent is to dupe his victims and thus to gain power over them.

With these three cases Franzos documents his view of the deforming power of Eastern European Jewish traditions on native high intelligence. He provides a summary of the reasons for these Jews' deformation and lack of true creativity, beginning with physical causes: the early marriages that work against individual desire; "oriental physical laziness"; lack of exercise and physical work that "allows the race to decay physically"; the "one-sided emphasis on the intellect" as a means of earning one's daily bread; and educational traditions that stress memory ("with the messenger it is the musculature of the legs, with the woodcutter the arms are overdeveloped, so too is it the brain of the Talmudist and the merchant" [59]). Jews' physical weakness is also the result of inheriting acquired mental gifts and dexterity over the centuries. The ghetto prodigies are the natural outgrowth of the living conditions of the people, and they are neither intelligent nor virtuous in the Western sense (59–60).

Franzos rereads Cesare Lombroso's idea that genius and madness are closely linked. For Franzos the internal and external conditions of the Eastern Jews, including their inheritance and living conditions, make them brilliant but easily destroyed. Here the Jewish prodigy is transformed into Woyzeck. As Woyzeck's nature is deformed by the social institutions that alter his body and his psyche, so too are these Jewish children. They, like Woyzeck, are the victims of the society in which they are compelled to live. And this difference of the psyche is inscribed on their sickly bodies, which will die because of the deplorable exploitation by the institutions that trap them. Alter the institutions, writes Franzos, and you have at least a chance of redeeming the Jewish superior intelligence in the East. But this must be done by redeeming the physical body and freeing the intellect ("denationalizing" it in Franzos's terms) from the constraints of the educational system (the Cheder) that destroys it.

Eastern Jews saw these arguments about Eastern Jewish difference as the first step to conversion, but Franzos stressed in his work that Eastern Jews could become as "western" as their German and Austrians fellow coreligionists.[20] In this light Franzos was a clear follower of Ludwig Büchner's view that Jews could and should abandon their mental and physical difference since the basis for Jewish difference was the Jews' cultural context, not their race.

Franzos's early enthusiasm for Georg Büchner's revolutionary writing stemmed from a similar understanding of the revolutionary potential of human beings. It was in the context of his reading of German and Russian high culture (Heine, Goethe, Gogol, Turgenev) that he discovered Büchner and read *Dantons Tod*. He saw Büchner as a "romantic realist" and read him as he wrote his own early books on the redeemable state of Eastern Jewry. But, according to Franzos, his advocacy of Büchner led people to comment that he wrote about "first crude people, then crude writers" (114). Franzos was asked in 1875 to compile the first complete edition of Büchner's works, which included the unpublished *Woyzeck*. He worked on Büchner from 1877 to 1886 in Vienna, where he earned a living as a journalist, freelance writer, and editor. The edition, which appeared in 1879, was the foundation for all editions used by scholars through the end of World War I, as well as for the libretto of Alban Berg's opera.

But Büchner's *Woyzeck* was a major difficulty for Franzos. Not only was the edition difficult—the manuscript, written in tiny script, was faded and difficult to read—but it also consisted of a number of drafts of the play. Franzos's reconstruction has been challenged often. According to Franzos, when he finally sent the deciphered text to Ludwig Büchner, Georg's brother wanted to excise the "cynicism," the "faulty expressions," and the "atheistic or excessively radical political" passages (121), which could have offended the reading public (and hurt the reputations of the remaining siblings). Ludwig also wanted to further censor Büchner's vulgarisms. Franzos had printed, for example, the Drum Major's explicit use of *Arschloch* [asshole] as A— loch [a—hole] while Ludwig wanted it reduced to A—. Ludwig Büchner was a "liberal," in the late-nineteenth-century sense of the word, who knew the proprieties of Wilhelminian literature, from which dirty words, politics, and religion must be banned. Franzos quickly arranged for journal publication in *Mehr Licht* (Berlin) and the *Neue Freie Presse* (Vienna), and the relatively uncensored *Woyzeck* saw the light of day.

At the *fin de siècle*, the "radical" materialist Ludwig Büchner, the revolutionary Georg Büchner, and the assimilationist Jewish journalist and novelist Karl Emil Franzos became linked in the public image of Johann Christian Woyzeck's crime and madness. *Woyzeck* became part of "Jewish" culture in Germany. With the rediscovery of Büchner's drama as a staple of German-language expressionism after its first performance in Munich in 1913, this association came to include the modern, which defined itself as radical and revolutionary, and was labeled by its detractors as "Jewish." Büchner, in the words of Julius

Bab in 1922, becomes the forerunner of German expressionism and *Woyzeck* his most contemporary drama.[21] Yet as early as 1904, Büchner had already been so labeled in an oblique manner by the protofascist critic Arthur Moeller van den Bruck, who observed that Büchner was a psychopath whose physical and mental instability was clearly reflected in his literary work. Indeed, even his death, according to Moeller van den Bruck, was "a crisis of nerves." In other words, in the connection between his physical and psychological degeneracy and his corrupt writing, he was just like the sick Jews in German culture.[22] As we noted in the previous chapter, the *fin-de-siècle* critic Ottokar Stauf von der March observed, "Jewry today finds itself at the stage of a physical and psychic decadence."[23] And this decadence is most marked for him in modern high culture.

Georg Büchner was thus linked to the image of the Jew as defined racially at the turn of the century. Here Büchner undergoes a radical re-reading. For his Jewish references, which could have been understood as examples of the influence of capital on the image of the Jew in the 1830s, come to be read as a sign of the Jew's inherent racial difference. Büchner's Jew and Büchner as a "Jew"—that is, as a revolutionary and a materialist—set the stage for a subtle rereading of the text when it is transformed into a libretto by the Viennese composer Alban Berg.

RECAPITULATION: ALBAN BERG

On 5 May 1914, Alban Berg saw Albert Steinrück as Woyzeck in a performance of Franzos's version of Büchner's play in Vienna. Berg was thunderstruck by the crudity and beauty of the piece. After seeing the drama on the stage, he read *Woyzeck* in light of its *fin-de-siècle* reception as a document of materialism and social criticism.[24] For his revolutionary materialism, Ludwig Büchner had come to represent the mindset of "the Jew" in turn-of-the-century Viennese culture. Otto Weininger summarized the feeling about the Jewish materialistic science in 1903, and Viennese intellectuals such as Ludwig Wittgenstein were still very much under the thrall of his views in 1914. Weininger wrote,

Alban Berg, the Jews,

> Because fear of God in the Jew has no relation with real religion,
> the Jew is of all persons the least perturbed by mechanical theo-
> ries of the world; he is readily beguiled by Darwinism and the
> ridiculous notion that men are derived from monkeys; and now
> he is disposed to accept the view that the soul of man is an evolu-
> tion that has taken place within the human race; formerly he was
> a mad devotee of [Ludwig] Büchner, now he is ready to follow
> [the chemist] [Wilhelm] Ostwald [1853–1932].[25]

Weininger would have seen Berg's fascination with *Woyzeck* as merely
a further example of the corruption of German culture by this materialism, "beguiled by Darwinism and the ridiculous notion that men
are derived from monkeys." For Weininger, being Jewish was a mindset rather than a racial designation—and even non-Jews such as Berg
(or, indeed, as Weininger noted, Wagner) could thus be "Jews."

Berg's sensitivity to this view can be read in an extraordinary letter he wrote to the director of the Brunswick Opera House prior to
the premiere of *Wozzeck* there in 1931. Evidently the director had demanded (in 1931!) that Berg prove his Aryan inheritance, and Berg
sent him a stack of documents to do so. In the accompanying letter
he observed that "it was a pleasure that he was given a chance to
prove his Aryan inheritance officially and thus to put to rest those
newspaper lies that had been haunting him ever more loudly over the
past years."[26] Those "newspaper lies" were that Berg, like his teacher
Arnold Schoenberg, was a Jew. Given that any product of high modernism, no matter what its provenance, was dismissed as "Jew-trash"
in Vienna, the question comes to be how Berg thought he could limit
the reading of his work as a "Jewish" opera.

Because of the racial politics of early-twentieth-century Vienna,
Berg shapes Büchner's drama into a libretto for his opera with the
notion of the Jewish associations of materialism, the modern, and
the negative meaning of Jewish superior intelligence firmly in mind,
making a series of overt alterations to the libretto to disguise the "Jewish" references. These racial politics implicated the very notion of the
creativity of the composer—for could Jews really be creative? And are
not all of the "moderns" simply Jews in their imitative mode of thinking? Was Berg the modernist not merely imitative of Schoenberg the

Jew, who by definition could never be truly creative because of his "mechanical" approach to music? How could Berg use this archmodernist text and still "put to rest those newspaper lies that had been haunting him ever more loudly"?

Berg does so by reworking Franzos's version of *Woyzeck* to distinguish between himself and his work of art. His alterations reflect two cuts that eliminate any overt references to the Jews and lessen any potential racial reading of the drama in the discourse of anti-Semitism. The Jew's scene, in which Büchner documented Woyzeck's madness, is cut completely, even though Berg had initially intended to set it and thought of the Jew as a role for a baritone.[27] Büchner used this scene as the touchstone for the question of Woyzeck's mental status in light of Clarus's interpretation of Woyzeck's moral insanity. For Berg, it could only be read as a racial reference to the *Schacherjude,* the exploitative Jew, one of the stock characters of turn-of-the-century anti-Semitism. In avoiding setting the Jew as a baritone, Berg also avoided associating the voice of the Jew with Wozzeck, the other baritone role in the opera. Wozzeck is therefore not to be heard as a "Jew," as he could have been in light of Franzos's understanding of Jewish superior intelligence. Throughout the opera the "degenerate" characters are carefully placed beyond racial identification in the amorphous world of "modernism." Such placement obscures the association between the modernism of the " 'racially' acceptable" Berg (to use Alexander L. Ringer's phrase) and the "Jewishness" of musical modernism and Arnold Schoenberg's twelve-tone scale.[28]

The other reference to the Jews Berg cut from *Woyzeck* is in act two, scene four, the final line in the mock-sermon held by the apprentice. "Now let's piss crosswise so that a Jew will die." (The aria ends with the penultimate line of the text: "as for my soul, it stinks of brandy wine" (33). This scene expresses an anti-Semitic fantasy rooted in sadistic omnipotence "associated with the jet of urine passed by the male." Karen Horney commented that "I can quote something I was told of a class in a boys' school: When two boys, they said, urinate to make a cross, the person of whom they think at the moment will die."[29] Thus the powerlessness of the apprentices is laid at the feet of the Jews, who are themselves only minor and marginal players in this materialistic world.

Alban Berg, the Jews,

At the turn of the century, *Woyzeck* was read—as by Franzos—to mean that the diseased, malformed body of the proletariat is produced by exploitation by the owners of capital (read: the Jews), and the body of the Jew is the marker of Jewish difference and self-defined uniqueness. When Berg, in the intense anti-Semitism of the 1920s, cut the specifically "Jewish" references from *Woyzeck,* he eliminated reference not only to the Jews' racial difference but also to the belief of their relation to the proletariat as oppressors. His editing of these scenes can also be viewed as a conscious attempt to eliminate anything that could be read as illustrating the truly weak position of nineteenth-century marginal Jews vis-à-vis German anti-Semitism.

But the most telling and subversive of Berg's cuts of the Büchner text are related to the Doctor and the *fin-de-siècle* image of the Jew and scientific medicine. He refigures the Doctor to deflect Weininger's accusation that the Jews have converted medicine into biochemistry: "The present turn of medical science is largely due to the influence of the Jews, who in such numbers have embraced the medical profession. From the earliest times, until the dominance of the Jews, medicine was closely allied with religion. But now they make it a matter of drugs, a mere administration of chemicals. . . . The chemical interpretation of organisms sets these on a level with their own dead ashes" (315). Here the critique of "modern" scientific medicine, interpreted by Büchner as a sign of the power the educated classes exert over the proletariat, comes to have a strongly anti-Semitic tinge. The Jew in Büchner's play, in a Viennese reading at the turn of the century, is represented not only by the shopkeeper's materialism but also by the "scientific" attitude of the Doctor. Berg alters the Doctor's central exchange with Wozzeck to maintain the Doctor's materialism but separates this materialism from what is seen, at the turn of the century, to be a specific sign of Jewish difference: placing the Doctor's voice in the lowest register, lower than both the tremulous, high-pitched "Jewish" voices of Wagner and Strauss and the "Jewish" baritone voice of Wozzeck.

A verbal leitmotif that runs through the exchange between Wozzeck and the Doctor reads on its surface as if Ludwig Büchner's anxiety about proper language affected Berg. He eliminates *pissen* [to

piss] from the Doctor's speech to Wozzeck and replaces it throughout with *husten* [to cough].[30] This change was read initially as Berg's
attempt to soften the "naturalistic roughness of expression" in the
text.[31] Recently, and in a much more convincing manner, the change
has been read autobiographically as reflecting Berg's own asthma.[32] I
would like to extend this "personal" reading to include the question
of the materialism of medicine and science, the *fin-de-siècle* Jewish reading of coughing and urination, and the meaning of coughing in the
opera at the turn of the century. For if Berg was indeed asthmatic, it
could be read as a sign of his Aryan racial identity, or at least as a sign
of his not being Jewish.

Büchner's original reference to pissing was a red herring in his reconstruction of the mock pellagra that was to have been caused by the
Doctor's prescribing peas to Woyzeck, because people suffering from
pellagra experience diarrhea, not polyuria, a fact Büchner acknowledges by having the horse defecate on stage early in the drama. Woyzeck's polyuria is more highly symbolic within Büchner's construction
of Woyzeck's somatic suffering than defecation would be. First, the
ancient practice of uroscopy, the physician's examination and tasting
of urine to find specific signs and symptoms of disease, is inscribed
in the text. This practice was still in use in Büchner's time, and associating the physician with urine was very much in line with Büchner's
representation of the Doctor's epistemology. Second, urination can
also be read as the public act of exposure of the male genitalia—like
that of the lower animals, as Büchner has his characters state in the
drama. This reference to exposure is echoed in the scene excised by
Berg in which the apprentices go offstage to urinate and "kill a Jew."

But the reason physicians from the Greeks to the early nineteenth
century tasted their patients' urine was to examine for the sweetness
that marks diabetes. Thus the polyuria that is present in that disease
becomes a public marker of diabetes. By the beginning of the twentieth century, diabetes had come to be understood as the essential
"Jewish disease." Jean-Martin Charcot, the famed Parisian neurologist,
noted the predisposition of Jews for specific forms of illness, such
as diabetes, where "the exploration [of the cause of the disease] is
easy." For Charcot, the cause of such illness is the intermarriage of

the Jews.[33] Charcot sees this intermarriage as exacerbating the Jews' inherited racial predisposition for diabetes.[34] This dismissal of Jewish ritual practices, such as endogenous marriage, was one of the clarion calls of liberals such as Charcot and Ludwig Büchner at the turn of the century. They believed in the inheritance of acquired characteristics and saw Jewish diabetes as a quality of the Jewish body that reflected the Jewish character.

Diabetes is, for the *fin de siècle* physician, the "Jewish" disease about which one can speak.[35] This disease, because of its evident association with the Jews, was seen as a sign of the Jews' racial degeneration. William Osler, visiting Berlin in 1884, reported on the work of the famed internist Friedrich Theodor Frerichs on diabetes: "With reference to race, it is remarkable that 102 of the [400] patients were Jews, which he attributes to hereditary excitability of the nervous system, the keen pursuit of business, and, above all, intermarriage."[36] Diabetes and its polyuria are thus as clear a sign of Jewish materialism as the Jewish shopkeeper in Büchner's *Woyzeck*. As late as the 1920s this view remained quite alive in German-language medicine. Diabetes was seen as the "sole result" of "the impact of the nervous excitement on the nervous system transmitted from the time of the ghetto."[37] It is the physical parallel to Franzos's representation of Jewish superior intelligence. For the Jewish male, diabetes provided an association of Jewishness and masculinity that stressed not only the diseased nature of the Jew but also his physical and social impotence. Both the mind and the body of the Jew are impaired because of the "perverse" sexuality of his "race" and his striving for the material aspects of life. This is the reason he (and the Jew is always a male in this discourse) believes the materialist Ludwig Büchner, according to Otto Weininger's account of the world. Thus the male Jew would indeed be marked by his "pissing on the street."

If Jews did suffer from diabetes, they did not suffer from tuberculosis except in very specific cases. The myth of a Jewish immunity to that most operatic of illnesses frames the discussion of coughing in Berg's opera. Tuberculosis marked the operatic body as different, even in the seemingly attractive fantasy of the female tubercular in Dumas's *Lady of the Camellias* (set to music in Verdi's *Traviata*) or Murger's Mimi (set to music in Puccini's and Leoncavallo's *Bohème*). Wozzeck is suddenly put into the line of these coughing female protagonists. His madness is marked by his coughing. Jews, unlike operatic protagonists, were believed to have had a natural resistance to tuberculosis. While some critics, such as Leroy-Beaulieu, evoked the tubercular bodies of Sarah Bernhardt and Rahel to characterize the Jewish male body as ill and effeminate, the counterview also existed. Jews, according to much of the technical and popular literature of the time, were spared the ravages of this great killer. Thus in 1911, in his *The Jews: A Study of Race and Environment,* a detailed study of the racial characteristics of the Jew, Maurice Fishberg stresses the view that the traditional hygienic virtues of Jewish law and family life enable Jews to have a lower incidence of tuberculosis through the inheritance of acquired characteristics.[38] Other views of the time stress the racial basis of this supposed resistance to tuberculosis. This racial argument was supported by anthropologists such as Georg Buschan, who wrote in the major popular geographic journal of the day that both increased predisposition and increased resistance as defining signs of racial identity.[39] For Buschan the "four to six times higher rate of mental illness" among the Jews must be the result of an inherited weakness of the central nervous system since Jews do not evidence any of the sociopathic etiologies such as alcoholism, which, according to him, causes mental illness. But if Jews can be predisposed to acquire certain illnesses because of their racial identity, they can also be immune from certain diseases for the same reason. He thus sees the relative immunity of the Jews from certain infectious diseases as a sign of the diseases' inherited biological nature.

Thus a coughing Wozzeck undermines and continues the play of stereotypes in the opera. For it is not only Wozzeck but also the Captain who coughs in the libretto. In act two, scene two, in which the Doctor uses his "scientific gaze" to diagnose both the Captain and a female passerby, the Captain is shown to be "quite out of breath." "He coughs with excitement and exertion, with the Doctor tapping him on the back to ease his cough. The Captain is moved almost to tears" (25–26). The tears come from considering his own demise. But both the Captain and Wozzeck cough in public. Berg can thus simultaneously label the cough as both "Jewish" (and as such feminizing) and "universal." Wozzeck is the representative victim, but certainly not the Jew in any of his particulars, including his baritone voice. In the mythmaking of the time, Jews don't cough; they piss.

The Doctor's materialism is removed from the contemporary discourse of Jewish difference. And Berg frees the libretto, he believes, from any potential rereading of Büchner's text as anti-Semitic. Once *Wozzeck* is performed, however, Berg's detractors see him, the twelve-tone composer, as one more in the line of diseased Jews who, like the stench of the canals, spread pestilence through the land. This quite literally is what Paul Zschorlich, the music critic in the *Deutsche Zeitung* (Berlin), wrote concerning the initial performance of the opera in 1925: "The work of a Chinese from Vienna. My name will be *Moses Kanalgeruch* [Canalstench] if this isn't a true swindle."[40] Zschorlich's use of the crypto-Jewish name in this "oriental" context places the opera firmly in the camp of the "Jewish modern." The image of the pestilence of the modern, associated with both Büchners and Franzos, is now associated with Berg. While attempting to repress all references to the Jews, no matter how tangential, Berg remains caught in the web of an anti-Semitic rhetoric that sees the cultural production of the modern as corrupt and corrupting. This is the essence of Berg's own reading of the Doctor, who in the opera is the embodiment of the materialism of Wozzeck's world. Even stripping the "Jewish" references in the text does not free Berg or the Doctor from this association. Berg's Doctor remains the worst of all possible diagnosticians, captured as he is by his notion of "big science" and "big medicine." In the drama he comes to be the embodiment of the cruelties of medicine rather than its solace. But this cruel materialism is a label placed on "Jewish medicine" by "scientific" racists, such as Otto Weininger, who claim that their science is simply better than that of the Jews, not that it is kinder. Given the fact that the racial science of the *fin de siècle* provides the basis for the Shoah, this claim turns out to be parody.

The role of science in providing the vocabulary of images for the Jew that Berg desires himself not to be is echoed in *Wozzeck*. From the voice of the Jew to the very body of the degenerate, the stereotypical model of Jewish differences provides alternatives that Berg chooses or rejects. Behind all is Berg's anxiety of being seen (or heard) as a Jew. Certainly Jewish composers, even converts such as Gustav Mahler, were anxious about their creativity and saw it in some way linked to their "Jewishness."[41] For Berg, being associated with the "Jews" in terms of their "modernism" and their "illness" would have drawn his own creativity into question. All this comes to be inscribed and projected onto the body of Wozzeck in the opera. Here the rereading of a non-Jewish text (Büchner's play) through a Jewish anxiety about original genius (Franzos) that came to constitute the original text as a text of modernity leads Berg to radically reformat the libretto and rethink his setting of it. The anxiety of being seen as "Jewish" frames the rethinking of the opera.

6

The End of Another Century:
The Image in American
Mass Culture

THE JEWISH BODY AND JEWISH SUPERIOR INTELLIGENCE
IN AMERICAN MASS CULTURE

OVING FROM the high cultural modernism of Alban
Berg's *Wozzeck* to American mass culture, especially cinema and television after the Shoah, seems a far leap.[1] Yet
it is in another work stemming from the "Golden Age" of the modern mass media, F. Scott Fitzgerald's fragmentary last novel *The Last
Tycoon,* that we can find our final set of criteria through which to comprehend yet another turn in the history of mythmaking about Jewish
superior intelligence. The movies are that imaginary space in which
Jews are seen as "geniuses" and where the studio system produced at
least one "genius." The view from the desk of Fitzgerald about what
constituted "true genius" placed him, the quintessential writer about
WASP culture in the 1920s, in contrast with the "genius" of Hollywood marked by Jewish superior intelligence.

Fitzgerald was working on *The Last Tycoon* when he died on 21 December 1940. He had been working as a screenwriter in Hollywood,
and this novel was to be dedicated to the world where he worked. The
studio that employed Fitzgerald was headed by the "boy genius" of
Hollywood, Irving Thalberg, who is transmuted into the character
of Monroe Stahr in *The Last Tycoon.* According to Ben Hecht, Thalberg was a genius.[2] Cecil B. DeMille also thought of him as a "genius"
in 1922, and Louis B. Mayer commented about his presence in Hollywood that "geniuses we have all we need" (221). The role of "boy
genius" in Fitzgerald's novel parallels Fitzgerald's own role in American letters during the 1920s, but Fitzgerald carefully distances himself
from his portrait of Monroe Stahr. The Jewishness of Hollywood,
the "Empire of Their Own" (the title of Neal Gabler's fine study of
Jews in Hollywood and a quote from *The Last Tycoon*), is evident in
Fitzgerald's account. And Fitzgerald provides, in the figure of Monroe Stahr, a way of understanding Jewish superior intelligence within
the American situation at the very moment of the Shoah.

Stahr is not only brilliant but sexy in a way that shapes the novel,
much of which is narrated by the teenage daughter of one of Stahr's

non-Jewish colleagues. The genius of the Jews in Hollywood is the sexiness of the Jew. For Stahr's sexual attractiveness is measured by the female narrator, herself a child of Hollywood, who sees Stahr as both "self-made" and sexy: "Though Stahr's education was founded on nothing more than a night-school course in stenography, he had a long time ago run ahead through trackless wastes of perception into fields where very few men were able to follow him. But in my reckless conceit I matched my grey eyes against his brown ones for guile" (17–18).[3] Her eyes are Irish-American; Stahr's entire physical presence is keyed to his Jewish genius and captured even in his gestures: "Stahr kept turning his ring so abstractedly that he made me feel young and invisible" (15). Part of the image of the Jew at the beginning of the twentieth century, rings are a sign of parvenu status. Stahr's ostentatious love of jewelry is a sign of how far he has come and how very far he must go to become a true member of modern society in spite of his Jewish superior intelligence. The rings mark the Jewish body as surely as any biological marker of the time, and the marked body of the Jew draws the image of the genius into question. Stahr's rings also mark the limits of his sexual attraction—for the plot of *The Last Tycoon*, as far as it was sketched out by Fitzgerald, ends in Stahr's death in a plane crash and his possessions being looted by scavengers. The material world is superficial by definition. No happy ending, no romantic resolution to the role of the Jew exists in Fitzgerald's Hollywood.

Stahr's manner of seeing the world is tied to his newly acquired Western rationality: "He was a rationalist who did his own reasoning without benefit of books—and he had just managed to climb out of a thousand years of Jewry into the late eighteenth century. He could not bear to see it melt away—he cherished the parvenu's passionate loyalty to an imaginary past" (118). This past is certainly not his. It is not the past of the Jew but that of Western civilization that, according to Fitzgerald, the Jew is acquiring like an ill-fitting suit. The Jew's genius is the genius of the ghetto, not of the university; it is the genius that is best applied to the world of Hollywood. But it is genius, and it is also not ubiquitous even among the Jews. Stahr is the parvenu as pariah. His attraction to the surface of culture is his entrance card to American society. His cultural world comes to be Hollywood, the

The Image in American Mass Culture

exemplary space where taste has vanished and art is converted into money. Stahr is the Jewish genius, but only as self-parody. He is truly quite distant from the world of true genius—that of the writer.

Stahr is very different from the other Jews in Hollywood who seem neither truly brilliant nor truly sexy. On the plane with Stahr are other Jews from Hollywood, such as "a middle-aged Jew, who alternatively talked with nervous excitement or else crouched as if ready to spring" (4). He was "staring, with shameless economic lechery" (6). "Mr. Schwartz was physically unmarked; the exaggerated Persian nose and oblique eye-shadow were as congenital as the tip-tilted Irish redness around my father's nostrils" (7). The nose is a sign of character, of the material nature of the Jew, just as the "redness" of the Irish nose implied the alcoholism ascribed to the Irish stereotype in American culture. All these physical characteristics are signs of the absence of virtue, of the pariah status of the parvenu who may mask his Jewishness and his lack of culture but who is surrounded by those who represent it.

Yet America does have the potential for reshaping the Jew just as it has the Irish and the Greek. Joe Popolos, a theater owner in the novel, "thought Jews were too fond of their own skins. But he was willing to concede that they might be different in America under different circumstances" (46). In America the old stereotypes were no longer completely valid; indeed they were often reversed. The material nature of the Jew was proven not by his "tightness" with money but by his parvenu attitude toward it. For Stahr "the literal sky was the limit. He had worked with Jews too long to believe legends that they were small with money" (42). American Jews, even Jews in Hollywood, are generous but always with a purpose. Their apocryphal meanness is precisely the opposite of the Hollywood reality—they are overly generous and indulgent, for they are parvenus who must show that they truly belong in the system. Their genius is thus not merely for making money but for reshaping themselves and the culture in which they live. And yet all is tainted by a sense of the unreality of the enterprise.

With limited historical insight, Fitzgerald frames his representation of the American image of the "smart Jew" in terms of the Shoah—or at least in terms of understanding the Jewish persecutions by the Nazis and fascists in 1940. While Stahr's world is extremely egocentric,

the external world, including the fate of his Jewish compatriots, im-
pinges itself upon him. At one point he picks up a stack of telegrams:
"a company ship was lost in the Arctic; a star was in disgrace; a writer
was suing for one million dollars. Jews were dead miserably beyond
the sea" (116). Stahr's world is the world that refuses to ignore his
Jewishness—the world from which he has escaped, the world of European Jewry. Hollywood becomes the site of refuge from destruction,
but it is fraught with the inability of the Jew truly to belong in its
brave new world. And yet Stahr attempts to transform himself into
an "American."

Central to Fitzgerald's project is that the Jewish genius, Monroe
Stahr, is an escapee from the ghetto of the mind. Thalberg's German Jewish ancestry was almost unique among the Eastern European
Jews of Hollywood. Fitzgerald plays off this in complex ways. For
Fitzgerald, Stahr is *the* Hollywood Jew—but also the example of a
native Jewish superior intelligence that is beyond education in the
Western/American tradition. His intelligence is the product of the
ghetto now adapted to the refinements of American commercial culture, and, unlike his compatriots in the novel, his body is not marked
by an "ethnic" physical taint. And yet his chronic illness marks his
body as different. Thalberg's reality was similar. He showed his "aqui-
line nose, his sculpted cranium, his fine features" (218) and reflected a
"tragic sense of mortality" because of his chronic heart problems (221).
Thalberg was, according to the producer Pandro Berman, "educated,
calm, cultured" (223). Stahr thus represents in Fitzgerald's fiction the
successful adaptation of the Jew to America. But the films (none by
Thalberg) made after the Shoah needed to see the Jew as smart and
adaptive but also as physically weak. Monroe Stahr has "a radiance
that is almost moribund in its phosphorescence" (139). His sickliness,
and his failure at love and sex compensate for his Jewish superior
intelligence, but, like his body, his creativity is also tainted, for Hollywood in Fitzgerald's eyes is the antithesis of "real" high culture.

Between the 1940s and the present, the representation of the "smart
Jew" in the mass media has taken up the figure of Monroe Stahr,
and the idea that Jewish superior intelligence compensates for Jewish physical weakness has remained. An African American author recently noted:

The Image in American Mass Culture

Another classmate said that while black people were gifted in sports and music, Jews had provided the world with intellectual genius. As proof, he ticked off three names: Freud, Einstein, Marx. I got very angry. For a long time I wondered whether the Jews were really chosen by God, as one of my Jewish classmates suggested. The argument seemed watertight. Wherever Jews were given the chance they have shown themselves to be smarter than anyone else. *Look how well we've done in America and everywhere else we've gone. Look at the Jews. Look.*[4]

This is a version of the myth of economic superiority as a sign of Jewish superior intelligence, but it also obscures the argument about compensation. If, in such a view, music and sports compensate for a lack of intelligence among Blacks, Jewish intelligence compensates for Jewish physical inferiority. Such images haunt the representation of the Jew in Hollywood. Remember Jose Ferrer as Barney Greenglass, Humphrey Bogart's lawyer, in *The Caine Mutiny* (1952)? Ferrer's "Jewish" body was dominated by the other military figures in the film. The relationship between "mind" and "body" in this view is extraordinarily powerful.

The representation of smart Jews in American cinema after the Shoah had been relatively rare until recently. In the movies, and by extension in television, Jews had been represented as victims, as "sensitive" or as "ethnic minorities," but rarely as Jews of exceptional intelligence. Of the triumvirate of smart Jews evoked above, Marx rarely appears in American popular culture, but Einstein and Freud do. (One might note that Moses, Jesus, Einstein, and Freud are the first four "Jews" listed in a recent tabulation of "the most influential Jews of all time." Marx shows up as number seven and Spinoza number ten.[5]) Einstein is the essential smart Jew in American popular culture. But his appearance in Stephen Herek's comedy *Bill and Ted's Excellent Adventure* (1989) or as the feature figure played by Walter Matthau in Fred Schepisi's film *IQ* (1994) is as the comic professor I discussed in chapter 1. He is asexual and only marginally aware of the reality around him. In the latter film, he serves as a matchmaker between his "too-smart" niece (played by Meg Ryan) and her proletarian boyfriend (played by Tim Robbins). Einstein, no matter what his actual reputation in late-twentieth-century biographies as a lover, never gets the girl in American popular film. Likewise, Freud seems to be ubiquitous in modern American culture, from the sensitive Freud (played by Montgomery Clift in the 1962 film biography) to the spectral Freud in Joshua Brand and John Falsey's television drama *Northern Exposure* in 1993. Unlike Einstein, Freud is rarely a comic figure in the presentation of his "insight," but despite the traditional association of Freud with sexuality, he is never a sensual figure.

The compensatory function of high intelligence in American mass and popular culture is clear when the theme is love and sex. Thus in the representation of mixed couples, the continuation of the image of the *Mischling,* the Jewish partner is always smarter and better educated. Perhaps this should be called "Annie Hall Syndrome," since the relationship between Woody Allen and Diane Keaton in that 1977 film set the pattern for the self-conscious exposure of failed intermarriage as "marrying down" in intellect.[6] Recently, in the television series *Chicago Hope,* Aaron Shutt (played by Adam Arkin) is a Jewish neurosurgeon who was married to a blond Catholic nurse. All such relationships fail. Indeed, Miles Silverberg (played by Grant Shaud), the Harvard-educated producer on CBS's *Murphy Brown,* embodies the ineffective Jewish intellectual who seems to have no sexuality at all. Silverberg is permitted to articulate his "Jewish" identity and his Jewish superior intelligence as part of the construction of his character's anxiety about his sexuality.

In the mass media, however, there seem to be no "dumb" Jewish women. Even if the image is not of Jewish superior intelligence but of the "maternal" woman (such as Gertrude Berg's *ur*-Jewish mother figure, Molly Goldberg), she is never represented in the same way as Diane Keaton's Annie Hall. Yet the image of Jewish superior intelligence is always linked to dysfunction that cuts across gender. Gender seems to be the significant variable when one speaks of "smart Jewish [male] doctors" and "dumb Gentile [female] nurses," but in *Prince of Tides* (1992), a Jewish woman, Susan Loewenstein (played by Barbra Streisand), is the stereotypically intelligent, educated, slightly neurotic New York psychiatrist. Thus gender depends on the category of "race," that is, "Jewishness" defines gender. In *Prince of Tides,* Loewenstein is a smart Jewish female psychotherapist, but her personal and professional life is a mess. She sleeps with her analysand, a problem that even the reviewers saw as reflecting on her role as a therapist in light of the discussion of sexual exploitation in therapy during the 1980s and 1990s.[7]

I. B. Singer's *Yentl* (1983) provides a further example of the problems seen in the presentation of Jewish superior intelligence on the screen. In order to fulfill her role as a "smart Jew" in this fiction of the Eastern European shtetl, Streisand's protagonist must disguise herself as a man. Such figures of the smart Jew run parallel to Streisand's early role as a bright social activist in Sidney Pollack's *The Way We Were* (1973), in which she plays her intelligence off against Robert Redford's "All-American" good looks. But here too unhappiness and the lack of personal fulfilment result from being too smart. You can't be happy and smart—especially if you are Jewish.

In spite of the fact that all smart Jews are alike (at least as represented in the mass media), the case of *Yentl* provides a model that implies the damaged masculinity of the "smart Jew." Yentl's Jewish superior intelligence can only be articulated in her masked state. In speaking about the constructed category of "the Jew" throughout this study I have gendered him male, as does the literature discussing him.[8] Thus Miles Storfer, in his 1990 study of Jews and their accomplishments, compiles lists of accomplished Jews who are exclusively male and stresses in his discussion of postwar American tests that Jewish males outperformed all other groups, including Jewish "girls."[9] This is contradicted by studies undertaken by women scientists such as Irma Loeb Cohen. Storfer's idealized account of Jewish Talmudic education is implicitly gendered, as only boys were permitted to study under the circumstances he describes (326–28). F. Scott Fitzgerald's world of Eastern European Jewry, the world out of which he imagines Monroe Stahr to spring, is the world of the Jewish male. And the attraction that the women in the novel have for Stahr, as well as his inability to stabilize such relationships, is a reflection of the powerful gendering associated with Jewish superior intelligence as a sign of flawed masculinity.

The myths about the masculinity of the Jew are historically defined by the Jew's body, specifically by his circumcised penis.[10] Indeed, the Talmudic rationale for circumcision is seen as a measure of the intelligence of the Jews. When the Roman general Turnus Rufus confronted Rabbi Akiba over the practice of infant male circumcision ("Why has God not made man just as He wanted him to be?"), Akiba answered, "Everything that God has created was purposely made incomplete, in order that human ingenuity may perfect it. Take, for instance, the acorn and the cake made from it; the cotton plant and the beautiful garments that are made from it. Man is born uncircumcised because it is the duty of man to perfect himself."[11] Jewish superior intelligence has completed God's plan for man's body.

In American society in the late twentieth century, the "Jewish" body, the circumcised body, becomes the measure of the body of all men, for infant male circumcision is ubiquitous if not universal in the United States. Here we could expect an extension of the nineteenth-century argument put forth by Miles Storfer, that Jewish ritual practices have direct health benefits and should be exported into the non-Jewish world to turn everyone into the exemplary Jew, and yet, of course, such arguments can no longer be heard. The relationship between the image of Jewish superior intelligence and the nature of the Jewish male body has become a mythic one as the idea of a specifically marked Jewish body becomes repressed.

For circumcision has come, in the current *fin de siècle,* to mark the body of the American male as the body of the victim. The columnist Dave Barry comments that the anticircumcision movement in the United States is a way of creating a new victim class: "I'm a middle-aged white guy, which means I'm constantly reminded that my particular group is responsible for the oppression of every known minority PLUS most wars PLUS government corruption PLUS pollution of the environment, not to mention that it was middle-aged white guys who killed Bambi's mother. So I'm pleased to learn that I myself am an oppressed victim of something. But no matter how hard I try, I can't get enraged about it."[12] Circumcision seems no longer to be a sign of radical difference that can easily be tied to the image of Jewish superior intelligence.

However, the late-twentieth-century American sense of the circumcised body as the "normal" body—as marking a sense not of difference but of identity—works only if you are in a society that does not understand the marked body of the circumcised male as a mark of inferiority. Here the alternative in German culture, even German cultural traditions in the United States, provides the counterweight. From 1964 to 1968 the Chicago playwright and singer Terry Abrahamson went to high school in Amundsen, Illinois, where he says that as a Jew he was somewhat of an oddity. "A lot of kids were children of people who had come over from Germany after the war, and they weren't the people with tattoos," Abrahamson says. "The only time I was a hero was in 1967 during the Six-Day War. These guys came up to me because the Jews had saved the Holy Land from Nasser. I was an anomaly in the locker room because I didn't have a foreskin, and these guys were saying, 'Hey! You guys really kicked ass over there!'"[13] And a contemporary German view of circumcision rereads anti-Semitism in Germany as an inversion of the orthodox Freudian theories of castration fear: "German" men envy Jewish men because the latter are circumcised and are therefore immune to castration anxiety and thus better lovers.[14] Such a reversal of the classic stereotype sets the male Jewish body apart as clearly as does the image of Jewish superior intelligence. These stereotypes continue to exist in 1995, when Jean-Charles Thomas, the bishop of Versailles, admitted that the *Bible for Christian Communities,* for which he wrote the preface, had an "anti-Semitic aspect" and had hurt the Jewish community. Some sixty thousand copies of that Bible have been sold in France and Belgium and eighteen million copies in English and Spanish have been distributed in South America since it was published in May 1994. Written in simple, straightforward language, it is the work of Bernard Hurault, a missionary based in Chile who planned to use it to combat the growing appeal of evangelical churches among the poor. According to the text, the Jewish people killed Jesus Christ because they "were not able to control their fanaticism." The text also reduces Jewish customs and rituals to "folkloric duties involving circumcision and hats." Only in

Europe (or, by extension, in the post-Shoah non-Jewish European Diaspora community in Chicago) does circumcision continue to set the body of the male Jew apart. Here the reading of good character and virtue into the Jewish body is linked to the reverse implication of circumcision.

The marked body of the Jew—not Dave Barry's American male—is in a European reading the body of the "tough Jew" or the image of the "Jewish lover."[15] Masculinity is thus reinscribed onto the body of the Jew: he is no longer just different but tough, which rereads the body in many new ways. For contemporary America, however, circumcision marks the body not of the Jew but of the male, given the ubiquitous practice of infant male circumcision. So it is another part of the Jewish body, the Jewish brain—or at least, in Miles Storfer's reading, the left side of the Jewish brain—that is marked by the myth of difference through "Jewish superior intelligence." And this difference sets him apart from the normal, from the two standard deviations from the center of the bell curve.

The image of Jewish superior intelligence becomes the means of articulating Jewish difference. It becomes the theme representing the difference in the Jew and is no longer linked in post-Shoah American culture explicitly to the image of circumcision or the materiality of the Jew.[16] Yet both qualities continue to be associated on a subliminal level with Jewish superior intelligence. In her insightful and critically acute autobiography, the Italian American writer Marianna de Marco Torgovnick added a complex response to this idea of the intellectual attractiveness of male Jews as life partners.[17] Here the parallel between Eastern European Jewish immigrants and their Italian contemporaries that haunts the literature on Jewish superior intelligence from the 1920s to the 1990s finally has a critical articulation.

In Torgovnick's account of growing up Italian in Bensonhurst, she notes that even with all the prejudices against the Jews, "the old Italian women admit" that Jewish men "make good husbands" (7). In this they are virtuous. These Jews, and Marianna de Marco Torgovnick marries one, are represented as smart and are thus a means of economic "upward mobility" (22), "a passport out of Bensonhurst" (15). Jewish males are thus "the only available models" for escaping the marginality of Bensonhurst (22). Indeed, she taunts her own father with these male Jews' intellectual superiority when she is threatened with being placed in a secretarial track in high school, "saying, if I were Jewish I would have been placed, without question, in the academic track" (14). Torgovnick thus self-consciously identifies with the "smart" Jewish men as a means of reconstructing a "smart" self-image for herself and her father. Virtually all the Jewish figures in Torgovnick's narrative, such as Dave, the man who provides piecework for her mother, are men. Yet the male Jews who haunt her memory are also Jews like Dave who "look Jewish": "Short, round, with his shirttails sloppily tucked into his pants and a cigar almost always dangling from his lips, Dave was a stereotypical Jew" (14). Dave's actions represent the absence of virtue; he is exploitative and crude. Thus the accomplishments (however limited) and the physicality of the Jewish male are linked much as they are in Storfer's account of left-hemisphere superiority.

Torgovnick's approach to her father enables her to persuade him to allow her to go on to college. But in her memory of her world, Jews, especially male Jews, do not have to persuade their parents. Torgovnick creates a category of the smart Jew that encompasses both men and women who had "culture" and intelligence:

> In Joan Karp's apartment, we talked about college and writing, listened to Vivaldi, and read Keats (with, in Joan's phrase, "sympathy and sorrow"). In David Sultan's Orthodox Sephardic household, we dabbled in kisses, debated the ethics of romance, and pondered the sources of religious thinking. These were important entries, my first participation with real people in intellectual life. Like all my Jewish friends, Joan and David simply expected to go to college; my Italian friends mostly did not. Gradually, through the high school years, I shifted alliances. (24–25)

The image that Jewish Americans are superior to Italian Americans haunts the literature on Jewish achievement from Seth Arsenian's discussion of bilingualism in chapter 2 to Seymour Martin Lipset's most recent book on American Jewry.[18] Torgovnick's "idealized, almost imaginary version of what it meant to be Jewish" (22) was a longing

The Image in American Mass Culture

not only for lost worlds but also for a sense of the accomplishments associated with the Jew, especially the Jewish male that she eventually marries. High culture and sex come to represent virtue in this world as Torgovnick associates such Jews with the civil rights movement of the 1960s. There is no anxiety about the parvenu in such narratives, and Torgovnick identifies completely with the goals of her Jewish classmates. Her sense of the positive nature of Jewish superior intelligence is that it may be copied, for her own academic success is proof positive that anyone following the "Jewish" model can become an intellectual.

Yet as an adult writing her autobiography, she is more than slightly ambivalent about the model of the "smart Jew," she has chosen. She sees it as "idealized, almost imaginary," a projection of her own desires. She is also aware of the coded nature of her message. Are Jews like "Dave" or her husband? Are they material or intellectual? The fact that they can be both or neither undermines her retrospective reconstruction of her earlier fantasies. The Jewish male body fulfills every purpose in her narrative. It is different, but it comes to be a difference located in the world of the intellectual with which she still wishes to identify.

This inarticulated anxiety about Jewish visibility and Jewish racial difference has dominated representation of Jews in the media. "Jewish superior intelligence" must be understood as an aspect of the question of Jewish visibility in post-Shoah America. The casting of Paul Newman (blue eyes, Jewish father, raised as a Christian Scientist) as the Jewish hero of the film based on Leon Uris's novel *Exodus* (1960) was one of the anomalies of this anxiety about the implied difference of the Jewish body. How could Jews be "racially" different if they looked like Paul Newman! Indeed, in Robert Mandel's *School Ties* (1992) the theme of "passing" works only because of the sports activities of Brandon Frasier. He is not quite able to "pass" in the snooty anti-Semitic private school he attends. Yet in *School Ties* the character is not only athletic but smart and compassionate. His athlete's body is not sufficient, within the narrative of the film, to enable him to be accepted, to pass successfully.

The ghost of the "smart Jew" haunts the representation of the Jew in Robert Benton's *Nobody's Fool* (1995), based on a novel by

The Image in American Mass Culture

Richard Russo. The following scene with the working-class protagonist, played by Paul Newman, takes place in a bar:

LAWYER: "Don't blame me, these aren't my holidays. I'm a Jew."
SULLY [played by Paul Newman]: "You're a Jew? I never knew you were a Jew." >*beat*< "How come you ain't smart?"[19]

Being smart and being Jewish are linked, even in the world of Paul Newman, the exemplary "Jewish" figure of the age of the "tough Jew." The images of the "tough Jew" and the "smart Jew" merge during the 1990s. In 1991, writer-director Barry Levinson made *Bugsy,* which was set in Hollywood's "golden age," the age of Monroe Stahr. James Toback's screenplay turned the aging Warren Beatty into the "smart Jew" as a powerful cultural icon. Benjamin "Bugsy" Siegel, the subject of Levinson's film, helped set up the West Coast headquarters of the New York City Mafia in 1935. In the mid-1940s, he built the Flamingo, the first luxury hotel-casino in Las Vegas. Out of the tawdriness of his life, Levinson and Toback tell the story of a "smart Jew" who makes his own vision of America come alive. Even Jewish criminals come to be "saved" by being shown to be smart (as well as tough).

Simon Louvish, the Anglophone Israeli British novelist, has one of his characters in *The Silencer* (1993), his novel about the charge of dual loyalties against American Jews, sketch the following history of modern Jewish identity formation in Israel:

When we met, when was it, 'sixty-nine? You'd just started on your work for the paper, and I was demobilized from the army magazine and was taken on as a reporter. The first years of the Occupation. The heyday of Golda Meir. "Who are these Palestinians? I've never met any." A neat and closed orthodoxy. Now it's all blowing in the wind. The great victory of 1967. The ship was sailing. The Americans came on board. Everybody admired us, except the Third World, that bunch of wogs, who cared? Everybody deserves an imperial hubris. Ours just happened to last half an hour. The warning signs of arrogance and presumption. The Yom Kippur War. Menachem Begin. Lebanon. No more invincibility. And then to twist the knife, *intifada*. Some people just can't take it, Joe. They want that half-hour back, to stretch for ever. They want the smart Jew, who pisses on everyone.[20]

Louvish's novel is the novel of American Israeli identity formation as seen from a British perspective. His history, however, collapses the image of the "smart Jew" with that of the "tough Jew." Here the transvaluation of the Diaspora "smart Jew" into the aggressive, powerful body of the Israeli as colonial aggressor (following a European model) provides a new reading of the "smart Jew," a Paul Newman figure who thinks he can think but, of course, really lacks any insight or intellectual acuity. This view was seconded by Ehud Barak, the retired Chief of Staff of the Israeli Defence Forces. Quoted in a 1995 essay in the *New York Times* on the "Israeli deglamourizing of the military," Barak championed the concept of "a smaller and more clever I. D. F."[21] As the "tough Jew" is seen in Israel and the United States to be more and more problematic, the desire for the "smart" or "clever" Jew returns, at least subliminally.

By the 1990s Jewishness and Judaism, Jewish identity and the different body of the "smart Jew," come to be interchangeable. With Gary David Goldberg's 1991 *Brooklyn Bridge* (based on Goldberg's childhood in Bensonhurst and attendance at the Bronx High School of Science) and Brand and Falsey's *Northern Exposure,* which appeared a year earlier, being Jewish is something that can be represented in American culture—but only as it equates to being smart. Thus Joel Fleischman (played by Rob Morrow), the protagonist of *Northern Exposure,* is brought to the wilds of Alaska because the inhabitants of the town of Cecily want a "smart Jew Doctor," since Jews are smarter than other people (implying that as doctors Jews are also more virtuous). This hint at a "biological" model for the smart Jew vanishes quickly and is made to seem an anomaly of the racial bias of the quirky character who uttered it, the multimillionaire ex-astronaut Maurice Minniefield (played by Barry Corbin). Yet it is an echo of the view that permeates American popular culture in the 1990s: Jews are smarter than everyone else because they are Jews! And yet Joel Fleischman's unhappy and ultimately unsuccessful attempt to enter the world of Cecily, to achieve happiness and fulfilment with Maggie O'Connell, the Gentile bush pilot from Grosse Point (played by Janine Turner), is the overarching plot of the series from 1990 until Fleischman returns to New York City in the winter of 1995. Fleischman thus proves his virtue by allowing himself to be physically and spiritually tested in the Alaskan outback, showing that he is now morally prepared to return to (his natural space?) New York City.

In the course of the series Fleischman's Jewishness is transformed into a highly ambivalent relation to his Judaism. In one episode, the same ex-astronaut, in order to keep his "Jew Doctor" happy, arranges to comb the wilds of Alaska for ten adult male Jews so that Joel can say "Kaddish," the prayer for the dead, for his uncle. The show ends with Joel abandoning his search for a *religious* community and saying the prayer in the church–cum–community center of Cecily, with the inhabitants of the town, people of all "races" and "religions," his new congregation. The countermoment in this series is an episode from 1991 in which Holling Vincouer, the French Canadian owner of the local bar/restaurant (played by John Cullum), decides that he must have himself circumcised in order to please his eighteen-year-old sweetheart Shelly (played by Cynthia Geary). His circumcision is divorced from ritual practice and associated with personal virtue — Jewish difference becomes masculine difference and virtue. Yet throughout the series Joel's physical insufficiency, his lack of hardiness (unlike Holling Vincouer, who single-handedly fights off a bear) is paralleled to his status as a "smart Jew," a Jewish physician. As in the war films of the 1940s and 1950s, such as *The Young Lions* (1958), the Jew's presence is marked as a sign of the plurality of American culture, and his physical insufficiency and religious identity seemed to be linked. They are, of course, but only by the reverse movement of the post-Shoah construction of Jewish religious identity out of the ashes of a secularized racism.

This brings us to three firm rules of contemporary American mass media for representing American Jews as "smart" as told to me by my friend Jo Miller:

1. All Jews are smart or at least clever.
2. All Jews are from New York.
3. Unless they are from Los Angeles, in which case they are movie

producers (who must nevertheless speak with New York accents to demonstrate their New York–Jewish roots).

"Jews" in post-Shoah American cinema are "smart," but this is not always a virtue. Indeed it often comes to be tied in complex ways to the victim status of Jews in popular myth, as parodied in Mel Brooks's *Blazing Saddles* (1974).

If the Jews are smart but victims, "Germans" are also represented as smart—yet with quite a different twist. For their genius is that of demented, evil intelligence, Moriarity to the Jew's Sherlock Holmes. This is the other side of the image of the scientist as intellectual. Thus Orson Welles in *The Stranger* (1946), Sam Jaffe as "the Professor" in *The Asphalt Jungle* (1950), Peter Sellers as Dr. Merkwuerdigliebe in Stanley Kubrick's *Dr. Strangelove* (1964), Hardy Krüger in *Flight of the Phoenix* (1965), or, indeed, Walter Slezak or George Sanders in any of their fiendish Nazi incarnations in the "B" movies made before 1945 are "evil." The evil "German" scientist is in many ways the extension of the idea of Jewish superior intelligence, now associated (as it was in the nineteenth-century literary stereotype) with the German scientist. Jews, if they are not victims, can be the equivalent of the "evil" German. Such an image of the smart yet destructive Jew can be found in Frederick Wiseman's character as a nihilist-anarchist in *Viva Zapata!* (1952), leading the Mexican children of nature to their doom apparently for the sheer pleasure of it.

Thus multiple versions of the myth of the "smart Jew" are to be found within the contemporary popular culture that spans the world of Herrnstein and Murray's *Bell Curve:* the myth of Jewish intellectual accomplishments stands in contrast to German American, African American, and Italian American expectations, but the myth of Jewish intellectual superiority is seen as compensatory for the imagined weaknesses of the Jewish body. Framing *The Bell Curve,* they show how alive and real the myth of Jewish superior intelligence and its relation to images of virtue remains.

The representation of Jewish superior intelligence in the mass media became a major theme of the mid-1990s with the appearance in 1993 of Steven Spielberg's Academy Award–winning *Schindler's List* and in 1994 of Robert Redford's *Quiz Show*. These films and the texts that parallel them present the question of Jewish superior intelligence as a moral moment in cultural representation. Both films question whether being "smart" is also being virtuous. Both films also present striking and complicated answers to the myth of Jewish selection and the meaning attributed to the Shoah in many popular cultural discussions of Jewish superior intelligence.

One can begin with the Australian author Thomas Keneally's novel *Schindler's Ark* (1982; released in the United States as *Schindler's List*). Given the reading of the absence of Jewish superior intelligence in Australia by Bill Rubinstein, to which I referred at the conclusion of chapter 3, it is fascinating to read an Australian author looking at this phenomenon in the world of Central European Jewry. Keneally's understanding of Jewish superior intelligence is framed by his sense of its exotic place of origin. Spielberg recasts Keneally's "outsider" perspective in terms of an American reading of Jewish superior intelligence and its implications for the reception of the Shoah. (One might note that Spielberg made number 94 in Michael Shapiro's *The Jewish 100: A Ranking of the Most Influential Jews of All Time*).

Keneally's historical narrative in fictive guise focuses on Oskar Schindler, the non-Jewish entrepreneur whose actions rescued the workers assigned to his factory in occupied Poland. As Keneally explains in the introduction, the central theme of the novel is "virtue."[22] It is a "strange virtue" (14) in that it is inexplicable at the beginning of Keneally's narrative, a historical preface in which he sets the stage for his own discovery of Schindler's story and his own rationale for writing this tale. (Spielberg begins his film at the historical beginning of Schindler's tale—in Cracow during the German occupation—and provides flashbacks to show how "ordinary" Schindler's life really was.) In the novel and the film, Schindler's ordinariness is contrasted with the idea of Jewish superior intelligence. Keneally observes that during childhood, Schindler went to school with the sons of his next-door neighbor in Zwittau, the liberal rabbi Felix Kantor, a modern Jew who wrote "articles not only for the Jewish journals in Prague and Brno, but for the dailies as well" (34). Kantor's views were that "we are secular scholars as well as sensible interpreters of the Talmud. We belong both to the twentieth century and to an ancient tribal race. We are neither offensive nor offended against" (34). He is an intellectual who sees himself as part of two intellectual cultures; even more, he is the father of "smart Jews": his children "become two of the rare Jewish professors at the German University of Prague" (34). Schindler, too, was "like the Kantor boys . . . a prodigy" (34). But his genius lay in the fact that he owned the only red Galloni motorbike in all of Czechoslovakia (35). This irony—comparing the image of Jewish superior intelligence with the acquisitive abilities of the teenaged Oskar Schindler—begins the tale. The novel and the movie present the story of the shaping of a "virtuous" man. The narratives serve to illustrate what this virtue was, how it evolved, and why it occurred. And this virtue is compared positively with Jewish superior intelligence throughout: for Schindler survives, but the Kantors move to Belgium in 1934 and vanish.

In the course of the film and novel Oskar Schindler remarkably comes to possess virtue—true virtue—while the Jews in the camp seem to possess only the qualities of victimhood, and a few of them, the products of perpetual victimhood, Jewish superior intelligence. Indeed, the central pairing of the natty Schindler (played by Liam Neeson) and his bookkeeper, Itzhak Stern (played by Ben Kingsley, physically reprising his 1982 role as Gandhi for which he prepared by losing 20 pounds) provides the contrast between an evolving sense of virtue on the one hand and the receding importance of intelligence on the other. Stern is a "Polish Jew," the bookkeeper in a fabric firm (44). He is initially introduced to resolve a problem: German soldiers had entered the firm and "bought" bolts of fabric with worthless Bavarian notes and World War I occupation money. How was the firm, now under "Aryan" management, to deal with this act without offending the German authorities or compromising the firm's profit? Stern suggests a Solomonic solution—he burns the offending currency and writes off the losses as "free samples" (44). Stern's "dry, effective style with the legal evidence" (44) is smart and direct.

Itzhak Stern's physicality defines him: "He was so thin, and there was a scholarly dryness to him. He had the manners of a Talmudic scholar, but also of a European intellectual" (44). When he is introduced he has a dreadful cold and we see him "blowing his nose and coughing harshly" (43). (Coughing now masks the Jew outside of the world of Alban Berg's opera.) In "the accountant's lean features" one saw "the complexities of Cracow itself, the parochial canniness of a small city" (44). It is "canniness" rather than Jewish superior intelligence that Stern represents, but it is a "canniness" of Cracow, not of the Jews. But Keneally moves from that generalization—small-town craftiness—to understanding Stern's intelligence in light of the Jewish experience and the body of the Jew—of Ben Kingsley's emaciated face.

Here the film's evocation of Ghandi with the casting of Kingsley and the emphasis on Stern's protruding ears should be mentioned. If Gandhi's emaciated body is the reflection of his revolt against colonialism, the Jew's body is a function of his Jewish nature. The old trope in European culture about the Jew's ears can be found in the anti-Semitic literature of the *fin de siècle*. It is also a major subtheme of Heinrich Mann's *Man of Straw* (1918).[23] In that novel, Mann's self-serving convert, Jadassohn (Judas's son?) "looked so Jewish" (85) because of his "huge, red, prominent ears," (86) which he eventually has cosmetically reduced. And while Jadassohn is only "witty" (87), other Jews in the novel are "too clever" (57). Stern's image in the film visibly contrasts the huge, dominant, masculine body of Schindler with the diminutive body of the Jew.

Itzhak Stern, like the Jews of Cracow (but unlike the other inhabitants of that small city), simply expects the Germans to disrupt their lives, even to "sporadically slaughter" them (45). But they assumed "the situation would settle; the race would survive by petitioning, by buying off the authorities—it was the old method, it had been working since the Roman Empire, it would work again. In the end the civil authorities needed Jews, especially in a nation where they were one in every eleven" (45). So much for the "cleverness" of the Jews. In retrospect we know that such an assumption was inherently false, for the Germans did not "need" the Jews—indeed they wished to destroy the Jews root and branch. The Jewish superior intelligence that understands the situation of the Jews proves to be not "canniness" but simply blindness.

In the novel, Stern sees in Oskar Schindler part of the age-old plan to rescue the Jews: "in men like Stern [there was] an ancestral gift for sniffing out the just Goy, who could be a buffer or partial refuge against the savageries of others" (46). Ignoring the image of the "sniffing" Jew and the "just Goy" (read: dog and master), Keneally clearly sees in Stern an inherent "canniness" that enables him to recognize Schindler as a useful tool—Stern is thus not a virtuous man. Yet Stern recognizes Schindler as different: "*This isn't a manageable German*" (44). Stern's Jewish superior intelligence meets its match; for Schindler does not easily fit into the mold of the "righteous" or even the "malleable" Gentile. Schindler is as different from the other Gentiles as he is from the Jews. His absence of intelligence is in fact a sign of his potential virtue.

For this "just Goy" was dumb where Stern was smart: "Stern spoke softly, learnedly. He had published articles in journals of comparative religion. Oskar, who wrongly fancied himself a philosopher, had found an expert. The scholar himself, Stern, whom some thought a pedant, found Oskar's understanding shallow, a mind genial by nature but without much conceptual deftness" (48). Stern, like Rabbi Kantor, is an intellectual who publishes learned articles. Oskar is a braggart whose intellectual ability is merely "shallow" and "genial." In the course of the narrative, Stern finds a like-minded Jew in the figure of the "young and black-bearded" Rabbi Menasha Levartov: "Stern, when it came to comparative religion, got greater pleasure out of talking to Levartov than he could even have received from bluff Oskar Schindler, who nevertheless had a fatal weakness for discoursing on the same subject" (207). Intellectual pursuits are not the strength of Schindler, but virtue is—and Keneally and Spielberg set these against each other.

The Image in American Mass Culture

Schindler is a seductive speaker. He has a "rowdy sense of humor" (18) and exudes an "easy magnetic charm" (19). His language is certainly unintellectual, evidently even when discussing comparative religion. According to Schindler, Jews such as Stern "could never make a straight statement or request unless it arrived smuggled under a baggage of talk of the Babylonian Talmud and purification rites" (221). This difference of intellect is inscribed on their bodies: unlike the "ascetic" Stern (77), Oskar is "big, sensual" (68). Stern is "clearheaded" (135) and yet his clearheadedness is valueless without Schindler's virtue. It becomes clear that intelligence will not rescue the Jews—the need is for virtue.

Virtue and intelligence are reinforced as antithetical. Neither Stern nor his friend Rabbi Levartov is rescued by his Jewish superior intelligence. Stern is saved from deportation to the death camps by Schindler, and Levartov is rescued by Schindler after the misfiring of the pistol held by camp commandant Amon Goeth (played by Ralph Fiennes). Schindler's virtue saves the Jews, even though retrospectively "some say, and there is some truth to it, that Emalia and Brinnlitz [Schindler's factories] succeeded in their eccentric way because of the acumen of men like Stern" (392). Stern's intelligent management of the company becomes the vehicle through which Schindler's virtue can act. Thus Stern comes to be "the only father confessor Oskar had, and Stern's suggestions had a great authority with him" (293). And yet Schindler's virtue gives meaning to Stern's "canniness."

In the novel and the film the smart Jew becomes an object needing to be rescued. Intelligence, especially when connected with the supposed superiority of the intellectual, is clearly an insufficient quality in this world. Stern, with his "canniness," recognizes that the "just Goy" is necessary to rescue the Jews and that his own intelligence should be harnessed to this vehicle. Yet this is Jewish "canniness," the learned protection of two thousand years of persecution.

Spielberg and Keneally also present the opposite assumption, that Jewish intellectual ability as measured by Western standards should serve to protect the Jews, in the case of Diana Reiter. An architectural engineer supervising the construction of the concentration camp barracks, Reiter demanded of a noncommissioned officer that the foundations of the building be torn down and rebuilt "correctly." Her argument attracts the attention of camp commandant Amon Goeth. Reiter approaches him with "the bogus elegance with which her middle-class parents had raised her, the European manners they had imbued her with, sending her—when the honest Poles wouldn't take her in their universities—off to Vienna or Milan to give her a profession and a heightened protective coloration" (167). She is the Jew as professional, certified by the institutions of Western culture as a member of the elite. She does not recognize the truth that European anti-Semitism does not provide any such role for the Jew—the Jew will always be the Jew and her intelligence will always be dangerous.

Spielberg adds a line when restructuring this scene for the film. Kneeling before a German soldier whose pistol is drawn, Elina Lowensohn, the actress who plays Diana Reiter, looks up at the camera—the viewer stands in the place of Amon Goeth—and states "it will take more than this."[24] That is, more than this to show that she is wrong, to destroy Jewish superior intelligence. Spielberg reads this scene as showing that it will take more than killing a single Jew to kill "the Jews." Reiter's death is thus transformed from a comment on the futility of Western acculturation as protective coloration for the Jew (or specifically the Jewish woman as intellectual) to a metacommentary on the Shoah. Thus Reiter's complaint that the foundation of the concentration camp barracks will subside because it is poorly built becomes in the film a symbolic statement that building the edifice of the Thousand-Year Reich on the murder of the Jews assures its destruction. Such a view certainly represents Spielberg's desire to give meaning to the death of the Jews, who through their martyrdom bring down the kingdom of evil. This is wishful thinking. Since no symbolic meaning can be assigned to the destruction of the Jews, no reading of their death can be understood as providing a rationale for it. In no case, except retrospectively, can the intelligence of the Jews give symbolic meaning to the Shoah.

The representation of Reiter in the novel and to a more modified degree in the film can be read in an ironic tone. After the Shoah, Max Horkheimer reflects on the anxiety about the false consciousness of Weimar Jews concerning their own intelligence:

The Image in American Mass Culture

WHY IT IS BETTER NOT TO KNOW ALL THE ANSWERS

One of the lessons which Hitler has taught us is that it is better not to be too clever. The Jews put forward all kinds of well-founded arguments to show that he could not come to power when his rise was clear for all to see. . . . The educated made it easy for the barbarians everywhere by being so stupid. The farsighted judgments, the forecasts based on statistics and experience, the comments beginning "this is a subject I know very well," and the well-rounded, solid statements, are all untrue.[25]

The representation of intelligence in the Reiter scene assumes that Jewish "cleverness" is dangerous—especially for the Jews. Being too clever, the standard calumny against the Jews, is now seen as the source of their own destruction.

In the novel it is the intelligence of the Jew—not her canniness, but her command of the discourse of the intellectual—that marks the Jew as dangerous. "She went on arguing the case, and Amon nodded and presumed she must be lying. It was a first principle that you never listened to a Jewish specialist. Jewish specialists were in the mold of Marx, whose theories were aimed at the integrity of the government, and of Freud, who had assaulted the integrity of the Aryan mind" (168). He orders her shot. And Keneally draws the appropriate lesson: "Miss Diana Reiter could not save herself with all her professional skill" (169). Jewish superior intelligence is a negative in this world; only "prompt and anonymous labor" seemed to count toward anything (167–68). And that too comes to be understood as false reasoning, for the ss understands that "the Jewish child is a cultural time bomb, the Jewish woman a biology of treasons, the Jewish male a more incontrovertible enemy than any Russian could hope to be" (174). Only total destruction can be the answer.

Genius plays no role in Keneally and Spielberg's image of the concentration camps and the Shoah: "While the pistol-waving Amon Goeth believes he maintains Plaszow by his special administrative genius, it is as much the bloody-mouthed prisoners who keep it running" (224). Virtue, the special realm of Oskar Schindler, turns the myth of Jewish superior intelligence into the reverse: the Jews are saved by their stupidity. Schindler manages to sabotage his own factory's war effort and lay the blame on "the stupidity of you damned people!" at least in the presence of the armament inspectors. "I wish they were intelligent enough to sabotage a machine. Then at least I'd have their goddamned hides! But what can you do with these people? They're an utter waste of time." (340). Indeed, the only mention of "smart Jews" in the novel comes at the very end. "Smart Jews" are those such as the man in the horsecar to Dachau who hangs the bodies of the dead from horse hooks to give more space to the living (354). Here intelligence and death are linked—yet intelligence cannot save lives, only virtue can.

In this text the Shoah gives the lie to Jewish superior intelligence—not intelligence but virtue is the way to survive, and survival is the proof of goodness. Schindler's virtue dominates the tale. The Jews he rescued and his own survival are proof of his value. Thus the tale of Schindler is the tale of survival and virtue; the tales of Stern and Reiter are of the uselessness of Jewish superior intelligence, unless it is connected to the virtuous act of the non-Jew.

It is a fortuitous association that Ralph Fiennes (who played the camp commandant Amon Goeth in *Schindler's List*) and Rob Morrow (Joel Fleischman in *Northern Exposure*) come to reprise versions of their characters in Robert Redford's 1994 film *Quiz Show*. This film illustrates quite a different tale of intelligence and virtue. For virtue is completely missing from *Quiz Show,* and its vanishing marks the dismissal of what passes (according to the film) for intelligence in the 1950s—the rote memorization of facts and their instant recall. The Redford film is the tale of the two central participants in the quiz-show scandals of the 1950s: the lower-class Jewish war veteran, Herb Stempel (played by John Turturro) and the upper-class Gentile academic, Charles Van Doren (played by Ralph Fiennes), son of critic Mark Van Doren. Stempel was the quiz-show contestant who blew the whistle on "Twenty-One" in 1959 before a congressional committee by revealing that he was bested by Van Doren in a fixed contest. Here Fiennes plays the Aryan as intellectual rather than madman. But here too race is directly and unmistakably inscribed into the film: according to one newspaper account, Van Doren is "the apparent embodiment of e.e. cummings's line 'more brave than me, more blond than you.'"[26] The conflict between Van Doren and the dark, working-class Stempel is described in Paul Attanasio's screenplay as the working out of post-Shoah anti-Semitism, a sort of retrospective *Gentlemen's Agreement* with Gregory Peck's role (a Gentile assuming the social identity of a Jew) now taken by a "real" Jew.

In *Quiz Show,* both Jews and Gentiles are shown to be neither smart nor virtuous, because the claim about innate intellectual ability comes to be a charade, a simulacrum of real intelligence. It is the IQ test writ large on the television screens of the day: memorize masses of meaningless material and you become a master of the medium. Yet Stempel's secret is not that he threw the final match to Van Doren—he rages that he knew the answer to the question "What film had won the Academy Award for best picture in 1955?" (*Marty*) and was made to look foolish because of the commonness of this information. Rather, Stempel is revealed to have been given answers all along, not just forced to throw the last match. Here he is revealed to be unlike Ernest Borgnine in *Marty,* a true working-class hero. Stempel's intelligence, like that of Van Doren, is not only compromised—in the scenes where Van Doren rattles off information to the producers, Stempel is shown to be slightly less clever and certainly less attractive than Van Doren.

In the film, all is corruption. Even the issue of class versus race—of the upper-class Gentile beating the working-class Jew—is revealed as part of the game, for neither Stempel nor Van Doren is virtuous. Only Richard N. Goodwin (played by Rob Morrow of *Northern Exposure*) recognizes the fix. Goodwin, whose Jewish identity is submerged in his desire to belong, to play the game, is shown to be the only character to have virtue. His wife accuses him of having been seduced by Van Doren's class status and calls him "The Uncle Tom of the Jews." Goodwin is an example of real Jewish superior intelligence, a top-of-the-class graduate of Harvard Law School who is confused between virtue and status. He eventually chooses virtue, and "intelligence" in the world of *Quiz Show* is revealed to be specious. The seduction of the truly smart Jew does not take place. Goodwin is tested—like Joel Fleischman—and is able to return to his world a better (and smarter) Jew. Unlike Stempel, Goodwin is the upper-class, educated American

Jew who seems not to need his Jewish identity to establish his victim status. Both the working-class Jew and the upper-class Gentile are revealed to be cheats; but the upwardly mobile Jew becomes the hero because of his tested virtue. He is not the parvenu but rather the virtuous American. Here the theme of virtue is manifest.

Sections from Richard Goodwin's memoir, *Remembering America*, served as a basis for the film script.[27] Goodwin's account, "a voice from the sixties" (the subtitle of the memoir), begins with his sense of the "anti-Semitism of Maryland" (15), which he first experienced when his father moved to Washington at the end of the Depression. His account of his vivid anger at being called a "Jew boy" (15) frames his sense of his own accomplishment when he graduates from Tufts University and is eventually admitted to Harvard. A member of the *Harvard Law Review* staff and eventually its editor, Goodwin graduates first in his class and goes on to clerk for Supreme Court justice Felix Frankfurter. Frankfurter becomes his idol, "an incarnation of the American dream. Born to Jewish parents in Vienna, Austria, he had arrived in New York at the age of twelve, unable to speak a word of English. A few years later he had plunged into the melting pot of City College and then gone to Harvard Law School, graduating with the highest honors" (27). Not a parvenu—certainly not Monroe Stahr—Frankfurter comes to represent the conservative, Republican establishment in Goodwin's text, even in regard to Goodwin's own politics during the Kennedy-Johnson era.

After his year of clerking for Frankfurter, Goodwin goes to the House Subcommittee on Legislative Oversight and begins his investigation of those "national heroes, living exemplars of American genius," the winners of the quiz shows. The key to the success of the quiz shows such as "The $64,000 Question" was the relation between money and the "hitherto secluded brilliance of fellow citizens" (44). Central to this most American of undertakings was Charles Van Doren, who was, according to signs at Columbia University, where he taught, "the smartest man in the world" (45). He was the American answer to the "soviet Sputnik," according to Goodwin, a "touch of class" (48). "Gifted with an extraordinarily retentive memory, widely read," Van Doren was prepared for his role by "a century of breeding" (48). His nemesis, the man he had defeated to become champion on "Twenty-One," was the "dark, Semitic" Herb Stempel. "He had come from a working-class background, a family in the anonymous lower reaches of the social structure, whose otherwise unremarked history had contained some dormant code of DNA gifting Stempel with a remarkably spacious memory, which he had furnished with an extraordinary collection of information" (49).

Intelligence for Goodwin—less so for Redford—is inscribed in the genes. Van Doren's "century of breeding" produces a brilliant though shallow intellectual; two thousand years of Jewish persecution produces in Stempel a recessive store of Jewish superior intelligence that appears in his generation. Both come to be parodies of the image of the "intellectual," but where Van Doren descends into this role, Stempel is raised into the realm of the pseudointellectual. He went from being an "unknown, unappreciated, unprivileged young man" to being an "instant celebrity" (50). And he was targeted to be defeated by someone "who, in Stempel's lucid, fevered imagination, had everything—privilege, breeding, aristocratic birth and manner—who seemed to possess every advantage that life had so cruelly and capriciously denied him" (50). Goodwin's identification with Van Doren, evident in the film, haunts his text. He is certainly not Stempel; yet he could see himself as Van Doren through Stempel's eyes. Yet there is an aspect of the loss of virtue in *Quiz Show* that is underplayed in Goodwin's account, one that appears in a text that certainly served as one of the intertexts for Goodwin's retrospective narrative.

Another reading of the quiz show problem and the image of Jewish superior intelligence in American mass culture appeared three years before the publication of Goodwin's autobiographical account of the 1960s. Philip Roth's novel *Zuckerman Unbound* (1985) provides an image of the failed contestant, evidently based on Roth's reading of Herb Stempel.[28] Roth calls the Stempel character, Alvin Pepler, "Pepler the Man of the People" and "Alvin the Jewish Marine" (197). Pepler is introduced to us and to protagonist Nathan Zuckerman as having written an account of the quiz show scandals in which he was defeated by Hewlett Lincoln, "the philosophical young county newspaperman and son of the Republican governor of Maine, and, while

The Image in American Mass Culture

he was a contestant, the most famous television celebrity in America" (198). The contrast between the "All-American" Lincoln and the "Jewish" Pepler is mirrored in the account of the scandals as represented in Redford's film and Goodwin's narrative. Yet it is clearly the mirroring of the Jewish writer in Roth's account that parallels Goodwin's own self-image, one that is heightened and ironized in Redford's film.

Alvin Pepler's account of his own fame is central to Roth's representation of Pepler's monomania. Pepler notes that he is not "an educated artist" but only "born with a photographic memory." He is not an example of Jewish superior intelligence but only a "smart Jew." With his performance on the quiz show, he had earned "the respect of the nation. If I have to say so myself, I don't think it did the Jewish people any harm having a Marine veteran of two wars representing them on prime-time national television for three consecutive weeks. . . . I wanted the country to know that a Jew in the Marine Corps could be as tough on the battlefield as anyone." The "tough Jew" has been transmuted into the "smart Jew." Pepler's performance becomes the touchstone for proving how "American" Pepler is. He is both soldier and intellectual, a "real" man at last (199).

In cheating on the show, or at least in being revealed to have cheated, he "harmed and left besmirched, all the millions I let down, Jews particularly" (200). Pepler's madness in the novel is externalized as his need to recuperate the shame he has caused the "Jews" rather than himself. This is, of course, the counterimage to Roth's protagonist, Nathan Zuckerman, whose pornographic novel (the very image of Roth's own *Portnoy's Complaint*) has been castigated by Jews in the text as the prime example of "nest dirtying." He has shamed the Jews by writing his book; Pepler wants to remedy his loss of virtue in publishing his own account of the fraud. But Pepler is also convinced that a Jewish conspiracy among the television executives has led to his downfall. The executives favor the Gentiles: "The bigger the goy, the bigger the haul" (215). And Pepler, like Stempel, is to stumble on the simplest of questions, one about American popular culture. Pepler "refused to let the Jewish people go down on prime-time television as not knowing their Americana" (216). Jews are real Americans in this mad fantasy only if they are strong and smart and virtuous.

202

The Image in American Mass Culture

The television executives sent Pepler to a Jewish psychiatrist, a Dr. Eisenberg. "This is how they were going to discredit me, by setting me up as a nut" (216). Back in New Jersey, according to Zuckerman's informants, Pepler is believed to have gotten a "Purple Heart. I think he got it in the head" (382). Pepler was understood as quite mad even before his public humiliation. Madness and intelligence are linked in the figure of Alvin Pepler—yet it is not real intelligence, merely a show-business simulacrum of intelligence. Pepler is in every way the failed Jew, the not-quite-intelligent-enough Jew whose public humiliation undermines the very existence of the myth of Jewish superior intelligence. Pepler is revealed to be as truly mad as everyone claims him to be when he threatens to kidnap Zuckerman's mother. It is a pointless threat that is not taken seriously by anyone but the already anxious Zuckerman.

It is, of course, Zuckerman who is the "real" example of Jewish superior intelligence. Yet his intelligence is not necessarily equated in the novel with virtue. For Zuckerman, a graduate of the University of Chicago, is really Franz Kafka's trained monkey: "I can just imagine what an enchanting little baboon you were at the University of Chicago. Pounding the seminar table, writing English on the blackboard, screaming at the class that they had it all wrong" (300). The process of creating a new Jew out of the old Jew is Kafka's process of acculturation into civilization: "to turn a jungle baboon into a seminar baboon is a cruel, irreversible process" (300). Likewise, Pepler's television exposure turns him into a television baboon. Stripped of his "natural" protection, Pepler is civilized man at his worst—a paranoid, which is what Zuckerman's friend accuses Zuckerman of becoming. Madness and the Jews is an old topic, but here it is keyed to the question of real or imagined Jewish superior intelligence and creativity.

Madness and creativity thus continue to be linked in the world of the paranoid schizophrenic. Roth's text provides the context for Goodwin's reading. Goodwin and Roth, the Jewish intellectuals, are not mad. And yet the link between Jewish creativity and madness is assumed in their world. Stempel and Pepler are represented as mad in the film and texts, and madness comes to stand for the state in which creativity takes place. In the mid-1970s there was a continuation of the debate about the meaning of Jewish "creativity" in the American psychiatric literature. After the Shoah, Silvano Arieti, certainly the most influential psychoanalyst after Sigmund Freud to deal with the question of creativity, provided a link between schizophrenia and creativity.[29] Arieti was fascinated by the relationship between "madness" in its mid-twentieth-century manifestation, schizophrenia, and the "creative."[30] Arieti examined the relationship between Freud's sense of creativity—stemming from the primary processes of psychic development as reflected in the mechanisms of the dream—and the higher forms of psychic organization. For Arieti, the clue to the meaning of creativity was in the psychopathological structures of the schizophrenic, who organizes the world along quite different structures than those of "normal" consciousness:

> The seriously ill schizophrenic, although living in a state of utter confusion, tries to recapture some understanding and to give organization to his fragmented universe. This organization is, to a large extent, reached by connecting things that have similar parts in common. Many patients force themselves to see similarities everywhere. In their relentless search for such similarities they see strange coincidences; that is, similar elements occurring in two or more instances at the same time or at brief intervals. By considering these similarities as identities they attempt to find some clarity in the confusion of the world, a solution for the big jigsaw puzzle.[31]

This is both Pepler and Zuckerman; both the madman who must understand his actions after the collapse of his television world and the author seen as mad by his world. It is the self-representation of neither Goodwin nor Roth.

But there is also an extraordinary subtext in Arieti's argument. For Arieti, an Italian Jew whose *The Parnas* is one of the most moving accounts of the psychological destruction of Italian Jewry, the Jew becomes the prototypical creative individual.[32] Arieti creates a category he labels the "creativogenic culture," which encourages the innovation of "creativity." Qualities such as the availability of cultural means, openness to cultural stimuli, emphasis on becoming (not just

The Image in American Mass Culture

on being), tolerance for diverging views, and freedom following repression all provide the matrix for "creativity." It is of little surprise
that for Arieti the exemplary "creative" individuals are the Jews. And
the exemplary Jews Arieti chooses as his examples of the truly creative are scientists, especially medical scientists. Arieti tabulates the
relationship of "Jewish" Nobel Prize winners to "German," "French,"
"Italian," and "Argentinian" winners and determines that "Jews exceed
in all categories with the exception of the Peace Prize, where they are
surpassed by the French and the Argentineans. If we examine the five
fields in which prizes are assigned, we notice that the greatest Jewish
contributions are in the fields of medicine and physics."[33] Here the
locus of Jewish superior intelligence is in the very field that defines
the author.

Arieti offers no working definition of the "Jew" and rejected any
biological definition of the "Jew." What he does instead is construct an
ontological category quite similar to that of Otto Weininger, simply
reversing the poles of Weininger's argument: the "creative" becomes
the Jewish state of mind, and the Jew, "creativity" incorporated. For
Arieti—and this is his self-definition—the image of the Jewish physi-
cian/scientist as intellectual defines Jewish superior intelligence.

Roth continues the saga of Zuckerman in *The Anatomy Lesson*
(1985). Here it is not Pepler who becomes the representative mad and
creative Jew, for he never publishes (or even writes) his account of the
quiz-show scandals, but rather Roth's surrogate, Nathan Zuckerman.
In *The Anatomy Lesson,* Zuckerman's mad desire is to return to the University of Chicago and begin to study medicine as a means of escaping
his tormented body. This is the next chapter in the further relationship
between Jewish superior intelligence and the decaying Jewish body:
the madness Roth locates in Zuckerman is the madness of the creative
Jew driven to the edge by the culture in which he dwells, a culture that
expects him to be the living exemplar of Jewish superior intelligence.

The anxiety about Jewish superior intelligence in modern culture is
rooted in the fear of the Jew as the embodiment of the different. As
Jean-Joseph Goux has observed about the Shoah, "The fatal inclination of such an aesthetic fiction of the political . . . is towards the elimination of all that seems misshapen, strange, unhealthy, and heteroge-

neous to the beautifully organized totality of the community—the extermination of the Jews."[34] The Shoah was to no small degree the result of German anxiety about heterogeneity, and no small part of that anxiety is expressed in the myth of Jewish superior intelligence. The continuation of this myth into the latter half of the twentieth century is the perpetuation of the anxiety about Jewish difference among American Jews. What is a Jew? Is Jewish difference absolute? Is the image of the Jews as Americans in doubt or can the qualities of Jewish difference be copied by others? Is virtue guaranteed by one or the other?

The continuation of the models of argument that began in the nineteenth century and continue into the late twentieth century seems to be a sign that there is little chance that the myth of Jewish difference, as represented by Jewish superior intelligence, will vanish after the millennium. The Jews—with or without their own state, with or without their being anchored in the Diaspora—have little likelihood of shedding their aura of difference. The image of the superior intelligence ascribed to the Jews is projected onto them by the cultures in which they live and internalized by them as if they are part of their own reality, as indeed, these qualities soon become. Are "the Jews" smarter than everyone else? How are "the Jews" different from everyone else? They are smarter and different only if the cultures in which they dwell need them to be smarter and different. That there are smart Jews is certainly true; that being Jewish is the equivalent to being smart is part of the construction of Jewish difference. And that is the hidden truth of both ends of *The Bell Curve*.

NOTES

1. A PROBLEM STILL

1. Richard J. Herrnstein and Charles Murray, *The Bell Curve: Intelligence and Class Structure in American Life* (New York: Free Press, 1994). The comments on Jewish superior intelligence are to be found on p. 275. On this comparison see Seymour B. Sarason, "Jewishness, Blackishness, and the Nature-Nurture Controversy," *American Psychologist* 28 (1973): 962–71.

2. Charles M. Madigan, "Race and I.Q.," *Chicago Tribune,* 16 October 1994, sec. 4, p. 1.

3. On the general questions of "race" and "intelligence" see Robert S. Albert, ed., *Genius and Eminence* (Oxford: Pergamon, 1992); Roger Pearson, *Race, Intelligence and Bias in Academe* (Washington DC: Scott-Townsend, 1991); Elaine and Harry Mensh, *The IQ Mythology: Class, Race, Gender, and Inequality* (Carbondale IL: Southern Illinois University Press, 1991); Wilhelm Quitzow, *Intelligenz, Erbe oder Umwelt? Wissenschaftliche und politische Kontroversen seit der Jahrhundertwende* (Stuttgart: J. B. Metzler, 1990); Paul Davis Chapman, *Schools as Sorters: Lewis M. Terman, Applied Psychology, and the Intelligence Testing Movement, 1890–1930* (New York: New York University Press, 1988); Raymond E. Fancher, *The Intelligence Men: Makers of the I.Q. Controversy* (New York: Norton, 1985); R. C. Lewontin, Steven Rose, and Leon J. Kamin, *Not in Our Genes: Biology, Ideology, and Human Nature* (New York: Pantheon, 1984), 83–130; Stephen Jay Gould, *The Mismeasure of Man* (New York: Norton, 1981); Michel Schiff, Richard Lewontin, et al., *Education and Class: The Irrelevance of IQ Genetic Studies* (Oxford: Clarendon Press, 1986); Brian Evans, *IQ and Mental Testing: An Unnatural Science and Its Social History* (London; New York: Macmillan, 1981); David Andrew Gersh, "The Development and Use of I.Q. Tests in the United States from 1900–1930" (Ph.D. diss., State University of New York at Stony Brook, 1981); Leon J. Kamin, *The Science and Politics of I.Q.* (Potomac MD: L. Erlbaum Associates; distrib., New York: Halsted Press, 1974); Thomas Pogue Weinland, "A History of the I.Q. in America, 1890–1941" (Ph.D. diss., Columbia University, 1970).

4. See Carl E. Pope, "Race and Crime Revisited," *Crime and Delinquency* 25 (1979): 347–57.

5. It also reflects the ambiguity of the image of the Jew in American his-

tory. See Louise Abbie Mayo, *The Ambivalent Image: Nineteenth-Century America's Perception of the Jew* (Cranbury NJ: Associated University Presses, 1988).

6. On the background of the idea of the Jewish race, see Raphael and Jennifer Patai, *The Myth of the Jewish Race* (Detroit: Wayne State University Press, 1989), and on the Jewish response see John Efron, *Defenders of the Race: Jewish Doctors and Race Science in Fin-de-siècle Europe* (New Haven: Yale University Press, 1994).

7. See Alan Ryan, "Apocalypse Now?" in *The Bell Curve Debate: History, Documents, Opinions* ed. Russell Jacoby and Naomi Glauberman (New York: Times Books/Random House, 1995), 14–29, here p. 23.

8. John M. Efron, "Scientific Racism and the Mystique of Sephardic Racial Superiority," *Leo Baeck Yearbook* 38 (1993): 75–96.

9. The most detailed and extensive study on Jewish superior intelligence is Raphael Patai, *The Jewish Mind* (New York: Jason Aronson, 1977). Patai divides the protagonists of this argument into philo-Semites, who believe that Jews are superior, and anti-Semites, who believe them to be "parasites." The case, as we shall see in this study, is much more complicated.

10. Moshe Zeidner, "Perceptions of Ethnic Group Modal Intelligence: Reflections of Cultural Stereotypes or Intelligence Test Scores?" *Journal of Cross-Cultural Psychology* 21 (1990): 214–31.

11. Heinrich Graetz, *History of the Jews* (Philadelphia: Jewish Publication Society of America, 1891–98), 5:4–5.

12. W. Petersen, "Jews as a Race," *Midstream* (February 1988): 35–37.

13. Jason DeParle, "Daring Research or 'Social Science Pornography,'" *New York Times Magazine* 9 October 1994: 48–80, here p. 52.

14. Steven Fraser, ed., *The Bell Curve Wars: Race, Intelligence, and the Future of America* (New York: Basic Books, 1995; hereafter cited as F). See also Jacoby and Glauberman, *The Bell Curve Debate.*

15. Jacoby and Glauberman, *The Bell Curve Debate*, p. 53.

16. On Jews and hypochondria see my *Franz Kafka: The Jewish Patient* (New York: Routledge, 1995), 62–68.

17. Jacoby and Glauberman, *The Bell Curve Debate*, p. 339.

18. On the models of resistance to the romanticization of the "Jewish intellect," see my "Appropriating the Idioms of Science: Some Strategies of Resistance to Biological Determinism," in *The Bounds of Race,* ed. Dominick LaCapra (Ithaca NY: Cornell University Press, 1991), 72–103 (with Nancy Stepan).

19. See the discussion in Charles Lane, "The Tainted Sources of *The Bell Curve*," *New York Review of Books*, 1 December 1994, 14–19.

20. On the history of circumcision see my *Freud, Race, and Gender* (Princeton: Princeton University Press, 1993), 49–93, and on the debates concerning ritual slaughter see the chapter on that topic in my *Franz Kafka*, 134–56.

21. Laura Otis, *Organic Memory: History and the Body in the Late Nineteenth and Early Twentieth Centuries* (Lincoln: University of Nebraska Press, 1994). See also my *The Case of Sigmund Freud: Medicine and Identity at the Fin de Siècle* (Baltimore: Johns Hopkins University Press, 1993), 11–69.

22. Mark Zborowski and Elizabeth Herzog, *Life Is with People: The Culture of the Shtetl* (New York: International Universities Press, 1952). The research on this book was completed in 1949.

23. See my "The Rediscovery of the Eastern Jews: German Jews in the East, 1890–1918," in *German-Jewish Symbiosis*, ed. David Bronsen (Heidelberg: Carl Winter, 1979), 338–65.

24. It is outlined in my *Jewish Self-Hatred: Anti-Semitism and the Hidden Language of the Jews* (Baltimore: Johns Hopkins University Press, 1986).

25. Immanuel Kant, *Anthropology from a Pragmatic Point of View,* trans. Victor Lyle Dowdell (Carbondale: Southern Illinois University Press, 1978), 101–2.

26. See my "The Indelibility of Circumcision," *Koroth* (Jerusalem) 9 (1991): 806–17.

27. P. M. Sheldon, "The Families of Highly Gifted Children," *Marriage and Family Living* 16 (1954): 59–61.

28. Armin Hermann, ed., *Deutsche Nobelpreisträger* (Munich: Moos, 1978). Compare, for example, Dorothea and Günter Stenzel, *Das grosse Lexikon der Nobelpreisträger* (Hamburg: Verlag Dr. Kovac, 1992); Asoke K. Bagchi, *Hinduja Foundation Encyclopedia of Nobel Laureates, 1901–1987* (Delhi, India: Konark, 1988); and William Breit and Roger W. Spencer, *Lives of the Laureates: Ten Nobel Economists* (Cambridge: MIT Press, 1990). For a further reading of the Nobel Prize question, see also Elisabeth T. Crawford, *Nationalism and Internationalism in Science, 1880–1939: Four Studies of the Nobel Population* (Cambridge: Cambridge University Press, 1992); and Lewis S. Feuer, "The Sociobiological Theory of Jewish Intellectual Achievement: A Sociological Critique," in *Ethnicity, Identity, and History: Essays in Memory of Werner J. Cahnman,* ed. Joseph B. Maier and Chaim I. Waxman (New Brunswick NJ: Transaction, 1983), 93–125, here pp. 107–9.

29. Compare Harold Uriel and Meir Z. Ribalow, *The Great Jewish Chess Champions* (New York: Hippocrene Books, 1986).

30. Nathaniel Weyl, *The Geography of American Achievement* (Washington DC: Scott-Townsend, 1989), 57–58.

31. Joseph Jacobs, "Are Jews Jews?" *Popular Science Monthly* 55 (1899): 507.
32. Gerald Krefetz, *Jews and Money: The Myths and the Reality* (New Haven: Ticknor & Fields, 1982).
33. Mark Twain, *Concerning the Jews* (Philadelphia: Running Press, 1985), 12. This edition has a good historical introduction. See also my essay "Mark Twain and the Diseases of the Jews," *American Literature* 65 (1993): 95–116; Carl Dolmetsch, "Mark Twain and the Viennese Anti-Semites: New Light on 'Concerning the Jews,'" *Mark Twain Journal* 23 (1985): 10–17; Guido Fink, "Al di qua della paroia: Gil ebrei di Henry James e di Mark Twain," in *Il recupero de testo: Aspetti della letteratura ebraico-americana,* ed. Guido Fink and Gabriella Morisco (Bologna: Cooperative Lib. Univ. ed. Bologna, 1988), 29–50. The best overall discussion of Twain's attitude toward the Jews is in Philip S. Foner, *Mark Twain, Social Critic* (New York: International Publishers, 1958), 288–307, which documents in great detail the critical reception of this piece, including its use in the anti-Semitic propaganda of the early twentieth century. On the overall question of the image of the Jew in nineteenth-century American culture, see Louis Harap, *The Image of the Jew in American Literature from Early Republic to Mass Immigration* (Philadelphia: Jewish Publication Society, 1974).
34. Among Storfer's publications prior to his book on intelligence are *Brain Research, Our Journey Has Begun: A Readers Guide to Brain Research Activities and Their Potential* (New York: Foundation for Brain Research, n.d.; *Characteristics of AFDC Families in New York State, May, 1969* (Albany: New York State Dept. of Social Services, 1970); *Characteristics of Home Relief Families in New York City, August 1971* (Albany: New York State Dept. of Social Services, 1972); with Edward Jove, *Characteristics of the Indigent Aged Population in New York City, 1980* (New York: City of New York Human Resources Administration, Office of Policy and Program Development, [1982]); with Kathryn Nocerino, *Characteristics of the Medicaid-Eligible Chronic Care Population* (New York: City of New York Human Resources Administration, Office of Policy and Program Development, Division of Policy and Economic Research, 1980); *A Comparison of New York State Welfare Benefit Levels for Families of Four with the Consumer Price Index, 1969–1978* (Albany: New York State Dept. of Social Services, Bureau of Program Forecasting and Economic Analysis, 1978); with Guy Florio, *Demographic Characteristics of Medicaid-Only Home Relief Adults* (New York: City of New York Human Resources Administration, Office of Policy and Program Development, 1983); *Effects of Federal Budget Cutbacks on Employed ADC Parents* (New York: City of New York Human

Resources Administration, Office of Policy and Program Development, [1983]); with Kathryn Nocerino, *Special Grants to Public Assistance Recipients, 1975 to 1979* (New York: City of New York Human Resources Administration, Office of Policy and Program Development, 1980) with Janet Wedel and Guy Florio, *Use of Medical Services by Supplemental Security Income Recipients Living in the Community* (New York: City of New York Human Resources Administration, Office of Policy and Program Development, Office of Policy and Economic Research, [1983]).

35. See my *The Case of Sigmund Freud* as well as David Lawrence Preston, "Science, Society, and the German Jews, 1870–1933" (Ph.D. diss., University of Illinois, 1971); Monika Richarz, *Der Eintritt der Juden in die akademischen Berufe* (Tübingen: J. C. B. Mohr, 1974); Monika Richarz, "Juden, Wissenschaft und Universitäten: Zur Sozialgeschichte der jüdischen Intelligenz und der akademischen Judenfeindschaft, 1780–1848," *Jahrbuch des Instituts für Deutsche Geschichte* 4 (1982): 55–74; and T. Schlich, "Der Eintritt von Juden in das Bildungsburgertum des 18. und 19. Jahrhunderts: Die jüdisch-christliche Arztfamilie Speyer," *Medizinhistorisches Jahrbuch* 25 (1990): 129–42.

36. Ryan, "Apocalypse Now," 28–29.

37. Jacobs, "Are Jews Jews?" 507.

38. Ernst Pawel, *The Nightmare of Reason: A Life of Franz Kafka* (1984; reprint, London: Collins Harvill, 1988), 205.

39. Martin Engländer, *Die auffallend häufigen Krankheitserscheinungen der jüdischen Rasse* (Vienna: J. L. Pollak, 1902), 11–12.

40. Paul Breines, *Tough Jews: Political Fantasies and the Moral Dilemma of American Jewry* (New York: Basic, 1990).

41. Alexander Bloom, *Prodigal Sons: The New York Intellectuals and Their World* (New York: Oxford University Press, 1986).

42. Gert Mattenklott, ed., *Jüdische Intelligenz in deutschen Briefen, 1619–1988* (Badenweiler: Oase, 1988); and Jost Hermand and Gert Mattenklott, eds., *Jüdische Intelligenz in Deutschland* (Hamburg: Argument-Verlag, 1988).

43. Michael P. Steinberg, "Jewish Identity and Intellectuality in Fin-de-Siècle Austria: Suggestions for a Historical Discourse," *New German Critique* 43 (1988): 3–33. See also Richarz, "Juden, Wissenschaft und Universitäten," 55–74, and Arthur Hertzberg, "The Jewish Intelligentsia and Their Jewishness," *Midstream* (November 1984): 35–39.

44. George L. Mosse, *German Jews beyond Judaism* (Bloomington: Indiana University Press; Cincinnati: Hebrew Union College Press, 1985).

45. See Heinrich Meier, *Carl Schmitt, Leo Strauss und "Der Begriff des Politischen": Zu einem Dialog unter Abwesenden* (Stuttgart: J. B. Metzler, 1988),

and Peter Graf Kielmansegg, ed., *Hannah Arendt and Leo Strauss: German Emigres and American Political Thought after World War II* (Washington DC: German Historical Institute; Cambridge: Cambridge University Press, 1995).

46. Dietz Bering, *Die Intellektuellen: Geschichte eines Schimpfwortes* (Stuttgart: Klett-Cotta, 1978), 48–49.

47. On the problem of "genius" and "race," see Jochen Schmidt, "Die kollektive Genialität der Rasse," in his *Von der Romantik bis zum Ende des dritten Reiches,* vol. 2 of *Die Geschichte des Genies-Gedanken in der deutschen Literatur, Philosophie und Politik 1750–1945* (Darmstadt: Wissenschaftliche Buchgesellschaft 1985), specifically on Herder, Gobineau, Wagner, Chamberlain, Hitler, Benn, Rosenberg, and "creativity." This book replaced the standard earlier study by Austrian Jewish philosopher-physicist Edgar Zilsel, *Die Entstehung des Geniebegriffs* (Tübingen: J. C. B. Mohr, 1926). Written with the encouragement and help of Theodor Gomperz, this volume assiduously avoids the discussion of any Jews or of Jewishness. See also George Becker, *The Mad Genius Controversy: A Study in the Sociology of Deviance* (Beverly Hills CA: Sage, 1978); and Penelope Murray, ed., *Genius: The History of an Idea* (Oxford: Blackwell, 1989).

48. Friedrich Nietzsche, *The Gay Science,* trans. Walter Kaufmann (New York: Vintage, 1974), 334. I have slightly amended the translation.

49. Ian Hacking, *Rewriting the Soul: Multiple Personality and the Sciences of Memory* (Princeton: Princeton University Press, 1995), 98.

50. Most recent scholarly studies and critiques of intelligence seem to avoid the question of "Jewish genius." General literature that reflects on the question of Jewish superior intelligence is Alphons Silbermann, *Was ist jüdischer Geist?: Zur Identität der Juden* (Zurich: Edition Interfrom, 1984); André Neher, *They Made Their Souls Anew,* trans. David Maisel (Albany: State University of New York Press, 1990); Shalom A. Singer, *The Sorokin Thesis: Jews in the Sensate Culture* (Princeton: Princeton Hillel Foundation, 1970). Of the older literature not discussed in this study, see Duncan Black Macdonald, *The Hebrew Philosophical Genius; A Vindication* (1936; reprint, New York: Russell & Russell, 1965); and A. A. Roback, *The Jew in Philosophy and Science. The Jewish Contribution to Art. Jewish Activities in Music. Jewish Physicians and Medical Discoverers. Jewish Genius in Literature. Jews in Law and Jurisprudence* (Boston: n.p., 1933).

2. THE ORIGINS AND FORMAT OF THE IMAGE

1. Madison Marsh, "Jews and Christians," *The Medical and Surgical Reporter* (Philadelphia) 30 (1874): 343–44. The association of the Jew with "intelligence" is an old American trope: see Mayo, *The Ambivalent Image.*

2. Steven Beller, *Vienna and the Jews 1867–1938: A Cultural History* (Cambridge: Cambridge University Press, 1989), 78–83.

3. Francis Galton, *Hereditary Genius: An Inquiry into Its Laws and Consequences* (London: Macmillan, 1869), 23 (on race); 4 (on Jews and Italians). Galton's views were critiqued in his own day because of his inability to consider class as a factor. See Frank Challice Constable, *Poverty and Hereditary Genius: A Criticism of Mr. Francis Galton's Theory of Hereditary Genius* (London: A. C. Fifield, 1905). On the persistence of Galton's views, see Frederick Osborn, "Galton's 'Hereditary Genius,'" *Eugenics Review* 44 (1952–53): 39–40. See also Ruth Leah Schwartz Cowan, "Sir Francis Galton and the Study of Heredity in the Nineteenth Century," (Ph.D. diss., Johns Hopkins University, 1969); Wolfgang Walter, *Der Geist der Eugenik: Francis Galtons Wissenschaftsreligion in Kultursoziologischer Perspektive* (Bielefeld: Universität Bielefeld, 1983); and Michael I. Kosacoff, "A Critical Examination of Some Assumptions of Psychometric Theory (Galton, Eugenics)" (Ph.D. diss., New York University, 1986).

4. Compare the somewhat earlier views of Lord Byron in Michael Scrivener, "'Zion Alone Is Forbidden': Historicizing Antisemitism in Byron's 'The Age of Bronze,'" *Keats-Shelley Journal* 43 (1994): 75–97.

5. Frances Galton, *Narrative of an Explorer in Tropical South Africa* (1852; London: Ward, Lock & Co., 1890), 53–54. On the Hottentot and her body see my "Black Bodies, White Bodies: Toward an Iconography of Female Sexuality," *Critical Inquiry* 12 (1985): 203–42, and Linda E. Merians, "What They Are, Who We Are: Representations of the Hottentot in Eighteenth-Century Britain," *Eighteenth-Century Life* 17 (1993): 14–39.

6. Cited (with photographs) in Joseph Jacobs, *Studies in Jewish Statistics* (London: D. Nutt, 1891), xl. These plates were reproduced from scholarly journals in *The Photographic News* 29 (17 April 1885 and 24 April 1885) as unnumbered insets, and as the frontispiece to vol. 16 (1886) of *The Journal of the Anthropological Institute,* which included the first publication of Joseph Jacobs's "On the Racial Characteristics of Modern Jews," and A. Neubauer, "Notes on the Race Types of the Jews." See Nathan Roth, "Freud and Galton," *Comprehensive Psychiatry* 3 (1962): 77–83. On the tradition of photographic evidence in the history of anthropology see Alan Sekula,

"The Body and the Archive," *October* 39 (1986): 40–55, and Joanna Cohan Scherer, ed., *Picturing Cultures: Historical Photographs in Anthropological Inquiry, Visual Anthropology,* (Special Issue) 3 (2–3), (1990). The image of race also plays a major role in the work of Lombroso. See F. Bazzi and R. Bèttica-Giovannini, "L'atlante fisiognomonico e frenologico del sig. Ysabeau tra quelli di Lavater e di Fall e quello di Lombroso," *Annali dell Ospedale Maria Vittoria di Torino* 23 (1980): 343–416, and A. T. Caffaratto, "La raccolta di fotografie segnaletiche del Museo di Antropologia Criminale di Torino: La fotografia come documento e testimonianza dell'opera di Cesare Lombroso," *Annali dell Ospedale Maria Vittoria di Torino* 23 (1980): 295–332. The tradition of fixing the racial gaze continues into the world of the scientific motion picture in the 1890s, such as the chronophotograph. See Elizabeth Cartwright, "Physiological Modernism: Cinematography as a Medical Research Technology," (Ph.D. diss., Yale University, 1991), 38.

7. Francis Galton, "Photographic Composites," *The Photographic News* 29 (17 April 1885): 243–46, here, 243.

8. Hans F. K. Günther, *Rassenkunde des jüdischen Volkes* (Munich: J. F. Lehmann, 1930), 70, on the physiology of the Jewish eye; pp. 210–11, Galton's photographs; p. 217 on the Jewish gaze.

9. Jacobs, "Are Jews Jews?" xxxiii.

10. Léon Poliakov, *The Aryan Myth: A History of Racist and Nationalist Ideas in Europe,* trans. Richard Howard (New York: Basic, 1974), 155–82.

11. Samuel R. Wells, *New Physiognomy, or, Signs of Character: As Manifested through Temperament and External Forms, and Especially in 'The Human Face Divine'* (1866; reprint, New York: American Book Company, 1871).

12. See Nancy Harrowitz, *Antisemitism, Misogyny, and the Logic of Cultural Difference: Cesare Lombroso and Matilde Serao* (Lincoln: University of Nebraska Press, 1994).

13. Francis Galton, *Hereditary Genius: An Inquiry into Its Laws and Consequences* (1892; reprint, London: Collins, 1962), 27.

14. Ernst von Schwartz, *Das Betäubungslose Schächten der Israeliten* (Konstanz: Ackermann, 1905), 37.

15. James Joyce, *Ulysses* (New York: Vintage, 1990), 687. See Harry Girling, "The Jew in James Joyce's *Ulysses,*" in *Jewish Presences in English Literature,* ed. Derek Cohen and Deborah Heller (Montreal: McGill-Queen's University Press, 1990), 96–112; Ira B. Nadel, *Joyce and the Jews: Culture and Texts* (Iowa City: University of Iowa Press, 1989); Ralph Robert Joly," Chauvinist Brew and Leopold Bloom: The Weininger Legacy," *James Joyce Quarterly* 19 (1982): 194–98.

Notes to Pages 41–45

16. Thurman B. Rice, *Racial Hygiene: A Practical Discussion of Eugenics and Race Culture* (New York: Macmillan, 1929), 13–14.

17. All references are to Anatole Leroy-Beaulieu, *Israel among the Nations: A Study of the Jews and Antisemitism,* trans. Frances Hellman (New York: G. P. Putnam's Sons, 1895). This work was first published as Anatole Leroy-Beaulieu, (Henry Jean Baptiste Anatole), *(Les) Juifs et l'antisémitisme: Israél chez les nations* (Paris: Lévy, 1893). This French edition went through at least seven printings in 1893 alone. Of his other works, see *La Révolution et le libéralisme: Essais de critique et d'histoire* (Paris: Hachette, 1890) and his pamphlet *Les immigrants juifs et le judäisme aux États-Unis* (Paris: Librairie Nouvelle, 1905). On his work, see Martha Helms Cooley, "Nineteenth-Century French Historical Research on Russia: Louis Leger, Alfred Rambaud, Anatole Leroy-Beaulieu" (Ph.D. diss., University of Indiana, 1971).

18. Thorstein Veblen, "The Intellectual Pre-eminence of Jews in Modern Europe," in his *Essays in Our Changing Order,* ed. Leon Ardzrooni (New York: Augustus M. Kelley, 1964), 219–31, here p. 219. (First published in *The Political Science Quarterly* [1919].) That this essay is a projection of Veblen's sense of his own "intellectual pre-eminence" was first discussed by Lewis Feuer, "Thorstein Veblen: The Metaphysics of the Interned Immigrant," *American Quarterly* 5 (1953): 99–112.

19. Veblen, "Intellectual Pre-eminence," 221.

20. Veblen, "Intellectual Pre-eminence," 221.

21. Veblen, "Intellectual Pre-eminence," 222.

22. Richard Wagner, *Richard Wagner's Prose Works,* trans. William Ashton Ellis, (London: Kegan Paul, 1912–29), 3:84–85. On Wagner's view of the Jews see Mark Weiner, *Richard Wagner and the Anti-Semitic Imagination* (Lincoln: University of Nebraska Press, 1995); Paul Lawrence Rose, *Wagner: Race and Revolution* (New Haven: Yale University Press, 1992); Dieter Borchmeyer, *Richard Wagner und der Antisemitismus* (Freiburg im Breisgau: Kroner, 1984); Manfred Eger, ed., *Wagner und die Juden: Fakten und Hintergrunde: Eine Dokumentation zur Ausstellung im Richard-Wagner-Museum Bayreuth* (Bayreuth: Druckhaus, 1985); Jacob Katz, *The Darker Side of Genius: Richard Wagner's Anti-Semitism* (Hanover NH: Published for Brandeis University Press by University Press of New England, 1986); Barry Millington, "Nuremberg Trial: Is There Anti-Semitism in 'Die Meistersinger'?" *Cambridge Opera Journal* 3 (1991): 247–60; Dieter David Scholz, *Richard Wagners Antisemitismus* (Wurzburg: Konigshausen & Neumann, 1993), as well as my *Jewish Self-Hatred,* 209–11.

23. Both are cited by Fritz Kahn, *Die Juden als Rasse und Kulturvolk* (Berlin: Welt Verlag, 1922), 226.

215

24. Friedrich Nietzsche, *Human, All Too Human,* trans. R. J. Hollingdale (Cambridge: Cambridge University Press, 1986), Book 1, sec. 475.

25. See my *Inscribing the Other* (Lincoln: University of Nebraska Press, 1991), 99–142.

26. Ludwig Woltmann, "Rassenpsychologie und Kulturgeschichte," *Politisch-Anthropologische Revue* 3 (1904/5): 350–57, here, p. 355.

27. See Peter U. Hohendahl and Sander L. Gilman, eds., *Heine and the Occident* (Lincoln: University of Nebraska Press, 1991).

28. Alfred Pfoser, *Literatur und Austromarxismus* (Vienna: Locker, 1980), 182.

29. Werner Sombart, *The Jews and Modern Capitalism,* trans. M. Epstein (Glencoe IL: Free Press, 1951), 320–22.

30. Beller, *Vienna and the Jews,* 78–83.

31. On the question of originality and "parasitism," see Alex Bein, "The Jewish Parasite—Notes on the Semantics of the Jewish Problem, with Special Reference to Germany," *Leo Baeck Yearbook* 9 (1964): 3–40, and Janet Lungstrum, "In Agon with Nietzsche: Studies in Modernist Creativity" (Ph.D. diss., University of Virginia, 1993).

32. Adolf Hitler, *Mein Kampf,* trans. Ralph Mannheim (Boston: Houghton Mifflin, 1943), 302–3.

33. Ernest Renan, *Histoire générale et système comparé des langues sémitiques* (Paris: Imprimerie Impériale, 1858).

34. Houston Stewart Chamberlain, *Foundations of the Nineteenth Century,* trans. John Lees, (London: John Lane/The Bodley Head, 1913), 1:418.

35. Sombart, *The Jews and Modern Capitalism,* 260.

36. Werner Sombart, *Die Zukunft der Juden* (Leipzig, Duncker & Humblot, 1912), 44.

37. Ellsworth Huntington, *The Pulse of Progress* (New York: Scribner's, 1926), 176.

38. Cyril D. Darlington, *The Evolution of Man and Society* (New York: Simon and Schuster, 1969), 187–89.

39. Arthur Landsberger, ed., *Judentaufe* (Munich: Georg Müller, 1912), 127. Compare the discussion of Weber's brother's views concerning the nature of the Jew as pariah. Arnaldo Momigliano, "A Note on Max Weber's Definition of Judaism as a Pariah-Religion," *History and Theory* 19 (1980): 313–18, and Gary A. Abraham, *Max Weber and the Jewish Question: A Study of the Social Outlook of His Sociology* (Urbana: University of Illinois Press, 1992).

40. Richard Weinberg, "Über einige ungewöhnliche Befunde an Judenhirnen," *Biologisches Centralblatt* 23 (1903): 154–62, with a summary of the older

literature beginning in 1882. See also his "K'ucheniu o forme mozga chel-veka," *Russian Anthropological Journal* 4 (1902): 1–34.

41. Richard Weinberg, "Das Hirngewicht der Juden," *Zeitschrift für Demographie und Statistik der Juden* 1 (1905): 5–10.

42. Günther, *Rassenkunde des jüdischen Volkes,* 202–3. Cited in the translation by Patai, *The Jewish Mind,* 304–5.

43. Lenz, cited by Patai, *The Jewish Mind,* 328–30.

44. Ernst Kretschmer, *Geniale Menschen* (1919; reprint, Berlin: Julius Springer, 1929), 73–108.

45. See Anson Rabinbach, *The Human Motor: Energy, Fatigue, and the Origins of Modernity* (New York: Basic, 1990).

46. H. H. Goddard, "The Binet Tests in Relation to Immigration," *The Journal of Psycho-Aesthenics* 18 (1913): 105–7, here, p. 105. See Leon J. Kamin, *The Science and Politics of I.Q.* (New York: Wiley, 1974), 16, and the rejoinder by Donald D. Dorfman, "Henry Goddard and the Feeble-Mindedness of Jews, Hungarians, Italians, and Russians," *American Psychologist* 37 (1982): 96–97. I have not used the figures attributed to Goddard by Kamin, though it is clear that Goddard's claim that he could identify the 95 percent of the "defectives" undiscovered by earlier methods reflects the tone of Kamin's statement.

47. C. C. Brigham, *A Study of American Intelligence* (Princeton: Princeton University Press, 1923), 190. See the discussion by Gould, *The Mismeasure of Man,* 225.

48. Katharine Murdoch, "A Study of Race Difference in New York," *School and Society* 11 (1920): 147–50.

49. Dorothy Wilson Seago and Theresa Shulkin Koldin, "The Mental Capacity of Sixth Grade Jewish and Italian Children," *School and Society* 22 (1925): 564–68.

50. May Bere, *A Comparative Study of the Mental Capacity of Children of Foreign Parentage,* Teacher's College Contributions to Education no. 154 (New York: Teachers College, Columbia University, 1924).

51. Lewis M. Terman, *Genetic Studies of Genius* (Stanford: Stanford University Press, 1925), 1:56. On Terman see Patai, *The Jewish Mind,* 321–24, and Henry L. Minton, *Lewis M. Terman: Pioneer in Psychological Testing* (New York: New York University Press, 1988).

52. Seth Arsenian, "Bilingualism and Mental Development: A Study of the Intelligence and the Social Background of Bilingual Children in New York City" (Ph.D. diss., Teachers College, Columbia University, 1937), 70.

53. Cited by Adrian Woolridge, "Bell Curve Liberals," *New Republic* (27 February 1995): 22–24, here p. 24.

3. JEWISH SCIENTIFIC RESPONSES TO THE IMAGE AT THE TURN OF THE CENTURY AND BEYOND

1. Ephraim M. Epstein, "Have the Jews Any Immunity from Certain Diseases?" *The Medical and Surgical Reporter* (Philadelphia) 30 (1874): 343–44.

2. D. Chwolson (Khvol'son), *The Semitic Nations,* trans. Ephraim M. Epstein (Cincinnati: Bloch & Co., 1874).

3. On the image of the Black in German culture see my *On Blackness without Blacks: Essays on the Image of the Black in Germany* (Boston: G. K. Hall, 1982).

4. Joseph Jacobs, *Jewish Contributions of Civilization: An Estimate* (Philadelphia: Conart, 1919), 46.

5. Adolf Jellinek, *Studien und Skizzen. Erster Theil: Der jüdische Stamm* (Vienna: Herzfeld and Bauer, 1869), 19.

6. Cesare Lombroso, *Genio e follia,* 6th ed. (Milan: Chiusi, 1864). All quotations are from the English translation: *The Man of Genius* (London: Walter Scott, 1901). See also Harrowitz, *Antisemitism, Misogyny, and the Logic of Cultural Difference.*

7. Wilhelm Wundt, *Grundzüge der physiologischen Psychologie* (Leipzig: Engelmann, 1887), 2:457.

8. Arthur Schnitzler, *Medizinische Schriften,* ed. Horst Thomé (Vienna: Paul Zsolnay, 1988), 233–39, here p.236.

9. See Joseph Jacobs, "Distribution of the Comparative Ability of the Jews" (1886), reprinted in his *Studies in Jewish Statistics, Social, Vital, and Anthropometric* (London: D. Nutt, 1891), xlii–lxix.

10. Cesare Lombroso, *Der Antisemitismus und die Juden im Lichte der modernen Wissenschaft,* trans. H. Kurella (Leipzig: Georg H. Wiegand, 1894), 43–50. Quotations in English are my translations of Kurella. The original is *L'Antisemitismo e le scienze moderne* (Turin: L. Roux, 1894).

11. Schnitzler, *Medizinische Schriften,* 236.

12. Joseph Jacobs, *Studies in Jewish Statistics* (London: D. Nutt, 1891), xli–lxix. On Jacobs see John Efron, *Defenders of the Race: Jewish Doctors and Race Science in Fin-de-Siècle Europe* (New Haven: Yale University Press, 1994), 58–90, and Patai, *The Jewish Mind,* 326.

13. Joseph Jacobs, *Jews of Distinction* (n.p., 1919), 10.

14. Lucien Wolf, "What Is Judaism? A Question of To-day," *The Fortnightly Review,* n.s., 36 (1884): 237–56.

15. [Goldwin Smith], "The Political Adventures of Lord Beaconsfield," *The Fortnightly Review* 23 (1878): 480 and 447–93. See also David Feldman,

Englishmen and Jews: English Political Culture and Jewish Society, 1840–1914 (New Haven: Yale University Press, 1993).

16. Alfred Nossig, "Die Auserwähltheit der Juden im Lichte der Biologie," *Zeitschrift für Demographie und Statistik der Juden* 1 (1905): 1.

17. *Wir Juden: Betrachtungen und Vorschläge von einem Bukowinaer Juden* (Zurich: Caesar Schmidt, 1883), 29–30.

18. Ernst Renan, *History of the People of Israel* (Boston: Roberts Bros., 1895), 5:9.

19. Werner Sombart, *Die Zukunft der Juden* (Leipzig: Duncker & Humblot, 1912), 44.

20. W. M. Feldman, *The Jewish Child: Its History, Folklore, Biology, and Sociology* (New York: Bloch, 1918).

21. Christian von Ehrenfels, *Sexualethik* (Wiesbaden: J. F. Bergmann, 1907), 362. This is reprinted in Christian von Ehrenfels, *Philosophische Schriften,* ed. Reinhard Fabian (Munich: Philosophia Verlag, 1982–90). On the question of the "higher" and "lower" races see his "Über den Einfluss des Darwinismus auf die moderne Soziologie," *Volkswirtschaftliche Wochenschrift* (Vienna) 42 (1904): 256–59, and *Die Wage* (Vienna) 7 (1904): 363–64, 382–85; see also *Philosophische Schriften,* 3:251–64.

22. On Ehrenfels's sense of his own Jewish ancestry see Max Brod, *Streitbares Leben* (Munich: Herbig, 1969), 211. See also Ehrenfel's review of Otto Weininger's monograph "Geschlecht und Charakter," *Politisch-anthropologische Revue* 3 (1905): 481–84.

23. Christian von Ehrenfels, "Rassenproblem und Judenfrage," *Prager Tageblatt* 36 (1 December 1911): 1–2. Reprinted in *Philosophische Schriften,* 4: 334–42, here p. 337.

24. Joseph Jacobs, *Jewish Ideals and Other Essays* (New York: Macmillan, 1896), 20–21.

25. Ehrenfels, *Philosophische Schriften,* 4:341.

26. Franz Kafka, *Tagebücher,* ed. Hans-Gerd Koch, Michael Müller, and Malcolm Pasley (Frankfurt: S. Fischer, 1990), 370–71.

27. Heinrich Singer, *Allgemeine und spezielle Krankheitslehre der Juden* (Leipzig: Benno Konegen, 1904), 25.

28. Felix A. Theilhaber, *Schicksal und Leistung: Juden in der deutschen Forschung und Technik* (Berlin: Der Heine-Bund, 1931).

29. Arthur Ruppin, "Der Rassenstolz der Juden," *Zeitschrift für Demographie und Statistik der Juden* 6 (1910): 88–92, here p. 91.

30. Arthur Ruppin, "Begabungsunterschiede christlicher und jüdischer Kinder," *Zeitschrift für Demographie und Statistik der Juden* 8/9 (1906): 129–35.

Notes to Pages 77–84

31. Arthur Ruppin, "Der Rassenstolz der Juden," *Zeitschrift für Demographie und Statistik der Juden* 12 (1910): 88–92.

32. Arthur Ruppin, *Die Juden der Gegenwart*, 2d ed. (Cologne: Jüdischer Verlag, 1911).

33. Here one sees the response to the claim of Sephardic intellectual and cultural superiority in the nineteenth century. See John Efron, "Scientific Racism and the Mystique of Sephardic Racial Superiority," *Leo Baeck Yearbook* 38 (1993): 75–96.

34. Maurice Fishberg, *The Jews: A Study of Race and Environment* (New York: Walter Scott, 1911).

35. Elisha M. Friedman, *Survival or Extinction* (New York: Thomas Seltzer, 1924).

36. Franz Boas, *The Mind of Primitive Man* (New York: Macmillan, 1911), 29. See also Andrew P. Lyons, "The Question of Race in Anthropology from the Time of J. F. Blumenbach to that of Franz Boas, with Particular Reference to the Period 1830 to 1890 (approx.)," (Ph.D. diss. Oxford University, 1974); Leonard B. Glick, "Types Distinct from Our Own: Franz Boas on Jewish Identity and Assimilation," *American Anthropologist* 84 (1982): 545–65; Carl N. Degler, *Culture versus Biology in the Thought of Franz Boaz and Alfred L. Kroeber* (New York: Berg, 1989); and Julia Elizabeth Liss, "The Cosmopolitan Imagination: Franz Boas and the Development of American Anthropology," (Ph.D. diss., University of California, Berkeley, 1990).

37. Cohen's thesis was published as *The Intelligence of Jews as Compared with Non-Jews* (Columbus: Ohio State University Press, 1927). Irma Loeb Cohen was born in 1901 and went on to have a distinguished career in the Jewish sorority movement. In 1927 she defended her dissertation, "Verbalization in the Solution of Problems of the 'Multiple-Choice Type'" (Ph.D. diss., Ohio State University, 1927).

38. Patai is self-identified as a Jew in this text.

39. Gottfried Benn, "Der neue Staat und die Intellectuellen," in his *Sämtliche Werke* ed. Gerhard Schuster (Stuttgart: Klett-Cotta, 1989), 4:12–20.

40. Arnold Zweig, "Rückblick auf Barbarei und Bücherverbrennung," in *Das Vorspiel: Die Bücherverbrennung am 10. Mai 1933*, ed. Thomas Friedrich (Berlin: LitPol, 1983), 43–45.

41. Primo Levi, *Survival in Auschwitz: The Nazi Assault on Humanity*, trans. Stuart Woolf (New York: Collier, 1976), 135; originally published as *Se questo è un uomo* (Milan: Einaudi, 1956).

42. Cited by Lewis S. Feuer, "The Sociobiological Theory of Jewish Intellectual Achievement: A Sociological Critique," in *Ethnicity, Identity, and*

History: Essays in Memory of Werner J. Cahnman, ed. Joseph B. Maier and
Chaim I. Waxman (New Brunswick NJ: Transaction, 1983), 93–125, here,
p. 100.

43. Berel Lang, ed., *Writing and the Holocaust* (New York: Holmes & Meier,
1988), 281.

44. Ernest van den Haag, *The Jewish Mystique* (1969; 2d ed., New York: Stein
and Day, 1977), 13–25. This thesis has come to infiltrate even the joke
books of the recent period: see Joseph Telushkin, *Jewish Humor: What
the Best Jewish Jokes Say about the Jews* (New York: W. Morrow, 1992). Van
den Haag identifies himself as "not Jewish" in the preface to this text.
Other works by Ernest van den Haag are *Education As an Industry* (New
York: A. M. Kelley, 1956); with Ralph Ross, *The Fabric of Society: An
Introduction to the Social Sciences* (New York: Harcourt, Brace, 1957); *The
War in Katanga: Report of a Mission* (New York: American Committee
for Aid to Katanga Freedom Fighters, 1962); *Passion and Social Constraint*
(New York: Stein and Day, 1963); with Emanuel Rackman and Miriam R.
Ephraim, *The Crisis in Values of the Young Adult in Our Society: Proceedings
[of] a One-Day Institute for Jewish Communal Workers* (New York: 92nd
Street YM-YWHA, 1964); *Political Violence and Civil Disobedience* (New
York: Harper & Row, 1972); with George C. Roche III, *The Balancing
Act: Quota Hiring in Higher Education* and, with Alan Reynolds, *Black
Studies Revisited* (LaSalle IL: Open Court, 1974); *Is Capital Punishment
Just?* (Washington DC: Ethics and Public Policy Center, Georgetown University, 1978); with John P. Conrad, *The Death Penalty: A Debate* (New
York: Plenum, 1983); *Smashing Liberal Icons: A Collection of Debates* (Washington DC: Heritage Foundation, 1984); *Deterring Potential Criminals*
(Social Affairs Unit, [1985]); *Must the American Criminal Justice System
Be Impotent?* (Washington DC: Washington Institute for Values in Public
Policy, 1985); *A Living Constitution?* (Washington DC: Heritage Foundation, 1987); *The U.N.: In or Out? / A Debate between Ernest van den Haag
and John P. Conrad* (New York: Plenum, 1987); *Pornography and the Law*
(Washington DC: Heritage Foundation, 1987); with Tom J. Farer, *U.S.
Ends and Means in Central America: A Debate* (New York: Plenum, 1988);
Punishing Criminals: Concerning a Very Old and Painful Question (Lanham
MD: University Press of America, 1991).

45. Lewis S. Feuer, *Scientific Intellectual: The Psychological and Sociological Origins of Modern Science* (New York: Basic, 1963), 308, and more extensively
in Lewis S. Feuer, "The Sociobiological Theory of Jewish Intellectual
Achievement." Feuer rebuts the Wiener/Haldane thesis in detail in his

work, yet he assumes that such a thing as Jewish superior intelligence does evidence itself in the history of modern science, but for purely sociological reasons.

46. Norbert Wiener, *Ex-Prodigy: My Childhood and Youth* (New York: Simon and Schuster, 1953), 11. Wiener evokes a conversation with Haldane that echoes Haldane's views as expressed in his Muirhead lectures at Birmingham University in February and March 1937 and published as J. B. S. Haldane, *Heredity and Politics* (London: Allen & Unwin, 1938), 162.

47. Telushkin, *Jewish Humor.*

48. Feuer, "The Sociobiological Theory of Jewish Intellectual Achievement," 121.

49. Francis Galton, *Hereditary Genius: An Inquiry into Its Laws and Consequences* (London: Macmillan, 1869), 357–58.

50. Charles Darwin, *The Descent of Man and Selection in Relation to Sex* (New York: H. M. Caldwell, 1874), 160. See Robert J. Richards, *Darwin and the Emergence of Evolutionary Theories of Mind and Behavior* (Chicago: University of Chicago Press, 1987).

51. The exchange on the Internet has been edited to remove names and affiliations. It took place in December 1994.

52. *The Geography of American Achievement* (Washington DC: Scott-Townsend, 1989). Other works by Nathaniel Weyl include *The Reconquest of Mexico: The Years of Lazaro Cardenas* (London: Oxford University Press, 1939); *Treason: The Story of Disloyalty and Betrayal in American History* (Washington DC: Public Affairs Press, 1950); *The Battle against Disloyalty* (New York: Crowell, 1951); *The Negro in American Civilization* (Washington DC: Public Affairs Press, 1960); *Red Star over Cuba: The Russian Assault on the Western Hemisphere* (New York: Hillman/Macfadden, 1961); with Stefan T. Possony, *The Geography of Intellect* (Chicago: H. Regnery, 1963); in collaboration with John Martino, *I Was Castro's Prisoner: An American Tells His Story* (New York: Devin-Adair, 1963); *The Jew in American Politics* (New Rochelle NY: Arlington House [1968]); *Traitors' End: The Rise and Fall of the Communist Movement in Southern Africa* (Cape Town: Tafelberg-Uitgewers [1970]); with William Marina, *American Statesmen on Slavery and the Negro* (New Rochelle NY: Arlington House [1971]); with R. Travis Osborne and Clyde E. Noble, eds., *Human Variation: The Biopsychology of Age, Race, and Sex* (New York: Academic Press, 1978); *Karl Marx, Racist* (New Rochelle NY: Arlington House, 1980).

53. Nathaniel Weyl, *The Creative Elite in America* (Washington DC: Public Affairs Press, 1966), 92.

54. Nathaniel Weyl and Marvin Weitz, "Ashkenazi Brainpower," *Midstream* 32 (February 1986): 22–25.

55. Dietz Bering, *The Stigma of Names: Antisemitism in German Daily Life, 1812–1933,* trans. Neville Plaice (Cambridge, England: Polity, 1992).

56. Sylvia Castleton Weyl and Nathaniel Weyl, "Jewish and Chinese Leadership in American Science," *Mankind Quarterly* 19 (1978): 49–62.

57. Kevin MacDonald, *A People That Shall Dwell Alone: Judaism As a Group Evolutionary Strategy* (Westport CN: Praeger, 1994), in the series "Human Evolution, Behavior, and Intelligence," edited by Seymour W. Itzkoff.

58. Hans Erman, *Berliner Geschichten, Geschichte Berlins: Historien, Episoden, Anekdoten* (Herrenalb: Verlag für Internationalen Kulturaustausch, 1966), 444.

59. Herbert Lindenberger, "Between Texts: From Assimilationist Novel to Resistance Novel," *Jewish Social Studies* 1 (1995): 48–68, here p. 51.

60. But MacDonald manipulates his sources rather shamelessly. For example, he uses my work to argue for a Jewish linguistic separation that was "an important force for maintaining genetic and cultural separation" (89). In fact, I argue quite the opposite: that in the late medieval and early modern period, Jews had linguistically integrated themselves into the cultures of Western Europe, and their separation was imposed on them because of this integration. MacDonald argues that my discussion of hysteria and its putative etiology in consanguineous marriages is proof that such marriages were common, rather than the obvious fact, which I stressed, that "incest" was and is a culturally defined category (107 n.23). He claims that my work supports the idea that Jews were diagnosed as having specific forms of mental illness and that this is an artifact of Jewish predisposition to such illnesses rather than a label placed on the Jews and their mental states (211).

61. Hillel Goldberg, "Jewish Genius," *Jewish Spectator* 55 (1990): 6.

62. Bill Rubinstein, "Genes and Genius," *Generation* 3 (1993): 12–24. I want to thank John Efron for calling my attention to this work.

4. *Fin-de-siècle* VIENNA AND THE JEWISH RESPONSE TO THE IMAGE

1. Quoted in Edmund Silberer, ed., *Sozialisten zur Judenfrage: Ein Beitrag zur Geschichte des Sozialismus von Anfang des 19. Jahrhunderts bis 1914* (Berlin: Colloquium, 1964), 292.

2. Robert Wistrich, *The Jews of Vienna in the Age of Franz Joseph* (Oxford: The Littman Library of Jewish Civilization/Oxford University Press, 1989), 205–6.

3. See the discussion of this concept, without any reference to the psychological or medical literature, in Steven Beller, *Vienna and the Jews 1867–1938: A Cultural History* (Cambridge: Cambridge University Press, 1989), 73–83.

4. Ignaz Zollschan, *Das Rassenproblem unter besonderer Berücksichtigung der theoretischen Grundlagen der jüdischen Rassenfrage,* 4th ed. (Vienna: Wilhelm Braumüller, 1920).

5. *Theodor Gomperz: Ein Gelehrtenleben im Bürgertum der Franz-Josefs-Zeit: Auswahl seiner Briefe und Aufzeichnungen, 1869–1912,* ed., Robert A. Kann (Vienna: Verlag der Österreichische Akademie der Wissenschaften, 1974), 384–90.

6. Wilfried Barner, *Von Rahel Varnhagen bis Friedrich Gundolf: Juden als deutsche Goethe-Verehrer* (Wolfenbüttel: Lessing-Akademie; Göttingen: Wallstein, 1992).

7. Leo Lensing, "Heine's Body, Heine's Corpus: Sexuality and Jewish Identity in Karl Kraus's Literary Polemics against Heinrich Heine," in *The Jewish Reception of Heinrich Heine,* ed. Mark H. Gelber (Tübingen: Niemeyer, 1992), 95–112.

8. Ottokar Stauf von der March, "Décadence," *Die Gesellschaft* (April 1894): 530.

9. Sigmund Freud, "Some Early Unpublished Letters," trans. Ilse Scheier, *International Journal of Psychoanalysis* 50 (1969): 419–27, here p. 426. On Freud and Jewish intellectualism see Akiva Ernst Simon, *Ha-im od Yehudim anahnu: Masot* (Tel Aviv: Sifriyat poalim; Jerusalem: ha-Universitah ha-Ivrit, Bet-ha-sefer le-hinukh, 1982).

10. Sigmund Freud, *Standard Edition of the Complete Psychological Works of Sigmund Freud,* ed. and trans. J. Strachey, A. Freud, A. Strachey, and A. Tyson (London: Hogarth, 1955–74), 8:56. This work is referred to hereafter as SE.

11. See the discussion in my *Difference and Pathology: Stereotypes of Sexuality, Race, and Madness* (Ithaca: Cornell University Press, 1986), 175–91.

12. On the history of this tradition of reading creative works, see John E. Gedo, *Portraits of the Artist: Psychoanalysis of Creativity and Its Vicissitudes* (New York: Guilford Press, 1983); Edward Hare, "Creativity and Mental Illness," *British Medical Journal* 295 (1987): 1587–89; John Hope Mason, "The Character of Creativity: Two Traditions," *History of European Ideas* 9 (1988): 697–715; and Albert Rothenberg, *Creativity and Madness: New Findings and Old Stereotypes* (Baltimore: Johns Hopkins University Press, 1990).

13. In this context see C. M. Hanly, "Psychoanalytic Aesthetics: A Defense and an Elaboration," *Psychoanalytic Quarterly* 55 (1986): 1–22, and D. M. Kaplan, "The Psychoanalysis of Art: Some Ends, Some Means," *Journal of the American Psychoanalytic Association* 36 (1988): 259–93.
14. See Barner, *Von Rahel Varnhagen bis Friedrich Gundolf.*
15. For a more extensive interpretation see Sarah Kofman, *The Childhood of Art: An Interpretation of Freud's Aesthetics,* trans. Winifred Woodhull (New York: Columbia University Press, 1988).
16. See the discussion by Janine Chasseguet-Smirgel, *Creativity and Perversion* (New York: W. W. Norton, 1984), on the relationship between object relations theory and "creativity."
17. On the uninterpretability of Jewishness and the feminine in Freud's writing see my *Freud, Race, and Gender* (Princeton: Princeton University Press, 1993), 34–37.
18. See Wilhelm Hirsch, *Genie und Entartung: Eine psychologische Studie* (Berlin: Coblentz, 1894).
19. In this context see Maurice Olender, *Les Langues du Paradis: Aryens et Sémites—Un couple providentiel* (Paris: Gallimard, 1989).
20. See the discussion of Freud's idealization of non-Jewish intellectuals in Peter Homans, *The Ability to Mourn: Disillusionment and the Social Origins of Psychoanalysis* (Chicago: University of Chicago Press, 1989), 88–95. The American Jewish psychoanalyst Abraham Aron Roback did address this question in an early popular paper, "The Jews and Genius," *American Hebrew* 40 (1919): 532, 576–78.
21. See also 3:201, and 7:160.
22. Theodor Reik, *Jewish Wit* (New York: Gamut Press, 1962), 12.
23. Quoted in Joseph Wortis, *Fragments of an Analysis with Freud* (New York: Jason Aronson, 1984), 145.
24. All quotations are from Otto Weininger, *Sex & Character,* trans. unknown (London: William Heinemann, 1906), here p. 303. On Weininger see my *Jewish Self-Hatred: Anti-Semitism and the Hidden Language of the Jews* (Baltimore: Johns Hopkins University Press, 1986), 244–51; Jacques Le Rider, *Der Fall Otto Weininger: Wurzeln des Antifeminismus und Antisemitismus,* trans. Dieter Hornig (Vienna: Löcker Verlag, 1985); Jacques Le Rider and Norbert Leser, eds., *Otto Weininger: Werk und Wirkung* (Vienna: Österreichischer Bundesverlag, 1984); Peter Heller, "A Quarrel over Bisexuality," in *The Turn of the Century: German Literature and Art, 1890–1915,* ed. Gerald Chapple and Hans H. Schulte (Bonn: Bouvier, 1978), 87–116; Franco Nicolino, *Indagini su Freud e sulla psicoanalisi* (Naples: Liguori editore, n.d.), 103–10.

25. Leopold Löwenfeld, *Über die sexuelle Konstitution und andere Sexualprobleme* (Wiesbaden: J. F. Bergmann, 1911), 146.

26. I am using the term "homosexual" throughout this and other discussions as a reflection of the debates about male and female gay identity within the medical literature of the period. While a number of different terms are used to represent male gay identity (including "homosexual" and "uranist"), it seemed clearest to reduce these to a single label. See in this context Richard Green, "Homosexuality as a Mental Illness," in *Concepts of Health and Disease: Interdisciplinary Perspectives,* ed. Arthur L. Caplan et al. (London: Addison-Wesley, 1981), 333–51, and G. Hekma, "Sodomites, Platonic Lovers, Contrary Lovers: The Backgrounds of the Modern Homosexual," *Journal of Homosexuality* 16 (1988): 433–55, as well as David F. Greenberg, *The Construction of Homosexuality* (Chicago: University of Chicago Press, 1988).

27. See, for example, the discussion in Carl Dallago, *Otto Weininger und sein Werk* (Innsbruck: Brenner-Verlag, 1912) and Emil Lucka, *Otto Weininger: Sein Werk und seine Persönlichkeit* (Berlin: Schuster & Loeffler, 1921), 37–80.

28. On this point, Fliess's letters are preserved and we can read both sides of the correspondence: Jeffrey Moussaieff Masson, ed., *The Complete Letters of Sigmund Freud to Wilhelm Fliess, 1887–1904* (Cambridge: Harvard University Press, 1985), 449–58.

29. Fritz Wittels, *Der Taufjude* (Vienna: Breitenstein, 1904). Ignaz Zollschan cites Wittels on Jewish intelligence: see Zollschan, *Rassenproblem,* 339.

30. See my *Jewish Self-Hatred,* 293–94.

31. Ernst Lissauer, "Deutschtum und Judentum," *Kunstwart* 25 (1912): 6–12, here p. 8.

32. Anatole Leroy-Beaulieu, *Israel among the Nations: A Study of the Jews and Antisemitism,* trans. Frances Hellman (New York: G. P. Putnam's Sons, 1895), 209.

33. Fritz Kahn, *Die Juden als Rasse und Kulturvolk* (Berlin: Welt Verlag, 1922), 208.

34. Quoted in *Minutes of the Vienna Psychoanalytic Society,* trans. M. Nunberg. (New York: International Universities Press, 1962–75), 2:387 (*Protokolle der Wiener Psychoanalytischen Vereinigung,* ed. Herman Nunberg and Ernst Federn [Frankfurt: Fischer, 1976–81], 2:351).

35. Alfred Adler, in *Minutes of the Vienna Psychoanalytic Society,* 2:288.

36. Otto Rank, "The Essence of Judaism," in Dennis Klein, trans., *Jewish Origins of the Psychoanalytic Movement,* Appendix C (New York: Praeger, 1981), 171.

37. Karl Abraham, *Traum und Mythus, eine Studie zur Völkerpsychologie* (Leipzig: F. Deuticke, 1909); all references are to *Dreams and Myths: A Study in Race Psychology,* trans. William A. White (New York: Journal of Nervous and Mental Disease Publishing Co., 1913).

38. Karl A. Menninger, "The Genius of the Jew in Psychiatry," *Medical Leaves* (1937): 127–32.

39. Beller, *Vienna and the Jews,* 205.

40. All references are to Leroy-Beaulieu, *Israel Among the Nations,* here p. 258.

41. Sombart, *Die Zukunft der Juden,* 44.

42. W. W. Kopp, "Beobachtung an Halbjuden in Berliner Schulen," *Volk und Rasse* 10 (1935): 392.

43. Ottokar Stauf von der March, "Décadence," *Die Gesellschaft* (April 1894), 530–36.

44. All references are to William Thackeray, *Vanity Fair* (London: J. M. Dent, 1912).

45. Max Warwar, "Der Flucht vor dem Typus," *Selbstwehr* 3 (30 April 1909): 1–2.

46. I draw for this discussion from two brilliant essays by Jens Rieckmann, "(Anti-)Semitism and Homoeroticism: Hofmannsthal's Reading of Bahr's Novel *Die Rotte Kohras,*" *German Quarterly* 66 (1993): 212–21, and "Zwischen Bewußtsein und Verdrängung: Hofmannsthals jüdisches Erbe," *Deutsche Vierteljahrsschrift für Literaturwissenschaft und Geistesgeschichte* 67 (1993): 466–83.

47. Cited by Reickmann, "(Anti-)Semitism," 214.

48. Quoted in Paul Peters, *Heinrich Heine "Dichterjude": Die Geschichte einer Schmähung* (Frankfurt: Hain, 1990), 159–60.

49. Cited by Reickmann, "(Anti-)Semitism," 214.

50. Jens Malte Fischer, "Rudolf Borchardt: Autobiographie und Judentum," in *Rudolf Borchardt 1877–1945,* ed. Horst Albert Glaser (Frankfurt: Peter Lang, 1987), 29–48, here p. 38. See also Willy Haas, "Der Fall Rudolf Borchardt: Zur Morphologie des dichterischen Selbsthasses," in *Juden in der deutschen Literatur: Essays über zeitgenössische Schriftsteller,* ed. Gustav Krojanker (Berlin: Welt, 1922), 231–40.

51. Rudolf Borchardt, *Der Krieg und die deutsche Selbsteinkehr* (Heidelberg: Richard Weissbach, 1915), 8.

52. Ursula Renner, "Leopold von Adrian über Hugo von Hofmannsthal: Auszüge aus seinen Tagebüchern," *Hofmannsthal Blätter* 35/6 (1988): 5–29.

53. Quoted in Walter S. Perl, ed., *Hugo von Hofmannsthal/Leopold von Adrian, Briefwechsel* (Frankfurt: S. Fischer, 1968), 44. Adrian's mother was the daughter of Giacomo Meyerbeer.

Notes to Pages 137–47

54. Beller, *Vienna and the Jews,* 205.

55. Cited by Reickmann, "(Anti-)Semitism," 218.

56. Frederic Raphael, in *Jewish Quarterly Review* 33 (1986): 124.

57. See Ranjit Chaterjee, "Judaic Motifs in Wittgenstein," in *Austrians and Jews in the Twentieth Century from Franz Joseph to Waldheim,* ed. Robert S. Wistrich (New York: St. Martin's, 1992), 142–53, and Ray Monk, *Ludwig Wittgenstein: The Duty of Genius* (New York: Free Press, 1990).

58. Brian McGuiness, *Young Ludwig: A Biography, 1889–1921* (Berkeley: University of California Press, 1988), 42.

59. Fania Pascal's comment about Wittgenstein's confession to her concerning his "Jewishness" was "Some Jew." Cited by Monk, *Ludwig Wittgenstein,* 369.

60. See Ludwig Wittgenstein, *Culture and Value,* ed. G. H. von Wright and Heikki Nyman (Oxford: Blackwell, 1980).

61. See Allan Janik, *Essays on Wittgenstein and Weininger* (Amsterdam: Rodopi; Atlantic Highlands NJ: Distributed in the U.S.A. by Humanities Press, 1985); Roberto Della Pietra, *Otto Weininger e la crisi della cultura austriaca* (Napoli: Libreria Sapere, 1985); and Nancy A. Harrowitz and Barbara Hyams, eds., *Jews & Gender: Responses to Otto Weininger* (Philadelphia: Temple University Press, 1995). For further Austrian readings see Ursula Heckmann, *Das verfluchte Geschlecht: Motive der Philosophie Otto Weiningers im Werk Georg Trakls* (Frankfurt; New York: Peter Lang, 1992).

62. All the following quotations from Wittgenstein are from Wright's edition of *Culture and Value,* and are cited by page (first number), text (letter), and date.

63. Tim Craker, "Remarking Wittgenstein: Mimesis, 'Witz,' Physiognomy, Fragmentation and Tempo in Wittgenstein's Remarks," (Ph.D. diss., State University of New York at Binghamton, 1991).

64. Frank Cioffi, "Wittgenstein on Freud's 'Abominable Mess,'" in *Wittgenstein Centenary Essays,* ed. A. Phillips Griffiths (Cambridge: Cambridge University Press, 1991), 169–92.

65. On this trope see Shulamit Volkov, "Die Erfindung einer Tradition: Zur Entstehung des modernen Judentums in Deutschland," *Historische Zeitschrift* 253 (1991): 603–28, here p. 609.

5. ALBAN BERG, THE JEWS, AND THE ANXIETY OF GENIUS

1. All references to the historical person and to Büchner's character are to "Woyzeck"; all references to Berg's opera and to his character are to "Woz-

zeck." The quotations from Büchner's play are from the translation by Henry J. Schmidt, *Georg Büchner: Woyzeck* (New York: Avon, 1969), which remains the best English version. The question of the organization of the play and its various editorial levels is unimportant to this paper except for the historical context of the libretto. This is well examined in Peter Petersen, *Alban Berg, Wozzeck. Eine semantische Analyse unter Einbeziehung der Skizzen und Dokumente aus dem Nachlaß Bergs* (Munich: text und kritik, 1985). The references to the English libretto are to the standard translation by Eric A. Blackall and Vida Harford, *Georg Büchner's Wozzeck: Opera in Three Acts* (New York: Associated Music Publishers, 1923).

2. I am grateful to Marc A. Weiner for his detailed comments on this chapter. The two best books on Büchner are Hans Meyer, *Georg Büchner und seine Zeit* (Berlin: Aufbau, 1959), and Henri Poschmann, *Georg Büchner: Dichtung der Revolution und Revolution der Dichtung* (Weimar: Aufbau, 1983). See also Ludwig Fischer, ed., *Zeitgenosse Büchner* (Stuttgart: Klett-Cotta, 1979); Sabine Kubik, *Krankheit und Medizin im literarischen Werk Georg Büchners* (Stuttgart: M & P, 1991); Albert Meier, *Georg Büchner, "Woyzeck"* (Munich: W. Fink, 1980); David G. Richards, *Georg Büchners Woyzeck: Interpretation und Textgestaltung* (Bonn: Bouvier, 1975); and Mario Regina, *Struttura e significato del Woyzeck di Georg Büchner* (Bari: Adriatica, 1976).

3. See Ian Hacking, *The Emergence of Probability: A Philosophical Study of Early Ideas about Probability, Induction and Statistical Inference* (London: Cambridge University Press, 1975), and Theodore M. Porter, *The Rise of Statistical Thinking, 1820–1900* (Princeton: Princeton University Press, 1986).

4. This is reprinted in Werner R. Lehmann, ed., *Georg Büchner, Sämtliche Werke und Briefe* (Hamburg: Christian Wegner, n.d.), 2:485–549, here p. 490.

5. See the discussion in Peter Uwe Hohendahl's chapter "Nachromantische Subjektivität," in his *Geschichte · Opposition · Subversion: Studien zur Literatur des 19. Jahrhunderts* (Cologne: Böhlau, 1993), 51–66.

6. Excerpted in Hans Mayer, ed., *Georg Büchner: Woyzeck. Vollständiger Text und Paralipomena. Dokumentation* (Frankfurt: Ullstein, 1993), 138–40.

7. Quoted from the review by Edgar Steiger of the 8 November 1913 production of *Woyzeck* from the excerpt in Dietmar Goltschnigg, ed., *Materialien zur Rezeptions- und Wirkungsgeschichte Georg Büchners* (Kronberg: Scriptor Verlag, 1974), 222.

8. Quoted in translation in Douglas Jarman, *Alban Berg: Wozzeck* (Cambridge: Cambridge University Press, 1989), 127.

9. Peter Gay, *The Cultivation of Hatred* (New York: Norton, 1993), 487.

10. See F. N. L. Poynter, *Chemistry in the Service of Medicine* (Philadelphia: J. B. Lippincott, 1963).

11. See the discussion in my *Jewish Self-Hatred*, 188–208.

12. The most striking contemporary account by a specialist in mental illnesses is Vincenzio Chiarugi, *Saggio di ricerche sulla pellagra* (Firenze: Presso Pietro Allegrini alla Croce Rossa, 1814). On the social history of the illness see Daphne A. Roe, *A Plague of Corn: The Social History of Pellagra* (Ithaca: Cornell University Press, 1973), and on the medical history see Kenneth J. Carpenter, ed., *Pellagra* (Stroudsburg PA: Hutchinson Ross, 1981).

13. Milton Terris, ed., *Goldberger on Pellagra* (Baton Rouge: Louisiana State University Press, [1964]).

14. Jarman, *Alban Berg*, 112.

15. Poschmann, *Georg Büchner*, 333.

16. Ludwig Büchner, *Am Sterbelager des Jahrhunderts: Blicke eines freien Denkers aus der Zeit in die Zeit* (Giessen: Emil Roth, 1898), 347.

17. On Franzos see Fred Sommer, ed., *Karl Emil Franzos: Kritik und Dichtung* (New York: Peter Lang, 1992); Maria Klanska, "Drei deutschsprachige Schriftsteller im nationalen Spannungsfeld Galiziens," *Österreich in Geschichte und Literatur* 34 (1990): 26–39; Carl Steiner, *Karl Emil Franzos, 1848–1904: Emancipator and Assimilationist* (New York: Peter Lang, 1990); Carl Steiner, "Deutscher und Jude: Das Leben und Werk des Karl Emil Franzos (1848–1904)," in *Autoren damals und heute: Literaturgeschichtliche Beispiele veränderter Wirkungshorizonte*, ed. Gerhard Knapp (Amsterdam: Rodopi, 1991), 367–87; Jörg Schönert, "Bilder vom 'Verbrechermenschen' in den rechtskulturellen Diskursen um 1900: Zum Erzählen über Kriminalität und zum Status kriminologischen Wissens," in his *Erzählte Kriminalität: Zur Typologie und Funktion von narrativen Darstellungen in Strafrechtspflege, Publizistik und Literatur zwischen 1770 und 1920* (Tübingen: Niemeyer, 1991), 497–531; W. G. Sebald, "Westwarts—Ostwarts: Aporien deutschsprachiger Ghettogeschichten," *Literatur und Kritik* 233–234 (1989): 161–77; Margarita Pazi, "Karl Emil Franzos' Assimilationsvorstellung und Assimilationserfahrung," in *Conditio Judaica: Judentum, Antisemitismus und deutschsprachige Literatur vom 18. Jahrhundert bis zum Ersten Weltkrieg*, ed. Hans Otto Horch and Horst Denkler (Tübingen: Niemeyer, 1989), 218–33; Ritchie Robertson, "Western Observers and Eastern Jews: Kafka, Buber, Franzos," *Modern Language Review* 83 (1988): 87–105; Andrea Wodenegg, *Das Bild der Juden Osteuropas: Ein Beitrag zur komparatischen Imagologie an Textbeispielen von Karl Emil Franzos und Leopold von Sacher-Masosch* (Frankfurt; New York: Lang, 1987);

Martha Bickel, "Zum Werk von Karl Emil Franzos," in *Juden in der deutschen Literatur: Ein deutsch-israelisches Symposion*, ed. Stéphane Moses and Albrecht Schöne (Frankfurt: Suhrkamp, 1986), 152–61; Claudia Albert and Gregor Blum, "Des Sender Glatteis neue Kleider: Judentum und Assimilation bei Karl Emil Franzos (1848–1904)," *Die Horen* 30 (1985): 48–92; Frederick Sommer, *"Halb-Asien"*: *German Nationalism and the Eastern European Works of Emil Franzos* (Stuttgart: H. D. Heinz, 1984); Mark H. Gelber, "Ethnic Pluralism and Germanization in the Works of Karl Emil Franzos (1848–1904)," *German Quarterly* 56 (1983): 376–85; Arno Will, "Karl Emil Franzos: Ein Beitrag zu den Gestalten der Polen in der osterreichischen Literatur des 19. Jahrhunderts," *Lenau Forum* 1 (1969): 46–57; Alexander Malycky, "A Note on the Writings of Karl Emil Franzos on Heinrich Heine," *Studies in Bibliography and Booklore* 6 (1963): 73–74.

18. Dieter Kessler, "Die deutsche Literatur des Buchenlandes und die Juden," in *Juden in Ostmitteleuropa von der Emanzipation bis zum Ersten Weltkrieg*, ed. Gotthold Rhode (Marburg a.d. Lahn: J. G. Herder-Institut, 1989), 295–309, here p. 297.

19. All references are to Karl Emil Franzos, "Wunderkinder des Ghetto," in his *Aus der großen Ebene: Neue Kulturbilder aus Halb-Asien* (Stuttgart: Adolf Bonz, 1888), 23–60. My translation.

20. See the long autobiographical introduction, written in 1893, to Franzos's last and most important novel, *Der Pojaz* (Stuttgart: J. G. Cotta, 1912), 5–14, here p. 13.

21. Julius Bab, "Durch das Drama der Jüngsten und Georg Büchners," excerpted in Goltschnigg, *Materialien*, 153–58.

22. Arthur Moeller van den Bruck, "Über Georg Büchner," excerpted in Goltschnigg, *Materialien*, 131–37.

23. Ottokar Stauf von der March, "Décadence," *Die Gesellschaft* (April 1894): 530.

24. On Berg see Siegfried Mauser, *Das expressionistische Musiktheater der Wiener Schule: Stilistische und entwicklungsgeschichtliche Untersuchungen zu Arnold Schönbergs "Erwartung," op.17, "Die gluckliche Hand," op.18, und Alban Bergs "Wozzeck," op.7* (Regensburg: G. Bosse, 1982); Guido Hiss, *Korrespondenzen: Zeichenzusammenhänge im Sprech- und Musiktheater: Mit einer Analyse des "Wozzeck" von Alban Berg* (Tübingen: M. Niemeyer, 1988); Siglind Bruhn, *Die musikalische Darstellung psychologischer Wirklichkeit in Alban Bergs "Wozzeck"* (Frankfurt; New York: Lang, 1986); George Perle, *The Operas of Alban Berg*, (Berkeley: University of California Press, 1980–85); Bo Ullman, *Die sozialkritische Thematik im Werk Georg Buchners*

und ihre Entfaltung im "Woyzeck"; mit einigen Bemerkungen zu der Oper Alban Bergs (Stockholm: Almqvist & Wiksell, 1972); James Martin Harding, "Integrating Atomization: Adorno Reading Berg Reading Büchner," *Theatre Journal* 44 (1992): 1–13.

25. All quotations are from Weininger, *Sex & Character*, here p. 315.

26. Quoted in Ernst Hilmar, *Wozzeck von Alban Berg: Entstehung—Erste Erfolge—Repressionen (1914–1935)* (Vienna: Universal, 1975), 66. My translation.

27. See Petersen, *Alban Berg*, 25.

28. Alexander L. Ringer, *Arnold Schoenberg: The Composer as Jew* (Oxford: Clarendon Press, 1990), 210.

29. Karen Horney, *Feminine Psychology*, ed. Harold Kelman (New York: Norton, 1967), 39.

30. In the score by Alban Berg, *Georg Buechners Wozzeck* (Partitur) (Vienna: Universal Edition, 1955), there are at least four points in this scene where Wozzeck's coughing is cited by the Doctor: "Ich habs gesehn, Wozzeck, Er hat wieder gehustet" (110); "(Husten müssen)" (114); "Er hat wieder gehustet" (120); and "Er hätte doch nicht husten sollen" (124). Not all of these appear in Jarman's English translation.

31. Rudolf Schäfke, "Alban Bergs Oper: Wozzeck," *Melos* 5 (1926): 267–83, here pp. 268–69. Jarman, *Alban Berg*, 31, calls this change "dramatically meaningless."

32. Petersen, *Alban Berg*, 55–56.

33. Toby Gelfand, " 'Mon Cher Docteur Freud': Charcot's Unpublished Correspondence to Freud, 1888–1893," *Bulletin of the History of Medicine* 62 (1988): 563–88, here p. 574.

34. Toby Gelfand, "Charcot's Response to Freud's Rebellion," *Journal of the History of Ideas* 50 (1989): 304.

35. There are references to diabetes as a Jewish disease in the standard textbook of internal medicine of the period, Adolf Strümpell, ed., *Lehrbuch der speciellen Pathologie und Therapie der inneren Krankheiten für Studirende und Ärzte* (Leipzig: Vogel, 1883–1912), excerpted as *A Text-Book of Medicine*, trans. Herman F. Vickery and Philip Coombs Knapp (New York: D. Appelton, 1893), 967. The "Jewish" nature of this disease is discussed widely in the medical literature of the period. In addition to Strümpell, Buschan and Charcot wrote on this question. See the literature summarized in E. Morpurgo, *Sulle condizioni somatiche e psichiche degli Israeliti in Europa*, Bibliotece dell'idea Sionisa 2 (Modena: Tip. Operai, 1903), 61–62. On the history of diabetes (without covering this topic) see Dietrich

von Engelhardt, ed., *Diabetes: Its Medical and Cultural History* (Berlin: Springer, 1989).

36. W[illiam] O[sler], "Letters from Berlin," *Canada Medical and Surgical Journal* 12 (1884): 721–28, here p. 723.

37. Dr. med. A. Kühner, *Arterienverkalkung heilbar! Neue Mittel und Wege* (Leipzig: F. W. Gloeckner, [1920]), 19.

38. Maurice Fishberg, *The Jews: A Study of Race and Environment* (New York: Walter Scott, 1911).

39. Georg Buschan, "Einfluß der Rasse auf die Form und Häufigkeit pathologischer Veränderungen," *Globus* 67 (1895): 21–24, 43–47, 60–63, 76–80, here pp. 45–46, 60–61.

40. Konrad Vogelsang, *Dokumentation zur Oper "Wozzeck" von Alban Berg* (n.p.: Laaber, 1977), p. 20.

41. K. M. Knittel, "'Ein hypermoderner Dirigent': Mahler and Anti-Semitism in *Fin-de-Siècle* Vienna," *19th-Century Music* 18 (1995): 257–76.

6. THE END OF ANOTHER CENTURY: THE IMAGE IN AMERICAN MASS CULTURE

1. On American films and the Jews see David Desser and Lester D. Friedman, eds., *American-Jewish Filmmakers: Traditions and Trends* (Urbana: University of Illinois Press, 1993); Lester D. Friedman, *Hollywood's Image of the Jew* (New York: Ungar, 1982), as well as his *The Jewish Image in American Film* (Secaucus NJ: Citadel Press, 1987); Lester D. Friedman, ed., *Unspeakable Images: Ethnicity and the American Cinema* (Urbana: University of Illinois Press, 1991); Sarah Blacher Cohen, ed., *From Hester Street to Hollywood: The Jewish-American Stage and Screen* (Bloomington: Indiana University Press, 1983); Judith E. Doneson, *The Holocaust in American Film* (Philadelphia: Jewish Publication Society, 1987); Patricia Erens, *The Jew in American Cinema* (Bloomington: Indiana University Press, 1984); Matthew Stevens, *Jewish Film Directory: A Guide to More Than 1200 Films of Jewish Interest from 32 Countries over 85 Years* (Westport CT: Greenwood, 1992).

2. Neal Gabler, *An Empire of Their Own: How the Jews Invented Hollywood* (New York: Crown, 1988), 218.

3. F. Scott Fitzgerald, *The Last Tycoon: An Unfinished Novel* (New York: Charles Scribner's Sons, 1941).

4. Joe Wood, "What I Learned about Jews," *New York Times Magazine* (10 April 1994): 42–45, here p. 44.

5. Michael Shapiro, ed., *The Jewish 100: A Ranking of the Most Influential Jews of All Time* (New York: Carol Publications Group, 1994). The list is as follows: Moses—Jesus of Nazareth—Albert Einstein—Sigmund Freud—Abraham—Saul of Tarsus (Saint Paul)—Karl Marx—Theodor Herzl—Mary—Baruch de Spinoza—David—Anne Frank—The Prophets—Judas Iscariot—Gustav Mahler—Maimonides—Niels Bohr—Moses Mendelssohn—Paul Ehrlich—Rashi—Benjamin Disraeli—Franz Kafka—David Ben-Gurion—Hillel—John Von Neumann—Simon Bar Kokhba—Marcel Proust—Mayer Rothschild—Solomon—Heinrich Heine—Selman Waksman—Giacomo Meyerbeer—Isaac Luria—Gregory Pincus—Leon Trotsky—David Ricardo—Alfred Dreyfus—Leo Szilard—Mark Rothko—Ferdinand Cohn—Samuel Gompers—Gertrude Stein—Albert Michelson—Philo Judaeus—Golda Meir—The Vilna Gaon—Henri Bergson—The Baal Shem Tov—Felix Mendelssohn—Louis B. Mayer—Judah Halevy—Haym Salomon—Johanan ben Zakkai—Arnold Schoenberg—Emile Durkheim—Betty Friedan—David Sarnoff—Lorenzo Da Ponte—Julius Rosenwald—Casmir Funk—George Gershwin—Chaim Weizmann—Franz Boas—Sabbatai Zevi—Leonard Bernstein—Flavius Josephus—Walter Benjamin—Louis Brandeis—Emile Berliner—Sarah Bernhardt—Levi Strauss—Nahmanides—Menachem Begin—Anna Freud—Queen Ester—Martin Buber—Jonas Salk—Jerome Robbins—Henry Kissinger—Wilhelm Steinitz—Arthur Miller—Daniel Mendoza—Stephen Sondheim—Emma Goldman—Sir Moses Montefiore—Jerome Kern—Boris Pasternak—Harry Houdini—Edward Bernays—Leopold Auer—Groucho Marx—Man Ray—Henrietta Szold—Benny Goodman—Steven Spielberg—Marc Chagall—Bob Dylan—Sandy Koufax—Bernard Berenson—Jerry Siegel and Joe Shuster. The last two are the creators of "Superman!"

6. Eric Lax, *Woody Allen: A Biography* (New York: Knopf; Distributed by Random House, 1991).

7. See the discussion in Clifford Pugh, "Psyched Up," *Houston Post* (10 March 1992), and "Psychiatrists Analyze Dr. Lowenstein," *New York Times* (19 January 1992).

8. Parallel questions have been raised concerning the role gender has in defining genius. See Christine Battersby, *Gender and Genius: Towards a Feminist Aesthetics* (Bloomington: Indiana University Press, 1990).

9. Miles D. Storfer, *Intelligence and Giftedness: The Constitutions of Heredity and Early Environment* (San Francisco: Jossey-Bass, 1990), 315.

10. See my *The Jew's Body* (New York: Routledge, 1991) and my *The Visibility of the Jew in the Diaspora: Body Imagery and Its Cultural Context. The B.G.*

Rudolph Lecture for 1992 (Syracuse: Program in Jewish Studies, 1992). More recently see Malek Chebel, *Histoire de la circoncision des origines à nos jours* (Paris: Balland, 1994).

11. *Pesiata Raba* and *Tanchuma on Tazria*.

12. David Barry, *Dave Barry Is Not Making This Up* (New York: Crown, 1994), 61.

13. Cited in Adam Lander, "Jack-of-All-Trades," *The Reader* (Chicago) (3 February 1995), 12.

14. Nicolaus Sombart, *Die deutschen Männer und ihre Feinde: Carl Schmitt —Ein deutsches Schicksal zwischen Männerbund und Matriarchats-mythos* (Munich: Hanser, 1991).

15. My reference here is to the study of the change in the popular image of the Jew in Anglophone mass and popular culture after the foundation of the state of Israel. See Paul Brienes, *Tough Jews: Political Fantasies and the Moral Dilemma of American Jewry* (New York: Basic Books, 1990).

16. Naomi Seidman, "Carnal Knowledge: Sex and the Body in Jewish Studies," *Jewish Social Studies,* n.s., 1 (1994): 115–46, quite correctly critiques my earlier work on this topic. She stresses that it is only because of the widespread American practice of medical circumcision that American Jews can view the debates about the physicality of Jewish difference with distance. Her view is that the hidden, unspoken question that middle-class American Jews cannot raise in the Academy is about the power of the economic stereotype.

17. Marianna de Marco Torgovnick, *Crossing Ocean Parkway: Readings by an Italian American Daughter* (Chicago: University of Chicago Press, 1994). On the parallel Jewish context see Jenna Weissman Joselit, *The Wonders of America: Reinventing Jewish Culture, 1880–1950* (New York: Hill & Wang, 1995).

18. See Seymour Martin Lipset and Earl Raab, *Jews and the New American Scene* (Cambridge: Harvard University Press, 1995), 17–27, on Jewish achievement in America. Lipset takes the view that this is a reflection of the immigrant ethos of upward mobility for the second generation.

19. *Nobody's Fool,* Paramount Pictures, Los Angeles, 1994.

20. Simon Louvish, *The Silencer: Another Levantine Tale* (New York: Interlink, 1993), 75.

21. Clyde Haberman, "Israelis Deglamourize the Military," *New York Times* (31 May 1995), sec. A, p. 9.

22. All references to the novel are to Thomas Keneally, *Schindler's List* (New York: Touchstone, 1993), here p. 14. See also Frank Manchel, "A Reel Wit-

ness: Steven Spielberg's Representation of the Holocaust in *Schindler's List*," *Journal of Modern History* 67 (1995): 83–100; Simon Louvish, "Witness," *Sight and Sound* 4 (1994): 12–15; Mordecai Richler, "Why I Hate *Schindler's List*," *Saturday Night* 109 (1994): 34, 68; Michael André Bernstein, "The *Schindler's List* Effect," *The American Scholar* 63 (1994): 429–32; Tim O'Hearn, "*Schindler's Ark* and *Schindler's List*—One for the Price of Two," *Commonwealth Novel in English* 5 (1992): 9–15; Michael Hollington, "The Ned Kelly of Cracow: Keneally's *Schindler's Ark*," *Meanjin* 42 (1983): 42–46.

23. Heinrich Mann, *Man of Straw,* trans. Ernest Boyd (London: Penguin, 1984). *Der Untertan* was first published by Kurt Wolff in Berlin in 1918. On the question of the reading of Jewish ears see Itta Schedletzky, "Majestätsbeleidigung und Menschenwürde. Die Fatalität des Antisemitismus in Heinrich Manns Roman *Der Untertan*," *Bulletin des Leo-Baeck-Instituts* 86 (1990), 67–81, here p. 74–76. See also the images of the "Jewish ear" in *Die Macht der Bilder: Antisemitische Vorurteile und Mythen,* ed. Jüdisches Museum des Stadt Wien (Vienna: Picus, 1995), 173.

24. *Schindler's List,* Universal Pictures, Universal City CA, 1993.

25. Max Horkheimer and Theodor W. Adorno, *Dialectic of Enlightenment,* trans. John Cumming (New York: Seabury Press, 1972), 209.

26. "The Enigma of 'Quiz Show': No Crowds," *New York Times* (12 February 1995), sec. H, p. 19.

27. Richard N. Goodwin, *Remembering America: A Voice from the Sixties* (New York: Perennial Library, 1989).

28. On Roth's trilogy *Zuckerman Bound* (of which *Zuckerman Unbound* is a volume) see Thomas Pughe, *Comic Sense: Reading Robert Coover, Stanley Elkin, Philip Roth* (Basel, Switzerland; Boston: Birkhauser Verlag, 1994); James D. Wallace, " 'This Nation of Narrators': Transgression, Revenge and Desire in *Zuckerman Bound*," *Modern Language Studies* 21 (1991): 17–34; Charles Berryman, "Philip Roth and Nathan Zuckerman: A Portrait of the Artist as a Young Prometheus," *Contemporary Literature* 31 (1990): 177–90; Stanley Trachtenberg, "In the Egosphere: Philip Roth's Anti-Bildungsroman," *Papers on Language and Literature: A Journal for Scholars and Critics of Language and Literature* 25 (1989): 326–41; Beverly Edwards, "*Zuckerman Bound:* The Artist in the Labyrinth" (Ph.D. diss., Lehigh University, 1987); Adeline R. Tintner, "Hiding behind James: Roth's *Zuckerman Unbound*," *Midstream* 28 (1982): 49–53.

29. Beginning with his essay "New Views on the Psychology and Psychopathology of Wit and the Comic," *Psychiatry* 13 (1950): 43–62, to his major

study *Creativity: The Magic Synthesis* (New York: Basic Books, 1976), Silvano Arieti's work focused on this question and the (for him) related question of the nature and meaning of schizophrenia.

30. See my discussion of the history and meaning of schizophrenia in *Disease and Representation: Images of Illness from Madness to AIDS* (Ithaca NY: Cornell University Press, 1988).

31. Silvano Arieti, *New Views of Creativity* (New York: Geigy, 1977), 7.

32. Silvano Arieti, *The Parnas* (New York: Basic Books, 1979).

33. Arieti, *Creativity: The Magic Synthesis,* 327–28.

34. Jean-Joseph Goux, "Politics and Modern Art: Heidegger's Dilemma," *Diacritics* 19 (1989): 10–24, here p. 19.

INDEX

Abraham, Karl, 143; *Dreams and Myths,*
 130–31
Abrahamson, Terry, 183
Adler, Alfred, 128–29
Adler, Victor, 103
Adrian, Leopold von, 136–37, 227 n.53
African Americans: considered as underclass, 4, 22, 34–35, 64; exclusion
 from intelligence studies, 57–58; and
 intelligence, 3, 9, 22, 29, 93, 179; in literature, 133; muscular development,
 23; race issues tied to, 3; as victims, 10
Agnon, S. A., 98
Aleichem, Sholem, 14
Allen, Woody, 19, 20, 180
Annie Hall, 180
anti-Semitic views: Jews as different, inferior, 49, 71, 106, 126; Jews lacking in
 imagination and creativity, 49–50, 75,
 104, 118, 132; linked to circumcision,
 183
anti-Semitism: Austrian, 103; and Freud,
 22, 121, 122; late-nineteenth-century
 discourse of, 45, 64, 165; responses to,
 75; weakness of Jews vis-à-vis, 166. *See
 also* Vienna, late-nineteenth-century
Arieti, Silvano, 204–5; *The Parnas,* 204
Arkin, Adam, 180
Arsenian, Seth, 57, 185
Ashkenazy, Vladimir, 18
Attanasio, Paul, 199

Bacon, Francis, 157
Bahr, Hermann, 137
Barak, Ehud, 188
Barry, David, 182, 184
Beatty, Warren, 187
bell curve: as complex model, 8–9;
 Galton's theory of, 34–35, 80; Herrn-
 stein and Murray's, 4–5, 206; Jews
 on, 5–6, 8–10, 22, 56; low end, 4, 22
Beller, Steven, 132
Benedikt, Moriz, 118

Benn, Gottfried, 83–84
Benton, Robert, 186
Bere, May, 57, 58
Berg, Alban, *Wozzeck:* characterized as
 Jewish modern, 170, 173; coughing
 in, 167, 168–69, 193, 232 n.30; influ-
 ence of local politics on, 163, 164,
 170–71; and modification of Büch-
 ner's *Woyzeck,* 164–70; use of baritone
 voice in, 165, 166
Berg, Gertrude, 180
Bering, Dietz, 25, 92
Berlin, Irving, 18
Berman, Pandro, 178
Bernhardt, Sarah, 48, 107, 169
Bible for Christian Communities, 183–84
Bill and Ted's Excellent Adventure, 179
Binet, Alfred, 55–56
blacks. *See* African Americans; Hotten-
 tots
Blazing Saddles, 190
Bloom, Alexander, *Prodigal Sons,* 24
Boas, Franz, *The Mind of Primitive Man,*
 79–80
Borchardt, Rudolf, 136
Börne, Ludwig, 70
Brand, Joshua, and John Falsey, 180, 188
Breines, Paul, 23
Breuer, Josef, 139, 141; *Studies in Hysteria*
 (with Freud), 112
Brigham, Carl, 56, 58, 80
Brooklyn Bridge, 188
Brooks, Mel, 190
Büchner, Ernst, 156
Büchner, Georg, 170; as physician and
 revolutionary, 147–48
—Works:
 Danton's Tod, 158, 161
 "The Hessian Reporter," 148
 Woyzeck: basis for, 148–49; first edi-
  tion of, 147, 157, 161–62, 163;
  and Jewish culture, 154, 162–63;
  performance of, 163; protagonist

Index

Büchner, Georg, (*cont.*)
characterized, 149, 154, 159; readings of, 166; role of medicine in, 149–54, 155–57, 166, 170. *See also* Berg, Alban, *Wozzeck*

Büchner, Ludwig, 150, 170; career and views, 158, 163–64, 168; and publication of brother's works, 157–58, 162, 166; *Force and Matter,* 158

Bugsy, 187

The Caine Mutiny, 179

Carey, John, 9

Chamberlain, Houston Stewart, 45, 50, 54, 77, 128

Charcot, Jean-Martin, 69, 118, 167–68

Chicago Hope, 180

Christianity: intelligence of Christian vs. Jews, 77, 86, 87–88, 91; and the Jews, 21–22, 183

circumcision, 12, 16, 129; contemporary German view, 183–84; in modern American society, 182–83, 184, 189

Clarus, Johann Christian August, report on Woyzeck, 148–49, 151, 154, 155

Clift, Montgomery, 180

Cohen, Irma Loeb, 220 n.37; studies of Jewish intelligence, 80–81, 181

conversion: and intermarriage, 106, 127–28, 132, 138; as mode of assimilation, 134, 161

Corbin, Barry, 188

criminality and intelligence, 4–5, 57

Cullum, John, 189

Dante Alighieri, 69

Darlington, Cyril D., 51–52, 84

Darwin, Charles, 33, 68, 88

degeneracy: of Jews, 46, 132–33, 163; Lombroso's concept of, 66–67; *Mischling* and, 132–34, 142; of working classes, 151

Delvaux, Paul, *The Awakening of the Forest,* 26

DeMille, Cecil B., 175

diabetes, 167

Dieß, Johann, 148

difference, Jewish: as biological, racial, 52, 74, 163; gaze as marker of, 33,

36–38, 51; modern anxiety about, 205, 206; as part of nature, 158, 161; signs of, 36; stereotypical model of, 170–71. *See also* intelligence, and the Jews; stereotypes of Jews

Disraeli, Benjamin, 70, 77

Dreyfus Affair, 25, 42, 84

Dr. Strangelove, 190

Dühring, Eugen, 45, 77, 106

Dumas, Alexandre, *Lady of the Camellias,* 168

Ehrenfels, Christian von, 73–75

Einstein, Albert, 17, 19, 76; in American culture, 179–80

Engländer, Martin, 23

Epstein, Ephraim M., 63, 65

Feldman, W. M., 73

females: black, 35–36, 133–34; and disease, 48, 168–69; and fantasy, 114–15; Jewish, 39–40, 48; intelligence of, 77, 81; as object of observation, 35–36, 39; portrayed in American mass media, 180–81; Weininger's attacks on, 124–25

Ferrer, Jose, 179

Feuer, Lewis S., 85–87

Fiennes, Ralph: in *Quiz Show,* 198; in *Schindler's List,* 195, 198

Fishberg, Maurice, 79, 80; *The Jews,* 169

Fitzgerald, F. Scott, *The Last Tycoon:* character of Monroe Stahr in, 175–78, 181, 200

Fleiss, Wilhelm, 123

Frankel, Moriz, 159–60

Frankfurter, Felix, 200

Franzos, Karl Emil, 97, 170; and Büchner's *Woyzeck,* 147, 161, 162, 163; studies of children of superior intelligence, 97, 159–61, 165; work and views on Büchner, 158–59, 161–62
—Works:
Aus Halb-Asien, 159
Die Juden von Barnow, 159

Fraser, Steven, 9, 20

Frerichs, Friedrich Theodor, 168

Freud, Sigmund, 17, 19, 104, 106, 109; in American culture, 179, 180; influ-

Index

ence of Weiniger on, 123–24, 126–27;
on Jews and creativity, 109–16, 143,
204; profession and role for, 22, 115,
116–17, 120, 131
—Works:
address to B'nai B'rith, 120–21, 122
"Autobiographical Study," 116
"The Claims of Psycho-Analysis to
Scientific Interest," 115
"Creative Writers and Day-Dreaming,"
113
"Dostoevsky and Parricide," 116
Jokes and Their Relation to the Uncon-
scious, 110
Moses and Monotheism, 121–22
Studies in Hysteria (with Breuer), 112
Totem and Taboo, 141
Friedman, Elisha M., 79

Gabler, Neal, 175
Galton, Francis, 34–35, 42, 64; backers
of, 52; definition of genius, 33, 34,
69, 92, 98; representation of Africans,
34–36, 80, 134; study of Jewish
character, 36–40, 46, 85–86, 108
gaze: Jewish, 36–38, 51; racial, photo-
graphing of, 36, 214 n.6; "scientific,"
169
Gay, Peter, 150
Geary, Cynthia, 189
genius, models of: Galton's, as heredi-
tary, 33, 34, 69, 92, 98; Jewish, denial
of, 124, 128; Leroy-Beaulieu's analy-
sis, 42–43, 45, 49–51; linked to the
insane, 38–39, 66–68, 126–27. *See also*
Lombroso, Cesare, *Genio e follia*
Gentlemen's Agreement, 199
George, Stefan, 135; circle of, 136
Glauberman, Naomi, 9
Glazer, Nathan, 10, 11
Gobineau, Arthur de, 46
Goddard, Henry Herbert, 56, 58, 77,
80–81, 217 n.46
Goebbels, Joseph, 84
Goethe, Johann Wolfgang von, 107, 112,
124, 128, 161
—Works:
Faust, 107
Torquato Tasso, 114

Goldberg, Gary David, 188
Goldberg, Hillel, 98
Goldberger, Joseph, 156
Goldhar, Pinchas, 98
Gomperz, Theodor, 103, 143, 212 n.47;
essay on Jewish intelligence, 106–9,
111
Goodman, Benny, 18
Goodwin, Richard, 199–200; *Remember-*
ing America, 200–203
Goux, Jean-Joseph, 205–6
Graetz, Heinrich, 7–8, 15
Grüner, Ruben, 160
Günther, Hans F. K., 37, 53–54

Hacker, Andrew, 9, 20
Hacking, Ian, 28
Haldane, J. B. S., 85–86
Hebbel, Christian Friedrich, 107
Hecht, Ben, 175
Hegel, G. W. F., 42
Heine, Heinrich, 161; as example of dis-
eased Jew, 68–69, 107, 129; as example
of Jewish genius, 34, 46–47, 64, 65,
70, 77, 118; negative assessments of,
124, 128–29, 132; poetry of, 108, 135
Herder, Johann Gottfried von, 124
Herek, Stephen, 179
Hermann, Armin, 17
Herrnstein, Richard J., 22, 92
Herrnstein, Richard J., and Charles
Murray, *The Bell Curve:* on African
Americans, 4–5; aim and subject
matter of, 4–5, 29–30, 92, 206; essays
on, 9, 20; Internet exchange about,
89–91; on Jews, 5–6, 8, 9, 22, 29,
57; reception of, 3–4, 9–12; sources,
11, 12. *See also* Storfer, Miles D.,
Intelligence and Giftedness
Herz, Henriette, 129
Herzl, Theodor, 7, 143
Herzog, Elizabeth. *See* Zborowski,
Mark, and Elizabeth Herzog, *Life Is*
with People
Hilberg, Raul, 84
Hintschmann, Eduard, 121
Hitler, Adolf, 197; *Mein Kampf,*
48–49, 84

Index

Hofmannsthal, Hugo von, 104, 139; anxiety about mixed identity, 135–37, 143
Horkheimer, Max, 196–97
Horney, Karen, 28, 165
Hottentots, 34–35, 64
Hugo, Victor, 128
Huntington, Ellsworth, 51
Hurault, Bernard, 183

intelligence, and creativity, Jewish, 5–6, 10, 29, 65–66, 75, 122, 204–5; American debate over, 204; anxiety about, 171, 205; and music, 43–45, 68, 70, 139, 165; in poetry, 47, 65, 107, 136; seen as limited, 139, 140. *See also* Freud, Sigmund
intelligence, and the Jews: canon of "smart Jews," 40, 64–65, 70, 107; catalogs concerning, 17–20, 98, 107–8, 141, 179, 233 n.5; as factor of difference, 25–26, 30, 40, 122, 127, 131–32; historical writing about, 24, 51–52; measurement/testing of, 16–17, 55–56, 59; as negative, 16–17, 27–28, 30, 45, 52–53, 190; as racial consideration, 5–8, 10–11, 13, 19, 23, 39, 41–42, 50, 55, 81, 95; self-doubt about, 103, 106–7, 143; studies on, 6–7, 12, 16–17, 56–59, 69, 80–82, 83–87, 98, 104–9, 159–61; theories about, 9–17, 33, 53–54, 69, 71–72, 77–79, 87–88, 92–97, 108, 130. *See also* genius, models of; Jewish intellectual; Jewish superior intelligence; virtue
IQ, 179
Israel, 20; absence of Jewish superior intelligence in, 98; population of, 6, 7, 8
Israel, Joseph, 78

Jacobs, Joseph, 19, 22–23, 65, 75; on Jewish gaze, 37–38; as source, 67
—Works:
  "The Comparative Distinction of Jewish Ability," 69–71
  Jewish Contribution to Civilization, 69
  Men of Distinction, 69
Jacoby, Russell, 9

Jaffe, Sam, in *The Asphalt Jungle*, 190
Janet, Pierre, 120
Jellinek, Adolf, 65–66, 107, 114, 127
Jensen, Arthur Robert, 3–4
Jensen, Wilhelm, 111
Jesus Christ, 21, 45, 128, 129, 179; as killed by the Jews, 183
Jewish intellectual, 29; and issue of intelligence, 23–26; portrayed as ineffectual, 180; and the scientist, 26–27; as special label, 78
Jewish superior intelligence: in American situation, 175–77; as insufficient and useless, 195–98; and the intellectual, 23–26; myth of, 6, 9, 33, 82–83, 91–92, 98, 184, 188, 203, 206; vs. physical weakness, 22–23, 178, 179; seen in terms of the Shoah, 177–78. *See also* intelligence, and the Jews
Jews
  assimilation for, 134, 159, 161
  Eastern European: acculturated, attitudes of, 159; immigrants, testing of, 56, 59; and intelligence, 160–61; linked to survival, 87; myths and images of, 14–15, 85
  essence of, 36–40, 141–42
  groupings of: Ashkenasic, 5, 6–7, as superior to Sephardic, 6, 13, 78; distinctions among, 7, 8; "Eastern" and "Western," 6
  in modern America: images of in today's culture and mass media, 179–81, 186, 190–206; in 1940s Hollywood, 175–77; presentation of, rules for, 189–90; as "smart," 177, 188; visibility of, 186
  professions for, 22, 131
  tabulations of: geniuses, 77–78; Nobel laureates, 17–18, 205; one hundred most influential, 191, 233 n.5; prize winners, 17 *See also* intelligence and the Jews; male(s), Jewish
Joachim, Joseph, 107
Joyce, James, *Ulysses*, 40–41

Kafka, Franz, 23, 75, 203
Kahn, Fritz, 128, 129

Index

Kant, Immanuel, 15
Kautsky, Karl, 103
Keaton, Diane, 180
Keneally, Thomas, *Schindler's Ark,*
    191–98
Khvol'son, Daniel Abramovich,
    assessment of Jewish intelligence,
    63–65, 68
Kingsley, Ben: as Gandhi, 192, 193; in
    Schindler's List, 192–93
Kleist, Heinrich von, 107
Koch, Robert, 26
Kohler, Josef, 78
Kraus, Karl, 107, 129
Kretschmer, Ernst, 53–54
Krüger, Hardy, in *Flight of the Phoenix,*
    190
Kubrick, Stanley, 190

Lacayo, Richard, 3–4
language of Jews, 15–16, 65; according
    to Wagner, 44–45; and intelligence,
    58; *Mauscheln,* 125, 129; Yiddish, 14
Lassalle, Ferdinand, 40, 70, 77, 129
Leonardo da Vinci, 111; *Holy Family,* 112
Leoncavallo, Ruggero, *La Bohème,* 169
Lenz, Fritz, 53
Leroy-Beaulieu, Anatole, *Israel among
    the Nations,* 127, 132; on Jewish
    intelligence, 42–43, 69, linked to
    nervousness, 46–47, 66, in music and
    theater, 43, 45, 48, principal features
    of, 49–51
Levi, Primo, 84
Levinson, Barry, and James Toback, 187
Lichtenberg, Georg, 149
Liebermann, Max, 118
Liebig, Justus, 150
Lindenberger, Herbert, 97
Lipset, Seymour Martin, 185, 235 n.18
Lissauer, Ernst, 127
Lombroso, Cesare: idea of degeneracy,
    66–67
—Works:
    L'Antisemitismo e le scienze moderne, 69
    Genio e Follia, connection between
        genius and insanity in, 38–39, 53,
        66, 116, 117, 161; linked to Jews and
        race, 66–67

Louvish, Simon, *The Silencer,* 187–88
Löwenfeld, Leopold, 123
Lowensohn, Elina, 196

MacDonald, Kevin, *A People That Shall
    Dwell Alone,* 95–98; use of sources,
    223 n.60
MacNaughton rule, 149
Madigan, Charles M., 3
Maimonides (Moses ben Maimon),
    25, 40
male(s), Jewish, 8; as carrier of superior
    intelligence, 94, 181; and circumci-
    sion, 16, 182; feminization of, 27, 48,
    49, 69, 124–26, 168–69; as good life
    partners, 184–85; as physically weak,
    22–23, 161, 168, 178; as tough, 184,
    188
Mandel, Robert, 186
Mann, Heinrich, *Man of Straw,* 193
Mantegazza, Paolo, 68
Marc, Carl Moritz, 149
Marsh, Madison, 33, 39, 63, 71
Marx, Karl, 17, 49, 70, 107, 129, 179
—Works:
    "On the Jewish Question," 155
    Das Kapital, 151
Mattenklott, Gert, *Jüdische Intelligenz in
    deutschen Briefen,* 24
Matthau, Walter, 179
Mayer, Louis B., 175
medicine: Jewish physician as different,
    131; in Germany, 148, 150; literary
    attack on, 149–54, 155–57, 166; scien-
    tific, 150, 156, 157; and treatment of
    madness, 149
Mendelssohn, Dorothea, 129
Mendelssohn, Moses, 40
Mendelssohn-Bartholdy, Felix, 40, 68,
    139, 141; as Jewish genius, 70, 77–78,
    107
Mendoza, Daniel, 40, 234 n.5
Menninger, Karl, 131
mental illness: and creativity, 68, 203,
    204; and genius, 38–39, 66–68,
    126–27; Jews and, 67, 69, 97, 169
Meyerbeer, Giacomo, 43–44, 68, 137,
    227 n.53
Michelangelo, 111

243

Index

Index

Ruppin, Arthur, studies of Jews, 77–79, 86
Rushton, J. Philippe, 3
Russo, Richard, 187
Ryan, Alan, 22
Ryan, Meg, 179

Sanders, George, 190
Schepisi, Fred, 179
Scherer, Wilhelm, 46
Schindler's List, 191, 192–93, 195–98
Schlesinger, Fritz, 136
Schmolling, Daniel, 148
Schnitzler, Arthur, 67, 68–69, 118
Schoenberg, Arnold, 164–65
School Ties, 186
Schopenhauer, Arthur, 124
Schreber, Daniel, 111
Schwartz, Ernst von, 40
scientist: evil, in movies, 190; Freud as Jewish, 120, 131; Jewish, as intellectual and strange, 26–27; and observation, 27, 33, 36, 40, 169; scientific positivism, 154
Seidler, Harry, 98
Seidman, Naomi, 235 n.16
Sellers, Peter, 190
sexuality: Freud's concept of, 117–18; Jewish, in American cinema, 175–76, 177; and Jews, 130
Shapiro, Michael, *The Jewish 100*, 191, 233 n.5
Shaud, Grant, 180
Sheldon, P. M., 16
Shoah: basis for, 170; communities spared from, 87; and Jewish intelligence, 11, 94–95, 96, 131, 198, 206; rationalizing of, 83-85
Shockley, William, 3–4
Singer, I. B., 181
Slezak, Walter, 190
Smith, Goldwin, 71–72
Sombart, Werner, 47, 50, 73
Sowell, Thomas, 9–10
Spencer, Herbert, 36, 52
Spielberg, Steven, 191, 194–97
Spinoza, Benedikt (Baruch): criticism of, 38, 49, 124; and Jewish achievement, 40; as model of Jewish superior

intelligence, 25, 45, 108–9, 118, 128, 179
Stanford-Binet tests, 16, 55–56
Stauf von der March, Ottokar, 133, 163
Steinberg, Michael, "Jewish Identity and Intellectuality in Fin-de-Siècle Austria," 24
Steinrück, Albert, 163
Stempel, Herb, 198–99, 201, 202, 203
stereotypes, of Jews: as adaptable and mutable, 24, 43, 47–48, 107–8, 125; blackness of, 133, 134–35; classic, reversal of, 177, 183–84; concerning health and illness, 33, 48, 75, 76, 142, 168, 169; as crafty, clever, 28, 38, 103, 133, 135; as degenerate, degenerating, 46, 52–53, 120, 132–33, 168; economic, 19–20, 47; as feminine, 39–40, 65–66; as mercenary and materialistic, 38, 154–55, 177; as overintellectualized, 52; as physically different, 52, 129, 134, 193, 205; and rationality, 176
Storfer, Miles D., *Intelligence and Giftedness*, 96; cataloging of Jews, 17–20, 181; on Jewish superior intelligence, 12, 20–21, 22, 33, 82, 93, 184, 185, 190; as source for *The Bell Curve*, 12; sources for, 14–15, 58–59
Strauss, Leo, 24–25
Strauss, Richard, 166
Streisand, Barbra, 180, 181

Terman, Lewis M., 12, 55, 57, 58–59
Thackeray, William, *Vanity Fair*, 133–34
Thalberg, Irving, 175, 178
Theilhaber, Felix A., 75–76
Thiérry, François, 156
Thomas, Jean Charles, 183
Torgovinick, Marianna de Marco, 184–86
tuberculosis: linked to male Jew, 48; myth of Jewish immunity, 168–69
Turner, Janine, 188
Turturro, John, 198
Twain, Mark, 19–20

Uris, Leon, *Exodus*, film based on, 186

van den Haag, Ernest, 85, 86–87, 91, 92, 98

245

Index